Tell Me Lies
About Vietnam

Tell Me Lies About Vietnam

Cultural Battles for the Meaning of the War

EDITED BY

Alf Louvre and Jeffrey Walsh

For the E.V.A.C. Research Group

OPEN UNIVERSITY PRESS
Milton Keynes · Philadelphia

1051302   7

Open University Press
Open University Educational Enterprises Limited
12 Cofferidge Close
Stony Stratford
Milton Keynes MK11 1BY

and

242 Cherry Street
Philadelphia, PA 19106, USA

First Published 1988

British Library Cataloguing in Publication Data

Tell me lies about Vietnam: cultural
  battles for the meaning of the war.
  1. English literature. American writings,
  1945–. Special subjects: Vietnamese wars –
  Critical studies
  I. Louvre, Alf.   II. Walsh, Jeffrey
  810.9′358
    ISBN 0-335-15594-4
    ISBN 0-335-15593-6 Pbk

Library of Congress Cataloging-in-Publication Data

Tell me lies about Vietnam: cultural battles for the meaning of the
  War/edited by Alf Louvre and Jeffrey Walsh.
      p.   cm.
  Includes index.
  ISBN 0-335-15594-4   ISBN 0-335-15593-6 (pbk.)
    1. Arts and society – United States.   2. Vietnamese Conflict,
  1961–1975 – United States – Art and the conflict.   3. United States –
  Popular culture – History – 20th century.   4. United States –
  Intellectual life – 20th century.   I. Louvre, Alf.   II. Walsh,
  Jeffrey.
  NX180.S6T43   1988
  700′.1′030973 – dc 19   88-22387   CIP

Typeset by Scarborough Typesetting Services
Printed in Great Britain by Biddles Limited, Guildford and Kings Lynn

10/06/92(D)

For Wilfrid Louvre,
knowing veteran of another war

Contents

Notes on Contributors

James Aulich: Lecturer in History of Art and Design at Manchester Polytechnic, whose subject specialisms include British and American Art, 1945 to the present, and Contemporary Graphic Design. He is Visual Arts Editor for the *New Manchester Review* and *City Life Magazine* and has published numerous reviews and articles in such journals as *Art Monthly* and *Artist's Newsletter*. He is co-editor of *Vietnam Images: War and Representation*.

Laurence Coupe: Lecturer and critic, he has written widely on modern literature. His work has appeared in *Critical Quarterly, P. N. Review, The Powys Review, Stand* and many other Journals; he has also contributed to books such as *British Literary Magazines* and *Jack Lindsay: The Thirties and Forties*. He is currently completing a doctoral thesis on modern poetics.

Antony Easthope: Wrote *Poetry as Discourse*, published in the Methuen 'New Accents' series in 1983, and a study of the masculine myth in popular culture, *What a Man's Gotta Do* (1986). An account of contemporary developments in theory, *British Post-Structuralism*, was published by Routledge in 1988, and a book on poetry and psychoanalysis, *Poetry, Phantasy and Gender*, is forthcoming from Cambridge University Press.

W. D. Ehrhart: The poet, novelist and essayist is one of the United States' best known writers about the Vietnam War. He served in Vietnam with the US Marine Corps from 1967 to 1968. He lives with his wife Anne and daughter Leela, and teaches English Literature at the Germantown Friends School.

Alan Fair: Was the research assistant for the EVAC project: he has taught both American Literature and Film studies at Sussex University and Manchester Polytechnic. He has since been appointed Arts Development Officer for the Trades Union Movement in Birmingham and is currently working on a book on images of the working class in popular cinema.

Jeffery Fenn: Received an M.A. in Dramatic Literature from the University of Calgary in 1983. He also has an M.A. in Chinese Studies from Soochow University, Republic of China, and a Ph.D. in Dramatic Literature from the University of British Columbia. He has taught English and Dramatic Literature at Soochow University, the University of Calgary, and the University of British Columbia. He is at present Senior Lecturer at Potchefstroomse University in South Africa.

Robert Hamilton: Is currently doing doctoral research at the University of Leeds into the roles of British Photographers during the Vietnam War. He teaches Art History at Manchester Polytechnic and has published several articles in scholarly journals.

David Huxley: Trained as a painter and has written and drawn for a range of British and American comics. He is currently researching for a Ph.D. on the history of British alternative comics.

Alf Louvre: Lectures in the department of English and History at Manchester Polytechnic. He is particularly involved in interdisciplinary courses combining literary/cultural studies and history. He has published on Cultural Studies theory, on nineteenth-century Chartist autobiography and is currently preparing a book on British working-class writing in the nineteenth and twentieth centuries.

John Storey: Teaches Drama and Cultural Studies at Manchester Polytechnic. A former Research Student at the Centre for Contemporary Cultural Studies, he is at present doing Doctoral research on Nineteenth-century Melodrama at the University of Manchester Drama Department. He has published on nineteenth-century Cultural Criticism and Contemporary popular culture.

Jeffrey Walsh: Who as Principal Lecturer in English at Manchester Polytechnic organized the First International Conference to study the cultural effects of Vietnam. He is author of *American War Literature: 1914 to Vietnam* and *A Tribute to Wilfred Owen*, and is co-editor of *Vietnam Images: War and Representation* and *The Vietnam Anti-War Movement: An International Perspective*. For many years he has taught part-time for the Open University.

Preface

More than a decade after the end of hostilities ⸤the Vietnam War continues to be a crucial litmus of American values⸥ The war of interpretation, the battle for ideological appropriation of the war, continues unabated, fuelled at one level perhaps by personal guilts and obsessions, at another by the need to promote versions of America's past that enhance its present status and – not least – by the promise of commercial gain. Vietnam is enduring trauma, opportunity for ⸤political image-making and good box-office all rolled into one⸥

We would be inclined – with an eye on this unceasing process of reassessment – to call this collection 'Reading Vietnam' were it not for the feeling that this phrase suggests too passive a process. 'Writing Vietnam' or 'making the war' might be nearer the mark – or any phrase that connotes the active assertion, intervention and resistance necessary to *construct* a version of such events, especially one departing from the dominant interpretation of the day.

Our chosen title, *Tell Me Lies About Vietnam* (a line from Adrian Mitchell's 1964 anti-war poem 'To Whom it may concern'), intends to suggest two basic motives. First, we wish to draw attention, singly and collectively, to the extent to which dominant depictions of the war serve as evasions, alibis, disavowals, distortion and lies. Much of our attention is therefore given to describing (in the major popular artefacts) those devices which attempted to sustain the myths of American dominance.

Secondly, through such critical evaluations of the major popular texts and by attending where we can to alternative and dissenting responses, we hope implicitly and explicitly to endorse the oppositional stance of the movement from which that poem of Mitchell's came.

In various ways, then, this collection rubs against the contemporary grain. By including several pieces about the perception of the war *outside* America it tries to go beyond a prevalent Americo-centrism. Equally, it questions the masculinism so prominent in many popular representations. And, recurrently, it insists upon the historical as necessary counter-force to myth.

Committed to interpreting the (continuing) *ideological* impact of the Vietnam War, we are inevitably drawn to the study of *popular* culture, site of the most dramatic and often the most significant ideological struggles. Artefacts that circulate by or among the millions do, after all, have a quantitative weight – hence the work here on film, on music, on best-sellers and on ephemera. But we are wary of any neat separation of the 'high' from the 'popular' arts, especially one that works to grant ideological immunity to the 'learned', to 'sophisticated' or 'minority' forms (as 'above the common struggle'). To concentrate exclusively on self-styled 'popular culture' can mean at once leaving such pretensions unchallenged and implicitly endorsing the notion that 'popular' means simple, transparent, reflexive, easily diagnosed. Opposing this divide, several essays consider the interrelations of popular and élite modes (between films and their novelistic antecendents, for instance, or between performance poetry and acknowledged poetic tradition).

The shape of this collection has been affected, too, by a sense of the work already done. As against specialist analyses (already well established in the area of 'literature' and especially 'the novel') we wished to explore a range of discourses, some of which have so far received scant attention (hence our concern for visual and aural as well as exclusively verbal modes – for cartoons, comics, songs and films as well as poetry and the novel). This range inevitably means that the collection offers sample studies, test cases and work-in-progress rather than the definitive scholarly last word. This is particularly the case when, in the Introduction, we try to recover something of the alternative voices so long marginalized or repressed.

We hope that students of this (massive) area will respond to these studies in the spirit they are offered – as attempts at an initial map of the ground, made to facilitate further study, analysis and commentary. Concerned to offer a critique of dominant images *and* to refer to a wide range of alternatives, this collection of necessity combines polemic and survey. While we have usually placed the broader 'overviews' early in the book and more singular case studies after, many essays predictably mix descriptive and polemic elements. This is most evidently true of our extended Introduction – but excusably so we hope in view of the number of issues it seeks to address. There, especially, but everywhere else in the book too, we hope readers will respond to what is speculative, partial or schematic by joining issue, by reading and writing more. The battle for meaning won't stop here.

Alf Louvre
Jeffrey Walsh

Acknowledgements

The publishers and the editors gratefully acknowledge permission to reproduce material from the following works:

The Virginia Quarterly Review for 'Soldier Poets of the Vietnam War'.
Prose Studies for 'The Reluctant Historians: American Culture Critics of the 60s'.

For comic illustrations in Chapter 5

D C Comics Inc. for figures 1 and 7 which are from *Our Army at War*, Nos. 236 and 250. These are trademarks of D C Comics Inc., New York. Illustrations © 1971; © 1972 D C Comics Inc. Used with permission.
Marvel Comics Group for figure 2 from *Sgt. Fury and his Howling Commandos*, No. 9.
Charlton Publications for figures 5 and 6 which are both from *Fightin' Marines*, 1967, No. 77 (November).
Last Gasp Press for figure 8 from *Nasty Tales*, No. 5, 1971.

For cartoon illustrations in Chapter 6

Evening Standard Co. Ltd. for figures 2, 9 and 10.
New Statesman for figure 1.
Syndicate International (1986) Ltd. for figures 16 and 17.
Mirror Group Newspapers (1986) Ltd. for figure 13.
The Daily Telegraph for figure 11.
The Sunday Telegraph for figures 4, 5, 6, 8, 12 and 14.
Ralph Steadman for figures 19 and 20.
Gerald Scarfe for figures 3, 7, 15, 16, 17 and 18.

The editors also wish to thank Ray Cunningham and the staff at Open University Press for their courtesy, encouragement and efficiency.

Many of the essays that are included in this volume originally arose from a project at Manchester Polytechnic called EVAC which studied the effects of the Vietnam War upon American culture and they were shaped by discussions at a research seminar hosted by the Department of English and History. In the running of this seminar and in the project generally, Alan Fair (who was the EVAC research assistant) played a major part: we are grateful for his scholarly contribution. Thanks also to Paul Vesty, Dave Olive, Liz Yorke, Theresa Wilkie, Tony Martin and Dave Harker who all contributed to the work.

For her patient and excellent typing, our sincere thanks to Kathy Wilk, and for other administrative help to Carole Burns and Jean Roebuck. A final acknowledgement to Michael Crompton who enabled the project to get started and to David Melling and John Hopkin who supported it.

Jeffrey Walsh and Alf Louvre

Introduction

Vietnam visions: then and now

The resurgence of interest in the Vietnam War has become an international
cultural phenomenon: shelves of bookshops stocked with Vietnam War fiction;
conferences in places as far apart as Manchester and Sydney; cinemas around
the world showing *Platoon, Hamburger Hill* and *Full Metal Jacket*; educational
courses and weekly magazines – all carry the images and narratives of Vietnam
into the minds of a generation of young men and women from Kentucky to
Vienna. The second phase of America's Indochina war is being fought, this
time not in jungles or on paddy fields but on cinema screens and in the pages of
comics and pulp novels. Vietnam, formerly a hated cause, has become at last
the world's most popular war if we measure it in commodity terms and
audience engagement. The Vietnam War remains ideologically significant
because it is box office, transmitting deeply resonant meanings throughout
Western culture. The battle for meaning continues.

The particular circumstances of the Vietnam War made it infinitely open to
interpretation and misinterpretation; it was a war of ambiguity, of irony and
paradox, fought for apparently abstract, intellectual reasons – no member of
the National Liberation Front (NLF) threatened Wayland, Massachusetts.
The material nature of the second Indochina war, involving not only Vietnam,
but Kampuchea and Laos, generated political and moral overtones that are still
evident decades later. Vietnam was a profusion of wars, as Alasdair Spark has
called it: an imperialist war fought by a superpower against an underdeveloped
country, a war of revolution, a civil war, a war for national reunification, a
guerrilla war and a media war. Because the Afghanistan and Iran–Iraq conflicts
have not caught the popular imagination, Vietnam has been resurrected to
serve as all our wars, and America's cultural power ensures its complex

reinventions are richly based, supplied with the full resources of its culture industry.

Vietnam, then, is synonymous with a spectrum of attitudes and remembrances: it may for former activists signify the heyday of the anti-war movement; for young men it may conjure up visions of élite Green Berets; for the movie-goer it may be associated with the internecine struggles of *Platoon*. Which of these attitudes and what kinds of remembrance have won or are now winning dominance is the essential theme of this book.

On the television screen of the 1980s Vietnam has become hot property. A recent episode of an American detective series, *The Equalizer*, for instance, was based on the clichéd theme of the man who is haunted by his Vietnam visions and turns to social violence. An advertisement on British television for Carling Black Label beer portrays GIs in a dug-out, called upon to volunteer to face 'The Goons' out in the jungle darkness. One man, significantly reading *War and Peace*, refuses to leave his trench, thereby causing the watching 'Goons' to surmise that it is he who drinks the magical lager, the drink that makes you a man. The terrain and its coding have become so familiar, so nostalgic in fact, that 'Vietnam' can sell beer. The war has been interiorized, made over into icons of dulling familiarity that utterly dehistoricize it and unashamedly exploit its commodity value.

Television supplies further evidence of the dominant 'Namstalgia' of the late 1980s: the complex and brutal 10-year war has been sanitized, deodorized by the programme-makers and made safe for children through such series as *The A-Team, Magnum, Miami Vice* and *Airwolf*. In prime television slots on American national networks the war provides the subtexts, narratives and character credentials for a series of chart-topping programmes.

There is, however, evidence that future TV representation will broaden out from the detective or trouble-shooter veteran stereotype into more 'serious' depictions which will, like their contemporary movie blockbusters, shelter under an anti-war umbrella.[1*] This would be no surprise, for the evolution of new motifs in TV and in popular culture is the norm not the exception. Despite its apparently seamless imagery – the visual litany of helicopters, vets, napalm, the Green Berets, men evacuating the gravely wounded – television has been the site for continual and sometimes rapid reinterpretation. We should beware, however, of making the contrasts between depictions 'then' and 'now' (the '1960s' versus the '1980s', say) too dramatic or too unilinear.

Daniel Hallin, in an impressive study of the impact of American TV on the prosecution of the Vietnam War, has reminded us that media coverage during the late 1960s and early 1970s was a two-edged sword.[2] His thesis is that news coverage tended strongly to support the official line, despite the fashionable hypothesis of revisionist academics (such as the 'Accuracy in Media' group) that the 'big story' of the Tet offensive caused the American public to turn against the war. He says television news stories continued to be consensually pro-war and usually reported US tactical successes. He finds little evidence for dissenting television reporting.

* Superscript numerals refer to numbered notes at the end of each chapter.

Other scholarly work by such writers as Braestrup and Gitlin[3] has, nevertheless, pointed up the television screen's importance as a site of ideological *tension.* Messages of American military victory and moral justification were implicitly challenged by juxtaposition with stories of anti-war protest, draft-dodging, saturation bombing and US-sponsored atrocities. Television (like newspapers and radio during the period 1965–75), if not a radical beacon, exemplified the war's divisiveness, with its capacity to polarize even members of the same family. For Americans, Vietnam has always been an ambivalent and fiercely controversial war, and this remains true even in the 1980s, as arguments about the merits of the Washington memorial make clear.[4]

Any discussion of the public depictions of the war 'then' and 'now', whatever the parallels, whatever the contrasts, should not forget that the 1960s and 1970s were characterized by a spectacular outpouring of protest art. In this book we discuss the features of some of this art – in Laurence Coupe's account of British underground poetry, in Jim Aulich's discussion of the anti-war cartoons of Steadman and Scarfe, in Alf Louvre's essay on the radical critics Mailer and Sontag, and in John Storey's examination of West Coast Rock and the protest movement. Anti-war forces generated a plethora of voices and forms which, taken collectively, comprise arguably the United States' most radical cultural moment: politics and art were fruitfully intertwined. Protest art evolved experimental modes and adapted older ones to express angry opposition – and much recovery work by historians and critics remains to be done so that this radical work is properly recognized. Of course, by its nature, its trajectory was different from more long-term projects; its protocols were less to do with 'immortality' than with urgent remedial action.

But many works of popular culture, as this book shows, were rich, elaborate and complex structures: during the time of Vietnam 'ephemeral' art and expression often took on a 'serious' stature. In every field of popular culture there were outstanding practitioners and productions. Those most readily remembered are Tomi Ungerer in poster art, Jules Feiffer, Ralph Steadman and Gerald Scarfe in cartoon, *The Pentagon Papers* and the work of David Halberstam and James Cameron in journalism; in photography, Larry Burrows, Philip Jones Griffiths, Tim Page and Don McCullin; in music Bob Dylan and Joan Baez; in agit prop and street theatre Megan Terry; in film documentary *The Anderson Platoon* and *Winning Hearts and Minds*; in popular poetry the work of Allen Ginsberg. The flavour of the period is detected in its characteristic manifestos and exposés – Angry Artists Against the War, the Winter Soldier Investigation, the scandalous *Pentagon Papers*, the anonymous satire *Report from Iron Mountain*. It was a period of visible radicalism and of a searingly critical art that exemplified the deep divisions of the culture. And it is, as ever, crucial to be historically aware of earlier radical and pacifist responses when faced with the view prevalent in the late 1980s, i.e. that Vietnam was a timelessly 'tragic' war with a kind of 'lost generation' glamour. Crucial because the suppression of memory, of remembered alternatives, is one means by which dominant views win their power.

Such (willed) amnesia can take various forms. The movies, comics, pulp novels and TV programmes purporting to tell the truth about Vietnam in the 1980s repeatedly suggest that Vietnam was an arcane and unique war absolutely distinctive in every respect. Yet there is usually little mention of what was *historically* specific – nothing about the Army of the Republic of Vietnam (ARVN), or the political origins of the war, or on the nationalist ideals of the North Vietnamese Army (NVA) and NLF – rather the movies and the comics focus more or less exclusively on what *are* allegedly unique (the rites of passage, the initiations of American boys). Such an approach ignores the contexts of the combat, its historical specificity *and* its resemblance to other conflicts.

For if the S.E. Asian conflict was in many ways distinctive (not least in its Cold War origins), yet in other ways it brings to mind other twentieth-century wars. For example, the Russian involvement in Afghanistan bears many resemblances: both are imperialist wars involving a superpower against an underdeveloped country; both indigenous populations are fiercely nationalistic, so making the war unwinnable for the occupying power; both are wars of attrition greatly dependent upon the outcome of guerrilla tactics ranged against helicopters. A recent article[5] has compared the problems that faced returning American vets with those encountered by Russian veterans; they suffer similar problems of re-entry into society, of marginalization, disorientation, post-traumatic stress and lack of approval. Indeed, Russian vets, in a curious irony, are privately collecting money to set up a memorial to their lost comrades. Like Vietnam in the 1960s and 1970s, Afghanistan, a far-off, confused and brutal war, carries no affirmative ideology for Russian soldiers in the 1980s. The point here is that Vietnam should be demystified and examined for what it is, a twentieth-century war with affinities to other wars, and not represented ahistorically as unique. The view often expressed in *Platoon*, for example, of its nature as a kind of universal epiphany of war, obscures its true character. Total American deaths in Vietnam, tragic and appalling as they were, were matched by British casualties sustained in the Battle of the Somme. It is important to retain such historical perspective and to resist the sometimes overwhelming pressures of contemporary mass culture to depict 'the Nam' as the 'ultimate' war, as uniquely horrific and special.[6]

The case of the veteran   *IMPORTANT*

It is essential, then, for those attempting a study of the war's cultural effects to sketch out a map of its changing representations, charting shifts and inflections. To observe the dynamics of these changes with their transitions, their fluctuating emphases and their suppressive silences, helps us to see the interactions of debate and myth-making. As ever, cultural images, whether dominant or subordinate, are constructed *and* constructive, both shaped by social circumstances and also an active agent in audience perceptions.

Vietnam has often been understood, as Harry Haines has argued,[7] by means of the 'sign' or metaphor of the Vietnam soldier or veteran, around whom a whole discourse has evolved. How this figure is perceived and constructed is of crucial significance as an index of ideology: narratives of his actions and thoughts are emblematic of meanings, values and attitudes in the wider culture. Indeed, we may claim that the cultural representation of the soldier and particularly the veteran is perhaps the single most influential ideological discourse of the war.

Formerly hegemonic genres such as the war film and the western would seem to bear out the argument that the Vietnam War threw established discourse into crisis – certainly the traditional war film had difficulties in representing Vietnam. John Wayne's *The Green Berets* (1968), a turgid, flag-waving version of Robin Moore's best-selling novel of 1965, is, as Antony Easthope shows, truly descended from *The Sands of Iwo Jima* (1949), the single most influential American film of the older 'realist' school. Apparently, Vietnam so traumatized this filmic form that it was not until 1978, a decade later, that a war film (Ted Post's *Go Tell the Spartans*) was produced dealing directly with combat in Vietnam. Only in the mid-1980s with Clint Eastwood's *Heartbreak Ridge* and Irvin's *Hamburger Hill* did the more recognizable, older war film resurface, albeit in a modified form. Vietnam had left its mark in the hard-bitten, anti-heroic overtones of both these movies and of Oliver Stone's *Platoon*.

Douglas Pye, in a seminal article,[8] has argued that a similar fate overtook the western: he coined the phrase 'Vietnam Western' to suggest the displacements that characterized a series of fine 1970s westerns seeking to allude obliquely to Vietnam. Films such as *Little Big Man, The Wild Bunch, Chato's Land, Ulzana's Raid* and *Soldier Blue* exemplified the tortured accommodations the western was then forced to make. Such movies reverse previous generic formulations and expectations by including scenes of massacres, rapes, mutilations and pillage carried out by white frontiersmen: hence the Indian population substitutes mythically for the Vietnamese devastated by Rolling Thunder. America is forced to confront its own genocidal past. The savagery that has now entered forever into the soul of the western, the noble heroic form of Randolph Scott, Gary Cooper and Alan Ladd, is henceforth seen in the violent post-Vietnam western of Clint Eastwood. Shane becomes High Plains Drifter. Americans can no longer psychologically lay legitimate claim to such a proud and dignified vehicle after the Vietnam conflict, and so the subsequent blood-spattered spaghetti westerns soullessly ghost for the real thing. American mass cultural innocence was the first casualty of Vietnam. Henceforth, other genres, such as the psychopathic thriller or the high-tech *Star Wars*, occupy the foreground: the Edenic pastures of American popular culture are defoliated.

As in the UK at present with regard to the Falklands conflict, popular culture in the US attempted to *ignore* Vietnam in the immediate post-war years. Writers such as the veteran W. D. Ehrhart have testified that it was virtually impossible for 10 years or so to persuade a publisher to take a book on the subject of the war. The reasons for such an absence from discourse are uncertain and one can only speculate upon the causes – guilt, despair, television overkill, the need for a period of mourning and contemplation, wounds inflicted upon the national psyche. A recent television interview with former president Gerald Ford is probably closer to the mark. He expressed his feelings of shame and helplessness in seeing his countrymen forced out of Saigon – such humiliation led perhaps understandably to a mood of collective amnesia. Whatever the validity of these speculations about why the war became marginalized, it is incontrovertible that the Vietnam veteran bore the brunt of the nation's impulse to forget. Veterans became a forgotten group in American culture and, in films and novels from, say, 1975 to 1982 (up to the time the memorial was inaugurated), they were represented as folk devils, demonized as psychotics, brutalized psychopaths and misfits.

As in most complex interactions between specific history and cultural myth the figure of the traumatized vet has some basis in fact. Various scientific studies have shown that the Vietnam veteran suffered a disproportionately high incidence of post-traumatic stress.[9] A new metaphor thus gained wide currency from 1972, that of the psychologized or troubled veteran who replaces or interacts with the earlier Green Beret figure. The earlier hero led an integrated platoon, but now a breed of loners or losers substitute for President Kennedy's Arthurian élite. Travis Bickle, the ex-marine of *Taxi Driver* (1976), and Rambo, the estranged hippie of David Morrell's thriller *First Blood* (1972), are vilified by society and changed into bad men, the detritus of a bad war. They both suffer marginalization, experience an identity crisis, are goaded into retaliation and eventually become versions of an older American literary type, the assailant victim. A whole series of movies such as the impressive *Tracks, Heroes, Cutters Way* and *Rolling Thunder* deploy such representations. In some of these figures, notably in Dennis Hopper's magnificent portrayal of the demented uniformed veteran in *Tracks*, the ideological contradictions of the war are symbolized most effectively. The cultural schizophrenia is expressed, for instance, in Scorsese's *Taxi Driver* in an ending equally as notable as that of *Tracks* or *Heroes*. Travis Bickle, his shaven head mohican-like, dies in an orgy of blood trying to cleanse the dirty streets of the city. This 'realist' ending is then subverted by a fantasy ending which expresses the vigilante Bickle's hopeless desire to be a real 'good guy' hero approved of by main street America, the sort of pure white Anglo-Saxon protestant (w.a.s.p.) figure who gets the girl and is admired by mothers and fathers as an exemplar for their children. Scorsese's contrary visions signify brilliantly all future Americo-centric versions of the war's after-effects: either the bloody truth of meaningless death or the presidentially approved fantasy of Rambo regeneration.

In 1978 three of the four most influential texts on the war appeared – Michael Herr's dazzling journalistic memoir *Dispatches*, and the academy award winning films *The Deer Hunter* and *Coming Home*. In 1979 *Apocalypse Now* appeared. As was the case in 1987, these texts seemed to create a kind of cultural moment, to signal a historical conjuncture when a new dominant vision of Vietnam began to emerge (a vision which lasted until the appearance of *Rambo – First Blood II* in 1985). The three films and Herr's impressionistic interpretation perceive the war in a radically different way. In place of the traumatized vet of, say, *Rolling Thunder* (1977) or the vigilante mafia-fighting vets of *Gordon's War* (1973) or *Mean Johnny Barrows* (1976), new overtones and associations are now evident of a broadly more sympathetic and complex kind. Hal Ashby's *Coming Home* is the least problematical of this new cluster of works, portraying principally the agonies of the physically disabled vet.

Dispatches explores different terrain, the war zones and the collective psychology of their inhabitants. It is often suggested that Michael Herr's ultra-subjective account of the war's craziness turned Vietnam into a 'post-modernist' war. Herr's book is a loose-leaf collage of impressions, individual insights and his personal interpretations of events. The effect is to stress the impossibility of arriving at fixed meanings or rational accounts of what was happening. Thus the conflict is, perhaps evasively, represented as atomistic and surreal. The material conditions under which *Dispatches* was first written may account in some measure for this. The book was initially a series of journalistic pieces for *Rolling Stone* hence the stress upon music, subcultural style, graffiti, argot and the semantics of dress. But as a representational model *Dispatches* has had some unfortunate consequences. This has probably resulted, through misappropriation and misunderstanding, in what Philip Beidler has aptly termed 'symbolic overkill', for example, in the surreal surfing scenes of *Apocalypse Now* or in the same film's rather pretentious ending when T. S. Eliot and Fraser's *The Golden Bough* are brought in as part of Kurtz's library. Interestingly, Michael Herr co-scripted the film (writing Willard or Martin Sheen's narrative) together with John Milius and Coppola himself. It has become obligatory, too, following Herr, to include rock'n'roll tracks in Vietnam movies – witness *Hamburger Hill* and *Full Metal Jacket* – and usually such movies feature reporters or news photographers. In *Dispatches* these new journalists and photographers, such as Tim Page or Sean Flynn, are treated as charismatic figures; in later movies such as *Hamburger Hill* they are reviled. Increasingly, commentators and commentary are thus placed in the fore-ground.

Both *The Deer Hunter* and *Apocalypse Now* tend to evade direct treatment of Vietnam in favour of more 'philosophical' considerations. The notoriously racist Russian roulette scenes of the former trivialize the war's impact, and its working class community is likewise symbolically unrepresentative. Coppola's *Apocalypse Now* like *The Deer Hunter* has some memorable scenes, yet it slides uneasily into a mythical mode equally as damaging as the earlier presentation that envisioned Vietnam as a war that screwed up veterans. It represents Vietnam, as does *Dispatches*, as a war for the initiated, whose arcane combat experience is mystically 'hip' and thrillingly complex.

The depiction of the veteran as a demented survivor haunted by drug addiction, fragging (the shooting of an officer by his own men) and loss of morale was remarkably persistent, but the 1978–9 films did begin to replace it. Steven in *The Deer Hunter* and the equally sympathetic disabled hero of *Coming Home* assist in the dismantling of the earlier stereotype.

Social interventions such as the Vietnam Veteran's Leadership programme and massive remedial work by ex-servicemen's groups and relief organizations laid the psychotic vet to rest (although he is exhumed from time to time, as in the recent *Equaliser* episode). Henceforth, the media constructs more positive images of vets such as Don Johnson of *Miami Vice* or the collective heroes of *The A-Team* or Thomas Magnum, for whom the war has been good therapy, turning them into well-adjusted, more rounded men.

In the early 1980s – from, say, 1982 to 1985 – a sequence of films and media shows revised an earlier codification of the war and placed the missing-in-action theme in the foreground, in which concerned and patriotic Americans tried to right former wrongs. Such a reworking is, of course, highly partial and usually consists of the rescue of GIs long incarcerated in Vietnamese prisoner of war camps. *Uncommon Valor* (1983), *Missing in Action* (1984), *Missing in Action II* (1985) and *Rambo – First Blood II* are the principal vehicles for this current of narrative (although pulp fiction, through such massively popular stories as Mac Bolam, draws heavily on it, as do TV serials such as *The A-Team*). Many of the recent gung-ho interventionist films coincide with early Reaganite doctrine and have affinities with the neo-cold war genre of anti-Russian movies such as Milius's *Red Dawn* (1985), *White Nights* (1985) and *Rocky IV* (1986). The most famous of these films (discussed at length in this collection), *Rambo – First Blood II*, depicts Vietnam as a client state of the Soviet empire.

From the veteran as psychopath through the veteran as hip, to the veteran as well-rounded and well-adjusted (he who has learned from not being broken by his experience of the war), and from the veteran as heroic avenger back (in present depictions) to anti-heroic visions of the poor bloody infantry – bitter, frustrated and mythically long-suffering – these multiple and accelerating changes in the dominant image of the man of battle signal at once an anxiety and a determination. The especially rapid shifts in the stereotype within the last 3 or 4 years (from the 'early' to the 'late' Reagan period) make dramatically clear what has always been evident; that is, that such depictions are an index of (shifting) attitudes toward the war in general, and hence of America's view of its own past . . . and future. It is to these broader underlying ideologies, particularly the powerful conservative perspectives of recent years, that we now turn.

Dominant meanings, dominant modes

In offering a chronology of different stages in the interpretation of the Vietnam War we run the risk of suggesting that each phase was self-contained, or vacuum-sealed. But, of course, the transitions from one phase to another and indeed the establishment of dominant views in any one period inevitably involve struggles between *contending* versions of what the war meant and why it mattered. In moving now to generalize about those representations of the war that secured wide popular assent, we must remember that this assent was neither easily nor immediately won and that dominant images and accounts even at their most powerful carry the marks of this struggle.

This was evident in two themes central to the conservative readings so prevalent in recent years. American manhood – so the Rambo sequence tells us – is innately equal even to the desperate tasks presented by Vietnam (given military and political will). But having to state and demonstrate what (before the defeat) would have been taken for granted, these texts make masculinity so prominent as to raise questions and doubts about it. Likewise, the depiction of an American community (on whatever scale) unified in purpose to prosecute the war or healed and restored afterwards, is possible only at the cost of forgetting real events and distorting the enemy. For confronting the facts of what was *done* to the *Vietnamese* threatens the values that the American community traditionally proclaims (not least the right of self-determination, i.e. independence).

The power *and* the instability, the confidence *and* the anxiety, in sum the ideological effortfulness of the process of winning dominance (for conservative, or any other views), is what concerns us next.

Being a man: 'Then I too will be a warrior'[10]

Cultural practices as different as the comic book and the fictive autobiography, the novel and the film are visited during the time of Vietnam by the same ghost – a masculinity so troubled but so defensively assertive that it seems appropriate (if ironic in view of established gender connotations) to call it hysterical.

The opening 'Then' of our quotation (the words of the son of a US soldier killed in Vietnam in the novel *Fields of Fire*) suggest a reflex action, determined by prior cause. The established Western myth, of course, is that a man's gotta do . . ., implying that the context, customarily some version of the struggle for survival at the frontier, forces his hand.[11] However reluctant the response, High Noon beckons.

Mailer's *Why Are We In Vietnam?* challenges the usual causal sequence suggesting that it is not necessary battles that make men, but men who make diversionary battles. Mailer shows American men, moreover, whose assertive masculinity routed into competition, combat, violence and at the end of the chain, warfare, masks homoerotic desires that cannot properly be confronted. Hence make war, not love, and its warrior, a product not of prior conflict embraced, but the desired embrace spurned. As usual in Mailer irony eventually undercuts bravado – the hero's decision to leave for the frontier of highest risk (Vietnam no less) stands as the signal of the profoundest cowardice. 'If there had been no Vietnam, he would have had to invent one',[12] so we are told of one of the characters in *Fields of Fire*: Mailer explores the nature of the necessity that fathers that invention.

Such repressed eroticism, however, returns – whatever attempts are made to disguise it – in battle dress. Figuratively (and in the case of comic drawing and contemporary popular film, literally), rippling muscles burst through the constraint of uniforms: a warrior made so by the denial of sexuality becomes himself the sexual object. As Rambo or Sergeant Fury, he becomes the male for our gaze, perilously close indeed to conventional homosexual pin-ups. Beyond rules, beyond culture, beyond women, this aims to be an exclusive world of spartan self-sufficiency, but it is one whose male strength and athleticism inevitably bring in their wake what they initially intend to avoid – male beauty.

The precariousness of 'masculinity' is evident elsewhere. In a narrative device frequently encountered in films, novels and comic stories, the querulous, detached observer, the man apart from other men, the critical noncombatant, is 'converted' by his experience into affirming the stance of the majority, and is effectively *enlisted*. Of the texts analysed in this volume, the comic tale 'The War Criminals' and the film *Who'll Stop the Rain?*[13] (like many others) thus wish away the figure of opposition; but to wish him away they must first present him. Importantly, the critical observer has two faces: he is seen as the dissenting voice, as a liberal, as the photographer or the writer, as the recorder rather than agent of the action, i.e. an intellectual; however, in a contaminated chain of association (because he is 'educated' and 'civilized'), he is also shown as being soft, as being out of touch with instinct, as being weak, thin, pale, cowardly, skinny, unmuscled, womanly, boyish. The frequency with which such figures and the mechanism of their conversion are met suggests the degree of disruption suffered by the inherited generic formulae at the time of Vietnam (whether of war film, novel or comic).[14] The confident pattern of assumed comradeship and coherence among military men (if traditionally qualified by a cynicism about the nous of higher officers) is now frequently at risk. The unmasculine dissident, for example Joker in *Full Metal Jacket*, often becomes, it seems, a necessary and central rather than marginal part of the formula. And so anxious and effortful are the interventions made in these fictions to contain this figure, that they unwittingly underline just what they would often deny, i.e. that masculinity is culturally constructed (and reconstructed) not 'natural'.

Anxieties about masculinity are also interwoven with class guilts. The observer-intellectuals (converted, as is the newspaperman in *The Green Berets*, in the course of the narrative) are usually middle class, lured in one way or another to participate in a war their brain or their conscience had told them to decline. The question that troubles them persistently and that otherwise might remain unanswered comes from the farthest reaches of ideology, beyond political beliefs and moral commitments, its source a construction of gender so naturalized that it presents itself only as the nagging reflex 'are you man enough'?

If, in a minor movement, there are working-class figures (grunts like Hicks in *Who'll Stop the Rain?*) who prove that as well as muscles they have intellect, then, in a more common crossing of boundaries, the intellectuals are determined to show their brute strength. Converse (the early hero of *Who'll Stop the Rain?*) and Hicks (his replacement) share an enthusiasm for Nietzsche – precisely the intellectual of intellectual renunciation. And outside of fiction (perhaps), Mailer himself – in *Why Are We In Vietnam?* so evidently conscious of the masculating pressures – is recurrently drawn into the role of the brawling brain, the best American novelist-cum-boxer. Significantly, this is particularly so on the occasion of his most sustained act of intellectual and moral dissent, the book of the march, *Armies of the Night*. Here, in a strategy akin to the saintly self-effacing catharsis conducted by Rojack in *An American Dream* (in his eyes delivering the nation of its bile, spleen and repressions), Mailer embodies all the qualities of populist masculinity. Gutsy, foul-mouthed, drunken, competitive, measuring himself against all-comers from Lyndon Johnson to Robert Lowell, he enacts, parodies and eventually explodes the prejudices that issue from the legendary, mid-west, small-town, hard-hat, all-American male.

Here, however, the observer – in this case the self-conscious narrator – remains at a distance, dissecting the masculine instincts of the protagonists from the sidelines.

Mailer is, of course, by no means the only narrator to retain his detachment. In many of the personal memoirs of the war and in the books of such writers as Larry Heinemann, Ward Just, Stephen Wright and David Halberstam,[15] as well as frequently in drama and poetry, we encounter those who voice disillusionment and scepticism, whose reluctance simply to do or say the manly thing gives the lie to the vision of unanimity conservative texts promote.

None the less, the power and appeal of this vision needs accounting for. The accommodation within conservative narratives of the erstwhile critic of the war, and his enlistment to 'the cause' is not to be seen merely functionally as a conspiratorial ploy to deceive the popular audience into forgetting the degree of opposition to the war. More significantly, we might recall Frederick Jameson's account of popular fiction[16] and suggest that these accommodations represent the Utopian desire for a genuine communality, for an organic unified action-in-concert where the antagonisms born of regional, racial and social differences – not least between intellectuals and 'the people' – cease to exist. Even in texts where the 'commentator' remains obstinately unconverted the same Utopianism can surface. And while texts may show the war was not, *in fact*, the occasion of organic cohesion, their protagonists can yet dream sorrowfully or in anger of how it could have been, if only. . . .[17]

This vision of social cohesion, so prominent in conservative depictions, is precisely what in legend, myth and ideology, war so often offers.

Losing memory: 'unencumbered by history'[18]

The cost of Utopian cohesiveness, with its exclusive concentration on the powers of the American man or the needs of the American community, is a corresponding neglect of Vietnam and the Vietnamese – the enemy becomes faceless, the war anonymous.

The enemy is 'faceless' because, in comics and cartoons, he is either literally missing from the frame, or imaged with features that signal only the familiar 'menacing' stereotypes, while in film he becomes merely the body for grotesque destruction. The war becomes anonymous because incidents depicted or recollected in popular fictions are so selected and selective that they appear chiefly as instances of *traditional* military heroism or competence.

The flashback scenes apparently obligatory in *The A-Team, Magnum P.I.* or *Airwolf* offer precisely conventional valour and expertise. The first comic devoted to the war – *The Nam* – does indeed name it: but this is possible only a decade after the war ended and in an inflection made nostalgic by distance, a distance that works to equate this war with others traditionally celebrated in that medium. The last *Rambo* film marks the limit of these tendencies: the account is so selective, the temporal distance so manipulative that the fact of defeat itself can be forgotten, the enemy now wishfully rendered only as countless corpses. In the poet Jan Barry's phrase, many popular fictions are 'unencumbered by history' – by the naming particularity that would bring in its wake the guilt, shame, self-accusation and the internal divisions that the national myths function by repressing.

The same might be said of some of the most prestigious artefacts to treat the war. Works such as Caputo's *A Rumor of War* or films – usually with a jungle setting – such as *Platoon* or *Apocalypse Now* offer a collective retreat into metaphysics, the view that war is to be seen as a darkness of the soul, an ordeal of the fallen, a version of hell, an apocalypse)

In stark contrast to such metaphysics (what Herr all too accurately called 'the Heart of Darkness trip') are those literally self-conscious writings which concentrate on closely observed immediate experience. Yet for all their 'authenticity', their naming of people and places, these personal memoirs and autobiographies often fail sufficiently to render Vietnam's alien context and inhabitants. Despite the wealth of personal information the autobiographical mode provides, its evident concentration on *one* individual's psyche limits the breadth and range of its witness. Kovic's *Born on the Fourth of July*, Mason's *Chickenhawk*, Caputo's *A Rumor of War* and Tim O'Brien's *If I Die In a Combat Zone* tend, in other words, to shade into what we might call the 'fictive realist' mode, perhaps the principal mode of discourse about the war.[19] Novels such as James Webb's *Fields of Fire* or John Del Veccio's *The Thirteenth Valley* and plays like *Tracers* give us (as can the memoirs) graphic recreations of drill, of drug-taking, of combat and intimate accounts of platoon-life, of weapons, of C-rations and the rest. Their central technique – *the* realist claim – is to offer an 'unmediated' slice of life, a window on reality. But such works, claiming to be unproblematical, to tell it like it was, actually constitute a clearly established, highly conventionalized fictional discourse whose recurrent scenes (the drill field, the first firefight) reveal the influence of *inherited* conventions and *common* ways of seeing over what is only apparently 'personal experience'.

Faced, then, with a range of discursive modes – from 'documentary' to 'fantasy', from the 'mythic' to the 'realist' – which all in one way or another seem to evade or conventionalize the actual incidents of the war and the identity of the enemy, it is easy to become pessimistic. But even looking back from the standpoint of the conservative late 1980s we would do well to remember the efforts of those radical film-makers, photographers, artists and writers who in one way or another sought to confront rather than evade the historical.

This confrontation occurs in some surprising places and is often absent where we might most expect to find it (as Jeff Walsh's comments on the *early* artefacts in the *Rambo* cycle and Robert Hamilton's investigation of photo-journalism, respectively, make clear). The quality of the radical contribution made by 'underground' comics (in the US) and by 'underground' poetry (in the UK) is, Dave Huxley and Laurence Coupe suggest, considerably at odds with the probable imaginings of popular memory: in fact the former addressed the war only rarely, the latter in a manner that often owed more to the continuing force of established poetic tradition than the demands of the moment. Perhaps, most strikingly of all, radical discourses are often made, so it seems, not by direct statement, by plain-speaking recognizably 'historical' narrative or moral denunciation, but by indirection (by parodic excess, surrealism, or understatement), by the self-conscious reluctance to mouth orthodox truths, by insistent reminders to the readers of the gulf between writing, reading and living the war.

If, in general, poster art, rock lyrics and Mailer's fictive and autobiographical outbursts typically follow the strategy of parodic excess (as do the novels of Vonnegut, Eastlake and O'Brien, and the plays of Terry and Heller), what is evident in the memoirs of Sontag, the novels of Stephen Wright and especially in the daunting particularity of the poetry of the veterans is the minimalist strategy that insists (explicitly in the prose, implicitly in the poetry) on the horrific magnitude of even a single event in this history. Against what was to become in the 1980s the glib fluency of reactionary nostalgia, these radical writers haltingly, stutteringly hold to their memory. Likewise, poets such as Balaban, Enright and Fenton forego personalized moral denunciation, instead sustaining a distance which allows them to see modern Vietnam in the redemptive contexts of longer histories and older cultures.

Faced with the dilemma John Balaban writes of, at a time when it is 'A lie to speak, a lie to keep silent',[20] radical interventions thus tend either toward an effusiveness whose exaggerations reveal the lies of normal political speech or toward statements whose evident omissions, whose partialness, whose reticent rather than expansive manner continually announce the dangers of an articulation that nevertheless must be attempted. Either way, the dominant effect is of a literally awful irony: the history that the myth so often represses returns with a vengeance. Across the radical poster using the photograph of bodies at My Lai is overprinted a simple extract from the command dialogue of that day 'Q: And children too? A: And children.'

Jan Barry's poem suggests that those who were once unencumbered will end up obsessed by history:

Unencumbered by history
our own or that of 13th-century Mongol armies
long since fled or buried
by the Vietnamese
in Nha Trang in 1962, we just did our jobs[21]

Wider perspectives: other visions, other voices

In the West the Vietnam War has usually been represented from the viewpoint of white American combat troops, its other participants frequently ignored or marginalized. If one antidote to dominant interpretations is to look *back*, to recall (as we have tried to do briefly) radical and counter-cultural interventions, another is to look *beyond*, to attend to more than the usual range of witnesses. It is time that we listened to alternative voices abroad and at home, to those outside the mythic community of happy American warriors and their stereotyped adversaries – to women, to blacks, to the Vietnamese themselves. (What follow can only be brief and schematic bibliographies, but these and the notes that accompany them will, we hope, help further study.)

Vietnamese voices

Martin Novelli has demonstrated that the depiction of the Vietnamese in American war films, with one or two meritorious exceptions such as *Go Tell the Spartans* (1978), is woefully racist and stereotyped.[22] In a succession of films ranging from Fuller's *China Gate* (1957) and Mankiewicz's *The Quiet American* (1957), extending through *The Green Berets* (1968) up to *The Deer Hunter* (1978) and *Rambo – First Blood II* (1985), Vietnamese civilians are usually shown as passive victims, prostitutes, or conniving with the enemy, while North Vietnamese soldiers or NLF guerrilla fighters are frequently drawn as cruel torturers or effeminate cowards, or represented as invisible save for the occasional evidence of their murderous deeds. In general, the attitude of the films is that the Vietnamese will not fight fairly in a direct 'manly' way. We may speculate that the ideology of such films speaks of several basic and widespread public attitudes toward the war; for example, that the ARVN were incompetent and pusillanimous, that the war was rightly waged against a worthless communist foe, that in its essentials it resembled the worthwhile war against those other 'slant-eyed' adversaries the Japanese in the Second World War and that militarily it was fought in an underhand, unAmerican way, i.e. if there had been set-piece battles, the US would have won hands down. Such attitudes die hard, and even in the excellent Kubrick film *Full Metal Jacket* (1987), there are deep contradictions in the representations of Vietnamese people. This film includes two stereotypical scenes showing Vietnamese prostitutes and one showing petty criminals, yet its conclusion sympathetically depicts a Vietnamese girl sniper portrayed as fighting for a worthy nationalist cause.

   The dominant racist characteristics of the Vietnamese in American feature films go back to such Second World War movies as *Batan* (1943). But, like other media, film too has another way of treating Vietnam and a cluster of alternative documentaries sensitively and humanistically bear witness to the reality of the conflict for the men, women and children of Vietnam. David James, in an essay called 'Vietnam and the Media',[23] has analysed several of these documentaries, of which Felix Greene's *Inside North Vietnam* (1968) is perhaps the most famous. Greene's film was censored, although initially backed by CBS. Emile de Antonio's *Year of the Pig* (1969) is discussed by James as a film which showed that Vietnam's history was 'the site of competing discourses rather than . . . a single unified text'. Nick Macdonald's *The Liberal War* (1972), James believes, is also technically interesting for its break with realism, its simple use of props, and its stark committed account of American war crimes, including genocide. Such films are diametrically opposed, ideologically speaking, to such feature films as *Rambo*.

A range of material other than documentary film exists for an understanding of the many Vietnamese voices and viewpoints. Apart from footage in such television documentaries as the acclaimed P.B.S. *Vietnam: A Television History*, there is a wealth of printed books and pamphlets. These may be separated conveniently into different categories: for example, the first-hand reports and memoirs of Western journalists and reporters, the writings and literature of Vietnamese people in translation, Vietnamese political pamphlets and manifestos of the period and, finally, academic and scholarly treatises upon the war and its impact.

The Vietnam War probably generated the best reporting of any war, journalists of many nations sending back a stream of impassioned and well-researched dispatches from the front. In the British press John Pilger (an Australian), James Cameron, David Leitch and Philip Knightley addressed such issues as saturation bombing, refugees and defoliation; on British television Brian Barron, Tom Mangold, Michael Charlton, Julian Pettifer and a host of other commentators brought 'the living room' war home. For the student of the period many of these first-hand accounts have been collected in book form. Taken collectively they provide a powerful source of evidence about how the United States devastated the Vietnamese countryside, villages and cities. Harrison Salisbury's *Behind the Line – Hanoi* (1967), John Gerassi's *North Vietnam: A Documentary* (1968) and John Pilger's *The Last Day* (1976) typify this genre of witnessing commentary. Its retrospective impact is deeply moving.

And there are, of course, texts voicing the thoughts and opinions of those people most profoundly affected by the conflict – the Vietnamese themselves – though it is, naturally, easier to find the views of the influential, of generals or senior politicians than those of ordinary villagers or foot soldiers. The commanders who fought on opposing sides – General Van Tien Dung of the Vietnam People's Army in *Our Great Spring Victory* (1977), or General Tran Van Don, an important military figure within Saigon, in *Our Endless War* (1978) – interpret the war, predictably, as liberation or tragic defeat. More valuable are anthologies of the conversations and first-hand accounts of Vietnamese peasants, mothers and farmers. At least two excellent collections of such oral history were published – Ly Qui Chung's *Between Two Fires: The Unheard Voices of Vietnam* (1970) and *We the Vietnamese: Voices from Vietnam* (1971).

Although difficult to obtain, translations of Vietnamese literature are now becoming available. One of the foremost translators and editors of such work is

the poet, John Balaban, whose *Ca Dao Vietnam* (1983) is a bilingual anthology
of Vietnamese folk poetry. Balaban is a considerable authority on Vietnamese
life and culture. His own work, especially his poems such as *After Our War*
(1974) and *Blue Mountain* (1982), and his novel *Coming Down Again* (1985),
recreate imaginatively the impact of the war both upon the Vietnamese and
Americans. Like *Ca Dao Vietnam*, an earlier anthology, *Of Quiet Courage*
(1974), edited by Jacqui Chagnon and Don Luce, includes impressive poetic
translations of Vietnamese poetry. Poetry is probably the most accessible
literary form for non-Vietnamese speakers, but there are also a number of
novels translated into English and written by Vietnamese. One of the most
interesting is that of the young woman novelist, Minh-Duc Hoai-Trinh (*This
Side . . . The Other Side*, 1980) which explores how Vietnamese fought each
other. The narrative is based upon the dramatic conflict between a daughter
compelled to become a Saigon 'hostess' and a son who fights in a communist
unit in the North. Other novels tend to be more overtly political, such as
Anh-Duc's *Hon Dat* (1969), which is a committed work espousing the cause of
the NLF. Clearly, it is valuable to read as much of this literature or oral history
written from the many Vietnamese viewpoints as possible.

Such reading provides a unique perspective on the war, and differs in tone
and character from the many novels written by Americans and Europeans
whose subject matter is often concerned with Asian life and culture.
Nevertheless, some such novels do offer a sympathetic and profound understanding of the situation of Asian men and women caught in the war zone and
through no fault of their own suffering great dislocation to their lives.
Outstanding among such fiction are novels by Graham Greene, Asa Baber,
David Halberstam, Smith Hempstone, Morris West, John Clark Pratt, Charles
McCarry, Loyd Little, Robert Olen Butler and Donald McQuinn.[24]

As this discussion has shown, there are varied perspectives upon the
Vietnamese struggle and eventual victory over the United States. It is a good
idea to concentrate on the ideological underpinning of the nationalist cause – a
biography of Ho Chi Minh will help here as will Douglas Pike's book on the
Vietcong[25] or Jeffrey Race's excellent exploration of ideological differences
between Americans and the NLF in *The War Comes to Long An* (1972). Le
Duan's *The Vietnamese Revolution* (1971) is perhaps the best single document
for an understanding of the revolutionary dimensions of the conflict.

It is useful, too, to consider the various phases of the war, to place Thich
Nhat Hanh's account of the Buddhist story in *Vietnam: Lotus in a Sea of Fire*
(1967) alongside Don Luce's exposé of the Saigon government's political
prisoners (see his *Hostages of War*, 1973) or Frances Fitzgerald's classic
historical account of Vietnamese life and culture (*Fire in the Lake*, 1972). Two
memoirs that treat the war's aftermath are Lady Borton's *Sensing the Enemy*
(1984), which narrates the author's involvement with the Boat People of the
early 1970s, and W. D. Ehrhart's *Going Back* (1987), which recounts the
author's return to Vietnam in the mid-1980s.

There is no shortage of well-written studies about the historical legacy of the
war for Vietnam and its people. There are biographies of most of the leading

political figures such as Ngo Dinh Diem, Thich Tri Quang and General Vo Nguyen Gap, accounts of atrocities such as Jonathan Schell's impressive *The Village of Ben Suc* (1967) and sensitively written analyses of Vietnam's social structure, economy, family life and customs (see Don Luce and John Sommer's *Vietnam: The Unheard Voices*, 1969).

Despite the abundance and intellectual quality of many of these commentaries the mass media have continued to misrepresent the war abysmally. The film industry, for example (with the honourable exception of *The Killing Fields*, which treats what is now Kampuchea under Pol Pot's Khmer Rouge), has not produced a single feature film sympathetically showing the endurance and heroism of the Vietnamese people. Even such television documentaries as have been made in the 1980s (although occasionally treating the refugee problem and Pol Pot's atrocities) tend to stress the unpleasant aspects of communist life under the Hanoi regime. Typical of such films is *We Can Keep You Forever*, made by Lionheart films and shown on British television in 1987, which reported sightings of American missing-in-actions (MIAs) and stressed the repressive cruelty of the Vietnamese. The culture industry, through its exploitation of the MIA theme in such films as *Rambo, Missing in Action* and *Uncommon Valor*, has not so far balanced such representations by narratives of Vietnamese, Kampuchean or Laotian casualties. Although new films such as *Full Metal Jacket* or *Platoon* are often admired for their realism, such 'realism' does not so far extend to allowing credence or recognition to the fact that the world's greatest superpower was defeated by a poor but resolutely organized small nation fighting for self-determination.

Women: the peaceable warriors

Popular myth has a nasty habit of perpetuating dominant ideologies, and it is not difficult to demonstrate how mass cultural representations of the Vietnam War have generally ignored the participation of women in the conflict. In popular television series such as the *A-Team, Magnum P.I., Air Wolf* or *Miami Vice*, whenever Vietnam is mentioned it is in the context of élite masculinity. With a few notable exceptions, such as *Purple Hearts, Coming Home* and the film based on C. D. Bryan's *Friendly Fire*, film versions of the war have similarly scaled down or excluded the part played in it directly or indirectly by women. In most film narratives, and this is true to an extent even of *Coming Home* or *Purple Hearts*, women are functionally included to supply romantic interest. Typical films include *The Deer Hunter* and *Rambo – First Blood II* where the women are depicted in subsidiary roles which emphasize the suffering or heroism of their men. If one were to judge solely from such productions it would appear that women's lives were only marginally affected by the war, but in the case of Asian women it has been estimated that there were 300,000 prostitutes in Vietnam to 'service' 500,000 American military personnel and ARVN soldiers – sexual contact seemingly bridged the culture gap.

For more truthful and authentic accounts of how women responded to and were affected by the Vietnam War it is necessary to consult a range of alternative sources and, of course, writings and interviews by women themselves. There is, fortunately, much rich primary material available, which is immensely valuable in recovering a forgotten and so far excluded history. Only by reconstructing a spectrum of women's voices and opinions may we begin to understand more comprehensively the wider and lasting cultural effects of the Vietnam years.

To be fair to male historians many of the best known oral histories of the Vietnam era, such as Mark Baker's *Nam* (1981) or Al Santoli's *Everything We Had* (1981), include accounts by women whose lives were deeply affected by the war. In recent years, too, there has been growing interest in collecting and recording exclusively women's experiences from a variety of class perspectives. The most impressive of these volumes is Kathryn Marshall's *In the Combat Zone* (1987), which is an oral history of American women who served in Vietnam in various capacities, as army personnel, hospital nurses, red cross volunteers, journalists, air force flight crew, doctors, etc. *In the Combat Zone* is typical of much of the best women's writing about Vietnam in its fusion of ironic recapitulation, humour and powerfully controlled emotional anger. It is an impressive record of first-hand experience and intelligent critical insight. Such first-hand women's accounts of the war are usefully supplemented by other witnessing, personal and group narratives such as Myra MacPherson's classic collective portrait of the Vietnam generation, *Long Time Passing: Vietnam and the Haunted Generation* (1984), and Gloria Emerson's tolerant and passionate *Winners and Losers* (1972). They form a humanistic, pacifist discourse against jingoistic, combat-centred stereotypes of the war. The power of many of these personal accounts by women is that they are unafraid to confront the depths of their feelings.

Women's autobiography and memoir, greatly in need of collection and evaluation, is able to provide an alternative perspective to the mainstream discourse of male veterans' personal accounts of the ordeal of combat. Contrastingly, most women's accounts of their experiences are concerned with the imperatives of preserving life, of enhancing its quality through medical work or involvement with refugee agencies and relief work. The best known of such works is Lynda Van Devanter's *Home Before Morning: the Story of an Army Nurse in Vietnam* (1983). Devanter's narrative typifies this genre of autobiographical recall. Like other works it laments the loss of life, deplores the masculine death instinct, and is sympathetic to Vietnamese casualties. Other authors such as Liz Thomas, Kate Webb and Philippa Schuyler echo Devanter's elegiac vision.[26] Kate Webb's *On the Other Side* (1972) is a magnificent account by a woman journalist of being captured by the enemy.

As Nina Adams has argued,[27] the Women's Liberation Movement was inextricably bound up with the anti-war movement in the US and, indeed, outgrew it. The number of feminist treatises that comment upon the war's ideologies and its impact upon women confirm Adams's hypothesis – Leah Fritz, Carol Lynn Mithers, Marge Piercy, Adrienne Rich, Pam McAllister, Susan Jeffords, Sheila Rowbotham and Susan Jacoby have all written interesting analyses of how Vietnam has radicalized consciousness in the Women's movement.[28] Non-violence has become a major feminist issue, and the Vietnam War has become a metaphor for other kinds of male violence, sexism and fantasies of sexual dominance, a point quickly evident to large numbers of women (often committed to a pacifist position) who participate in courses on the war.

Women's writing has sought to challenge the neat literary categorization so beloved in belletristic male surveys of the 'war and poetry' category. It is appropriate, therefore, to approach a territory provisionally marked out as 'the war and women's writing' in as open and flexible a way as possible, allowing the work of art critics such as Lucy Lippard or literary critics such as Marilyn Butler legitimate entry. The field of women's writing and the war is extremely interesting and virtually unexplored from both a literary and socio-historical angle. The area stretches from popular fiction to intellectual polemic. Both Evelyn Hawkins's *Vietnam Nurse* (1984 – 'She was a woman in a man's war'), a souped-up version of Della Field's earlier *Vietnam Nurse* (1966 – 'Natalie was needed by many men, but she needed a very special man in a Green Beret'), exemplify that genre of romantic fiction which forces women into sexual stereotypes and exploits the frissons created by women among large numbers of men. Such fiction is light years away from the radical political writing of Susan Sontag in *Trip to Hanoi* (1969) or the three Vietnam reports by the critical novelist Mary McCarthy.[29] Interestingly, other women of a politically high profile who opposed the war – in the US Jane Fonda and in the UK Vanessa Redgrave – have been demonized by men. Jane Fonda, in particular, is a folk she-devil and *bête noire* of paramilitary cultists in the US, as William Gibson has recently shown.[30] To be a woman *and* an outspoken radical like Jane Fonda is clearly more than many military-inclined men can bear.

It is unhelpful, then (to repeat an earlier point), to separate out ostensibly 'literary' pieces, such as Bobbie Ann Mason's fine novel *In Country* (1984), perhaps the best novel to explore the war's impact from a woman's point of view, from other kinds of writing. Such a novel benefits (because of its US post-war setting) from being read alongside earlier more topical pieces of a historical nature, because they restore some of the gaps in Bobbie Ann Mason's novel of enquiry and search. (Here we think of the analytical writing of Frances Fitzgerald in *Fire in the Lake* (1972) or the engaged, image-laden prose of Gloria Emerson in *Winners and Losers*.) What is needed is a catholic and uncanonical critical review that does not focus solely on narrowly-defined generic slots but on a range of writing. This archive might usefully take in such works as the anti-war poetry of Adrienne Rich, Denise Levertov and Diane de Prima as well as the Vietnam pieces of the journalist Judy Coburn (*Mother Jones*); it should accommodate easily both the experimental drama of Megan Terry in *Viet Rock* (1967) and Adrienne Kennedy's *An Evening with Dead Essex*, as well as the sensitive autobiographical memoir of Barbara Evans (*Caduceus at Saigon*, 1968), which relates her medical mission to Vietnam. There are many such works by women, sadly relatively unknown, such as Corinne Browne's moving memoir of the war's effects (*Casualty*, 1981).

The potential richness of this archive may be adjudged by the change of direction exhibited by women's writing about Vietnam in recent years. The earlier romance fiction (and there is astonishingly a third, early version of *Vietnam Nurse*, this time by Suzanne Roberts in 1966) has given way in the 1980s to serious works more concerned with material reality, such as Jeanne Holm's *Women in the Military* (1982). Replacing earlier romances such as *Love to Vietnam* (1968), *Games of Love and War* (1976), *Miranda* (1978), *A Boat to Nowhere* (1980),[31] in the 1980s we encounter a profound concern to recover women's history and authentic experience of the war. Many writers have clearly defined aims and projects to counter the 'shit, I was there' masculinist verité school. Doreen Spelt, Patricia Walsh and Lydia Fish, for example, wish to put the record straight once and for all about the mythic Vietnam nurse, commemorating the fact that at least ten women nurses died in Vietnam.

Arlene Eisen, in similar proselytizing vein, follows her earlier book about the women of Vietnam, and echoes the current widespread feminist commitment to solidarity with her Asian sisters in her book *Women and Revolution in Vietnam* (1984). Feminism is thus displayed in its true internationalist and anti-war colours. Another work which shows an identical internationalist and feminist trajectory is the collaboration between Wendy Larsen and Tran Thi Nga in *Shallow Graves: Two Women and Vietnam* (1986).

This efflorescence of women's writing about the war since 1984 suggests that women writers are once again finding Vietnam a significant site for discourse, ideological enquiry and personal expression. The recent work has usually taken two routes, the fictional and the oral-historical: Jayne Ann Phillips's splendid novel *Machine Dreams* (1984) follows the former path and *A Piece of My Heart: The Story of 26 Women Who fought in Vietnam* (edited by K. Walker 1986) the latter. Such works challenge the recently dominant male revisionism of the war expressed in such movies as *Rambo* or television series such as *The A-Team*, and threaten to blow it apart. Vietnam is perhaps the supreme test case for women's writing: if the women's movement can win the battle for meaning and show that the war affected women as much as it affected men then a citadel of male ideology – the combat fiction – will be taken.

'The black man's true subject'

The involvement of black Americans in the Vietnam War is inextricably bound up with the Civil Rights movement and the struggle against racism. Such racial discrimination was encountered in essentially two ways; first, in how the Draft was administered and, secondly, the day-to-day living of black soldiers in Vietnam. In the first instance, the Draft was inherently discriminatory. A research study has shown that in 1966 only 1 per cent of Draft Board members were black.[32] As Baritz has illustrated in *Backfire* (1985), his excellent study of the war's impact upon American society, 'poor black Americans were swept into the fighting war in "disproportionate" numbers'.[33] They thus had a far greater chance of being killed in action than better educated white soldiers. Research has demonstrated that, along with Hispanics and other ethnic minority groups, black Americans were given fewer opportunities for vocational training and were assigned to tougher and more dangerous jobs than their white counterparts.[34] Their fate clearly demonstrates both racism and the class system in action and, predictably, most works of popular culture, especially films, ignore the statistically large relative numbers of black soldiers in Vietnam. One film, *Hamburger Hill*, does portray a large percentage of black troops, but other representations, like the super hero, Mr T. of the *A-Team*, or the black sergeant in the comic *The Nam*, fit the stereotype of blacks as muscle-bound heavies.

As well as difficulties from the Draft itself, many blacks encountered racial discrimination within the military while in Vietnam, as Wallace Terry has verified from contemporary surveys. Terry's main point is that after 1969 black soldiers were far more radical and rebellious in spirit than those of 1966 and 1967. The effects of black power, the impact of the Civil Rights struggle and the resurgence of black subcultural style, expressed through dress, language and gesture, had been exported to the war zone. Many black brothers trained in weaponry confided to Terry that if conditions did not improve 'back in the World', then their skills in fighting would be at the disposal of such radical groups as the Black Panthers. What the war did was to intensify the process of their radicalization and heighten black consciousness.

Clyde Taylor's *Vietnam and Black America: An Anthology of Protest and Resistance* (1973) captures the sweep and energy of the great historical movement for Civil Rights in the 1960s and 1970s. Taylor's anthology offers a spectrum of voices including those of the most prominent Civil Rights leaders such as Martin Luther King Jr, Malcolm X, Eldridge Cleaver, Huey P. Newton and Stokely Carmichael. All of these leaders vigorously opposed the war, although advocating different strategies of resistance, from the non-violent protest of King to the more radical stance of the revolutionary activist Newton who offers, in a famous public letter, the support of his Black Panthers to the National Liberation Front of South Vietnam. As Taylor's collection demonstrates, within black consciousness the war was widely perceived as a racist one waged against Asian brothers: this attitude was strikingly prevalent among ordinary black grunts (infantrymen). *Vietnam and Black America* suggests the depth and comprehensiveness of black opposition to the war from intellectuals such as James Baldwin, sportsmen such as Muhammed Ali and writers such as Julius Lester and George Davis, author of *Coming Home* (1982), one of the key texts for understanding the black veteran.

David Pinchney has remarked that Vietnam 'is the black man's true subject', and the war undoubtedly acted as a focal point for black struggle and identity.[35] A series of studies has explored this from specialist political, social or psychological points of view, such as Robert W. Mullen's *Blacks and Vietnam* (1981) and Wesley Brown's *Tragic Magic* (1972). It is interesting to study the opinions and thoughts of black soldiers through the relatively new cultural form of oral history, and there is a first-class source book available here in Wallace Terry's *Bloods: An Oral History of the Vietnam War by Black Veterans* (1984). Such accounts of the lowly soldier may be usefully read against more revolutionary interpretations of the period such as Julius Lester's *Revolutionary Notes* (1969). What appears common in virtually all black accounts of the war is that the stance is oppositional, a position which is illustrated in Stanley Goff's seminal *Brothers: Black Soldiers in the Nam* (1982).

For black Americans Vietnam was one more example of oppression and inequality to include within the prevailing climate of injustice. Such a hypothesis may be confirmed from other sources and analyses. A search through the back numbers of *Ebony, Time, Life, Newsweek* and *Rolling Stone*, for example, yields verification. From such illustrated stories the philosophy and practice of black struggle may be gleaned as the resonances of the war years return, together with people, places and events that helped to shape the perceptions and values of black culture's opposition to the war – Angela Davis, Watts, Detroit, Cassius Clay, Alabama, the Fort Jackson 8, the deaths of Martin Luther King and Robert Kennedy, for example.

It is useful in complementary fashion to try to piece together snapshots of black combat experience 'over there' in Vietnam. A range of sources may be consulted: video material, of course, is valuable, as is (unexpectedly perhaps) war photography, which is generally exceptionally sympathetic to the causes of black Americans. The work of Felix Greene, Mark Jury, Tim Page, Larry Burrows, Don McCullin and, above all, Philip Jones Griffiths details visually the dilemmas of black soldiers in the various phases and situations of the war.

In literature the enterprise of representing the war experience of black Americans seems to have proved more difficult to achieve and, in some ways, is less successful than, say, the photographic records or the oral histories. Many works are nevertheless of great interest for their poetic insights and narrative pattern. There are, for example, a number of novels, such as Walter Kempley's *The Invaders* (1979), John Crowther's *Firebase* (1975), Ray Cunningham's *Green Eyes* (1976), Thomas Taylor's *A Piece of This Country* (1970) and John A. Williams's *Captain Blackman* (1972). Poetry is represented in Clyde Taylor's anthology by the work of such poets as Lance Jeffers, Imamu Amiri Baraka, Etheridge Knight and Askia Muhammed Touré. Such reading can be supplemented by two classics that record aspects of the black experience of Vietnam, David Parks's *G.I. Diary* and George Davis's much admired *Coming Home*.

As Mary Ellison has shown,[36] perhaps the least dramatic but most influential way that black America addressed itself in the Vietnam era was through its own musical culture. Ellison has demonstrated how the lyrics and styles of music performed by black artists articulated both a powerful undercurrent of protest against the United States' involvement in the war and also a deep sympathy for the plight of black veterans.

It is necessary then to examine other voices and other views if we are to address meaningfully the true histories of the Vietnam era. It is important that the particularities of evidence be uncovered and given due attention, and that this evidence be held in opposition to the ideologies of, say, the blockbusting film. For now *Rambo* is seen overseas in non English-speaking countries with sub-titles that equate the Vietnamese with the Japanese, the Russians with the

Nazis. The transformations of such an artefact show how ideological power is waged – even the slender historical referents it once made have now been wholly replaced by myth, cliché and stereotype. Such arrogant contempt for history is profoundly dangerous.

Reading culture: some notes on method

As should by now be apparent, a collection of essays that aims (among other things) to assess the impact of Vietnam on American culture faces daunting problems. On what grounds do its studies argue for the significance, the representativeness and the sufficiency of the texts examined? And what is meant by 'American culture'? These are directly related questions, for the range, quantity and nature of the texts taken for study will imply an approach to and a definition of 'culture'. In one inflection, 'American culture' connotes what is usually studied (the familiar selection of 'achieved' artefacts), in another, what is lived (the analysis of which might include texts of a different sort – the popular, the ephemeral and indeed the endless range of symbolic activities more familiar to the anthropologist than the critic).

At the outset, then, it may be useful to distinguish our approach from some current modes of cultural analysis. For instance, while several essays are concerned with prose fiction we do not offer a sustained specialist account along the lines of 'The American novel and Vietnam'. In our view that approach tends to overemphasize formal matters and in tracing developments in *one* genre can beg the question as to the significance of *this* genre in relation to others (among which other prose modes such as the memoir or diary come to prominence at the time of Vietnam). Traditionally, this kind of specialist generic study is untroubled by broader questions regarding institutional matters such as the circulation and the readership of its chosen texts. In a familiar sleight of hand, the 'achieved' text is taken to speak for its 'culture' regardless of popularity.

To this kind of idealism which shrinks cultural to conventional literary study, a cultural study stressing the data of the historical moment might seem a welcome alternative. Yet historically based empirical surveys of popular culture bring their own difficulties. Moving beyond the canonical artefacts, interested in the creative depictions of war-related events and incidents throughout the culture, such studies can replace the disciplined formal analysis that is the virtue of orthodox literary study with a reductive thematics. Countless artefacts can simply be seen as direct reactions to the events described in a historical discourse that is taken as unproblematic. A chronology is constructed, say, of the 'phases of the war' and texts read reflexively in relation to it. Such surveys can feature artefacts that speak more directly to and of American culture than those often found in literary-critical analysis. But historical surveys of the culture's 'shifts in mood' can take too much for granted. They can overlook the revision of the 'history' itself, one aspect of which has been the evident power of cultural *artefacts* retrospectively to confront and alter prior perceptions about, say, the nature of American engagement. In sum, such surveys may underestimate the *discursive power* of texts to alter the contours of the 'primary' (historical) account they are too easily read as merely reflecting.

Even the national referent in the phrase '*American* culture' cannot be taken as self-explanatory, for 'American culture' and the ideological assumptions it produces and promotes, is not geographically bound to the States of the Union, but is relentlessly exported and hence functions within and is of concern to the international (especially the Western) community. The need to consider the impact of the Vietnam War on the status and effectiveness of American culture and Americanism *abroad* adds further complications to our study. But, in view of the significance Vietnam held as a focal point for dominant ideologies concerning America's 'world role' as well as a rallying-cry to those radical oppositions evident in London and Paris as well as Washington, these considerations must be made.

We attempt to avoid at least some of the pitfalls described above. Sustained formal analysis of complex literary and film texts is prominent but we have sought to go beyond exclusively literary study by examining verbal, visual and aural artefacts in avowedly popular modes (hence we discuss popular novels, comics, newsphotos and songs). More 'conventional' literary material is, in any case, studied before its calcification into 'the canon' (most evidently in the work on the poetry of combatants). And, whether 'high' or 'low', we attempt to read texts in relation to the commercial and ideological pressures at work in different cultural institutions – novel, film and record production, newspaper and comic publication – not simply as autonomous statements from author, artist or singer. By *situating* texts in relation to these institutions, whose power relative to each other and whose capacity to resist or respond to radical intervention is of central interest to us, we hope to avoid the homogenizing tendencies of the survey, which flattens out the material distinctiveness of different institutions and different discourses in the search for thematic similarities.

There is a pronounced comparative tendency in this volume, with groups of two or three essays exploring different dimensions of novel production (from critically acclaimed 'post-modernist' texts to commercial blockbusters and film sequels), different aspects of film production (from conservatively realist to subversively allegoric modes) and the different trajectories of poetic discourse (whether of the British underground or the Vietnamese battleground). Still images are examined in several essays (on comics, newsphotos and cartoons), but here the temptation to compare *directly* and cross-reference must, as always, be tempered by an awareness of the particular pressures operating in each institutional context. Cumulatively, these related studies will, we hope, suggest something of the complex contours of different cultural practices. In opposition to a free-ranging survey where numerous aspects of cultural production are singularly read as constrained by nothing but the historical event they are finally seen to 'reflect', we offer several clusters of cognate pieces where the constitutive powers of given discourses, their relative capacity for originating the meanings and values circulating in the culture is at least tentatively suggested.

Working through these selective case studies will, we hope, also allow recurrent problems to be identified and analysed in a *multidisciplinary* way. For example, the range and effectiveness of anti-war protest is better understood if its various expressions are considered together: the writings of east coast intellectuals juxtaposed with the music of wést coast bands; political cartoons in Britain studied together with the news photograph that might have been published in the same newspapers; the poetics of the British underground set against American underground comics. It is thus possible to construct links and to begin to make comparisons between different artistic forms and genres.

Attempting such a synthesis, moving beyond specialist analysis to offer readings of a culture in 'crisis' (as this collection implicitly does) means, of course, taking up a position rather than offering 'neutral descriptions'. The periodization of analysis, the exact selection of texts, the questions addressed to them, the contextual setting in which they are placed are matters of choice, are constructions of critical commitment. The focus of *these* essays individually and cumulatively is on the ideological conflicts that accompanied the war, and their cultural representation.

We consider the struggle between contending versions of community as depicted in novel, film and song (where oppositional and alternative life-styles vie with a disillusioned liberal individualism and where both confront a traditional, conservative and, in America, a wishful vision of an organic society unified by the adversity of war). And we try to assess how far a traditional American precept, the belief in individual autonomy, survives the successive frustrations of American designs in Vietnam. In their formal and informal versions, American ideologies invest massively in individualism – in the transformative powers of political will, or inventive talent or military daring (each potentially a Lincoln or a Franklin or a Patton). But, as several essays attest, this belief was profoundly shaken by the intractable problems of Vietnam, a place where military and political initiatives ran aground and where inventive talent, accordingly, could take perverse and unheroic forms (of the sort *Catch 22* earlier made famous).

Reminding readers of these moments of personal and national doubt, of the critical interrogation of traditional wisdoms that was occasioned by the war is, we think, a necessary intervention when strident and chauvinistic revisions of America's role and the war's significance are still much in evidence.

Finally, we should make clear that whatever positions these essays collectively endorse, they adopt no single house-style nor any uniform method. There are a variety of critical approaches here and some inevitable tensions between them. Three kinds of method are perhaps most prominent.

Several essays (such as those on *Rambo*, on Sontag and Mailer and on Hollywood) adopt a predominantly formalist strategy: they seek to move from the scrutiny of a small number of 'texts' to generalization about the impact of Vietnam on a given cultural practice. As such, they most acutely confront the problem of 'typicality' or 'representativeness': do the chosen texts have the significance assigned them, are they a reliable index either in terms of the breadth of their popular appeal or subsequent developments in their genre?

Each of these essays emphasizes *mutation*; they explore those extradiscursive pressures and/or those interior contradictions as a result of which the genres and discourses *change* (whether progressively as in the films breaching the constraints of Hollywood realism or in reactionary fashion as in the *Rambo* cycle). Examining such transformations, these pieces draw attention to the possibilities of conflict and change even within powerful genres and discourses of a highly conventionalized kind.

In tracing the developments within a given cultural practice, in mapping the ideological and commercial pressures at work and in trying to specify in detail the *range* of reactions to, say, poetic, musical or graphic innovations, some of the essays here work through cumulative survey rather than selective formal scrutiny. (See, for example, John Storey on 'West Coast Rock', Laurence Coupe on 'British Underground Poetry' or Dave Huxley on 'American War Comics'.) This second mode of analysis attempts to supplement the contrasting 'positions' that feature in formalist schemata ('realist', 'modernist', 'post-modernist') by attending to the sometimes gradual, piecemeal and contradictory processes by which 'positions' are eroded and/or constructed. The development of new novelistic, poetic, lyric and graphic modes does not simply 'happen' by the natural unfolding of inherent formal possibilities, it requires active social interventions, creative and/or academic and/or commercial. Weighing the relative significance in such a process of artists, performers, reviewers, critics and polemicists as against commercial entrepreneurs as against the audiences (whose modes of consumption may also involve innovations – the rock 'festival' for example), is a necessary but difficult task. And, one equally necessary whether one examines 'popular' or 'high' culture. Indeed, *only* possible if one examines the full range of artefacts (since the mutual borrowings and corruptions of élite and popular forms are a frequent aspect of generic innovations at all 'levels').

This is one reason for the range presented in this volume. Another, closely connected is the necessity of examining popular as well as élite modes if discussion of the ideological impact of the war (our major concern) is to mean more than simply reading those singular artefacts ('great' poems, novels or plays) assumed to be the antennae of shifts in public mood. Attempts to define the ideological meanings at work in a culture, this is to say, to chart the changing patterns of dominance and resistance, must attend to their *material* circulation (to institutional matters of the conditions of production, distribution and consumption). This is our third kind of critical concern. Sometimes (especially in the study of ephemeral material, e.g. comics or cartoons) such a focus is an established component of the cultural survey.

Such *material* dimensions of cultural production about Vietnam almost inevitably give rise to subverting (and sometimes devastating) ironies. Textually, *Apocalypse Now* can be read as a critique of the logic-cum-psychosis of imperialism: the filming of it *reproduced* the conditions and relationships its statement (some say) attacked, i.e. from defoliation of the forest to the exploitative occupation of foreign territory. Evidently, the most profoundly difficult aspect of cultural resistance and innovation is, precisely, changing the material relations in the production and consumption of the 'artefact'.

This collection of essays is, of course, liable to the self-same ironies, because its attempt to offer alternatives to the contemporary rightward revision of the war in America is, in the end, inevitably compromised. To mean anything at all, to enter the discursive arena, like all the other representations of the war – its photographic images, its written histories, its filmic, novelistic and poetic recreations, its day-to-day reporting – it must first assume the ubiquitous shape of the commodity.

Notes

1. For example, the series *Tour of Duty* on US television.
2. Daniel Hallin, *The Uncensored War: The Media and Vietnam*, Oxford: Oxford University Press, 1986.
3. Peter Braestrup, *Big Story: How the American Press and Television Reported and Interpreted the Crisis of Tet in 1968 in Vietnam and Washington*, New Haven: Yale Press, 1983.
   Tod Gitlin, *Inside Prime Time*, New York: Pantheon, 1983.
4. See, for example, C. Howeth, 'The Vietnam Veterans' Memorial: Public Art and Politics', *Landscape*, 1985, **28** (2), p. 4.
5. Angus Roxburgh, 'Afghanistan Veterans to Build Moscow Memorial', *Sunday Times*, 22 November 1987.
6. This tendency is evident not just in popular culture but also in contemporary criticism. For example, for all the intelligence of its commentaries the special edition of *Cultural Critique* addressed to American Representations of Vietnam (No. 3, Spring 1986, edited by Richard Berg and John Carlos Rowe), recurrently represents the war as being not just conventionally meaningless but uniquely meaning-less. This seems to betray either a lack of historical imagination about how other participants felt about other wars, or an implicit imperialist claim to have produced the war to end all wars, a post-structuralist best of 'the worst'.
7. Harry W. Haines (Trinity University, San Antonio, Texas), unpublished doctoral thesis, 1986, p. 211 of Conclusion, 'Repositioning the Subject'. The thesis is especially concerned with revisionist theories of the Vietnam war and especially the A.I.M.S. response to the P.B.S. series *Vietnam: A Television History*.
8. Douglas Pye, 'Ulzana's Raid', *Movie*, 1981, 27/28 (Winter/Spring), p. 79.
9. Tom Williams (ed.), *Post Traumatic Stress Disorders of the Vietnam Veterans*, Cincinnati, Ohio: Disabled American Veterans, 1980.
10. The phrase 'then I too will be a warrior' is from James Webb, *Fields of Fire*, New York: Bantam, 1981, p. 389.
11. For an interesting discussion of masculine myths in popular culture, see Antony Easthope's *What A Man's Gotta Do: The Masculine Myth in Popular Culture*, London: Paladin, Grafton Books, 1986.
12. *Fields of Fire*, p. 34.
13. Released in UK as *Dog Soldiers*.

14. A version of this figure is found in Steven of *The Deer Hunter*, and in recent movies such as *Platoon, Full Metal Jacket* or *Hamburger Hill*; sensitive, innocent boys are turned reluctantly into killers. The popular comic *Nam*, is in essence devoted to the project of showing boys and adolescents that the Vietnam War was sadly inevitable but also heroic and, therefore, made you 'a man'. In fiction novels such as C. S. Stone's *The Coasts of War* (1966), William Wilson's *The L.B.J. Brigade* (1966), Donald E. McQuinn's *Targets* (1981) and the much acclaimed John Del Veccio's *The Thirteenth Valley* (1982) represent versions of the myth in widely differing forms.

15. Larry Heinemann, *Close Quarters*, New York: Farrer Straus and Giroux, 1977.
    Ward Just, *Stringer*, New York: Little Brown and Co, 1974.
    Stephen Wright, *Meditations in Green*, New York: Charles Scribners, 1983.
    David Halberstam, *One Very Hot Day*, Boston: Houghton Mifflin, 1968.

16. For his discussion of the Utopian aspects of popular cultural texts, see the conclusion of Frederick Jameson's *The Political Unconscious*, the closing sections of *Marxism and Form* and his article on 'Dog Day Afternoon' in *College English*, Vol. 38, No. 7 (March 1977), reprinted in *Screen Education*, No. 30 (Spring 1979).

17. This is, of course, the complaint and lament of John Rambo when he says in essence 'you wouldn't let us win' in *First Blood* (1982).

18. This phrase is from Jan Barry's 'In the Footsteps of Genghis Khan', included in the excellent anthology of veterans poetry, *Winning Hearts and Minds* (eds Jan Barry, Basil T. Paquet and Larry Rottman), New York: First Casualty Press, 1972.

19. Rather than give an extended note on novels of the war we refer the reader to valuable studies which contain bibliographical material and discussions of fictional modes. These are Philip D. Beidler, *American Literature and the Experience of Vietnam*, Athens, Georgia: University of Georgia Press, 1982.
    Merritt Clifton (ed.), *Those Who Were There: Eyewitness Accounts of the War in Southeast Asia, 1956–75, and Aftermath*, Paradise, CA: American Dust Series, Dustbooks, 1984.
    John Hellman, *American Myth and the Legacy of Vietnam*, New York: Columbia Press, 1986.
    Timothy Lomperis and John Clark Pratt, *Reading the Wind: The Literature of the Vietnam War*, Durham: Duke University Press, 1987.
    John Newman, *Vietnam War Literature*, Methuchen, N.J.: Scarecrow Press, 1982.
    Jeffrey Walsh, *American War Literature: 1914 to Vietnam*, London: Macmillan, 1982.

20. From 'Saying Goodbye to Mr and Mrs My, Saigon 1972', in *After Our War*, Pittsburg: University of Pittsburg Press, 1974, p. 80.

21. This phrase is also from Jan Barry's 'In the Footsteps of Ghengis Khan'.

22. Martin Novelli, 'The Depiction of Vietnamese in American War Films', Paper given at Popular Culture Conference, Toronto, 29 March 1984.

23. David James, 'Discourse of Presence/Presence of Discourse: the Vietnam Documentary', *Wide Angle 7*, 1985, No. 4 pp. 41–51.

24. For example, Graham Greene, *The Quiet American*, Harmondsworth: Penguin, 1955.
    Asa Baber, *Land of a Million Elephants*, New York: William Morrow, 1970.
    David Halberstam, *One Very Hot Day*, New York: William Morrow, 1965.
    Robert Olen Butler, *The Alleys of Eden*, New York: Horizon Press, 1981.
    Donald E. McQuinn, *Targets*, New York: Tom Doherty Associates, 1980.

Charles McCarry, *The Tears of Autumn*, New York: E. P. Dutton, 1975.

25. Douglas Pike, *Viet Cong: The Organisation and Techniques of the National Liberation Front of South Vietnam*, Cambridge, Mass.: M.I.T. Press, 1966.

26. Liz Thomas, *Dust of Life*, New York: E. P. Dutton, 1978. (The story of a nurse who worked before, during and after the Communist takeover in the South.)

Philippa Duke Schuyler, *Good Men Die*, New York: Twin Circle, 1969.

27. Nina S. Adams, 'The Woman Who Left Them Behind: Speculations on the Impact of the Vietnam War on Female and Male Politics', Paper given at EVAC conference, Manchester Polytechnic, September 1986.

28. See, for example, Leah Fritz, *Thinking Like a Woman*, New York: Win Books, 1975.

Carol Lynn Mithers, 'Missing In Action: Women Warriors in Vietnam', *Cultural Critique*, 1986, No. 3 (Spring), pp. 79–90 (especially recommended).

Marge Piercy, *Vida*, London: The Women's Press, 1980.

Adrienne Rich, 'Vietnam and Sexual Violence', in *On Lies, Secrets and Silence*, London: Virago, 1980.

Pam McAllister, *Reweaving the Web of Violence: Feminism and Non Violence*, Philadelphia: New Society, 1982.

Susan Jeffords, 'Friendly Civilians: Images of Women and the Feminisation of the Audience in Vietnam Films', *Wide Angle 7*, 1985, No. 4, pp. 13–22.

Sheila Rowbotham, *Women, Resistance and Revolution*, New York: Vintage, 1974.

Susan Jacoby, 'Women and the War', in *The Wounded Generation: America After Vietnam* (ed. A. D. Horne), New York: G. P. Putnam, 1981.

29. Mary McCarthy, *The Seventh Degree*, New York: Harcourt Brace Jovanovich, 1974.

30. James William Gibson, 'Paramilitary Culture and the Reconstruction of Vietnam', in *Vietnam Images: War and Representation* (ed. J. Walsh and J. Aulich), London: Lumiere Macmillan, 1988.

31. Pamela Sanders, *Miranda*, Boston: Little Brown, 1978.

Dina Brooke, *Games of Love and War*, London, Jonathan Cape, 1976.

Edith Morris, *Love to Vietnam*, New York: Monthly Review Press, 1968.

Maureen Crane Wartshi, *A Boat to Nowhere*, Philadelphia: Westminster Press, 1980.

See also, Maureen Crane Wartshi, *A Long Way From Home*, Philadelphia: Westminster Press, 1980.

32. See Martin Binkin and Mark J. Eitelberg, *Blacks and the Military*, Washington, D.C.: The Brookings Institution, 1982, p. 33.

33. Loren Baritz, *Backfire*, New York: William Morrow, 1985, p. 284.

34. This research from Charles Moskos Jr's book, *The American Enlisted Man*, is cited by Wallace Terry in 'The Black Soldier', an essay in *Vietnam and Black America: An Anthology of Protest and Resistance* (ed. Clive Taylor), Garden City, N.Y.: Anchor Press/Doubleday, 1973, p. 211.

35. We have, unfortunately, been unable to locate the source of this opinion expressed by David Pinchney but see also some key sociological texts of the period, such as Nancy Zaroulis and Gerald Sullivan's *Who Spoke Up: Protest Against the War in Vietnam 1963–1975*, New York: Doubleday, 1984.

36. Mary Ellison, 'Black Music and Vietnam', in *Vietnam Images: War and Representation* (ed. J. Walsh and J. Aulich), London: Lumiere Macmillan, 1988.

Antony Easthope

1

Realism and its Subversion: Hollywood and Vietnam

In Hollywood you can make any kind of film you want – so long as it's naturalistic (Francis Coppola in BBC interview, 1982)

We won't lose – 'cause we're Americans (Soldier in *Go Tell the Spartans*, 1978)

Coppola is right. Liberal and pluralist as it appears, Hollywood's commitment to cinematic realism is an imposition and a form of dogmatism, for it promotes certain values and proscribes others. Hence Vertov's attack on Hollywood as providing 'cinema-nicotine' and Godard's criticism in *Wind from the East* that 'Nixon-Paramount' has always 'made the same film, for fifty years'. Perhaps, but this essay will argue that the most interesting Hollywood films about Vietnam had to undermine the usual realist form in order to deal with the contradictions posed by the war and the American presence in it. I'll begin by trying to define and place American Vietnam War films in contrast both with a text from another culture, an Australian film on Vietnam, and one from an earlier historical period, a traditional American Second World War film.

Australia: 'Sands of Iwo Jima'

Australia fought in Vietnam from 1966 until August 1971, when the withdrawal of Australian troops was announced. According to Peter Pierce, the 'sustaining legend of the Australian troops' was that 'they were the finest in Vietnam . . .' both at killing the enemy and minimizing their own casualties.[1] In a commitment proportionately one-quarter of the size (for a smaller country) of the American involvement, over 500 Australians were killed in the war; the province they died for was called Phuc Tui. An Australian film about the war,

The Odd Angry Shot, was directed in 1979 by Tom Jeffrey and tells the story of four soldiers from the Special Air Service Regiment on a 12-month tour. Some get wounded, some killed, some survive. The message of the film is signalled unmistakeably in a discussion between the central character, Harry (Graham Kennedy), and one of his mates about the meaning of the war:

> Do you reckon we're doing much good here, mate?
> Not much.
> What are we doing here then?
> Well everyone's got to be somewhere and you're here, so you better get bloody used to it.

I don't believe that either in content or tone this exchange could have occurred in an American film. It is characterized by a fatalism and pessimism that marks it as European and specifically a derivative of British working-class culture: a stoical acceptance of suffering is compensated for by the solidarity of the male bond. In contrast, as the man says in *Go Tell the Spartans*, Americans expect to win.

In my second contrasting example they do. Allan Dwan directed *Sands of Iwo Jima* in 1949 and it represents well the war genre of that time. Sergeant John Stryker (John Wayne) welds his men, from many different backgrounds, into a fighting unit, despite the resistance of Private Conway (John Agar). On Iwo Jima the men come to value Stryker's leadership and raise the flag on Mount Suribachi. When Stryker is killed by a sniper Conway is ready and able to take his place: 'I was John Wayne in *Sands of Iwo Jima*', says Phillip Caputo of his arrival in Vietnam.[2]

Four features distinguish the Second World War genre. The enemy, especially if Japanese, are simply an inhuman other ('little lemon-coloured characters' as Stryker calls them) and the film has no hesitation about the way they are enthusiastically wiped out with flame-throwers. Secondly, the leadership is tough but trustworthy ('Sergeant, I'm scared'; 'So am I'). Stryker is a father figure and Conway, the symbolic son, conflicts with him in that endless and familiar negotiation between fathers and sons which, of course, earns Conway the right to take Stryker's place at the end. Thirdly, the narrative shows the men being transformed from civilians into soldiers, from individuals differentiated by class and region into an effective 'fighting unit'. And, finally, the mission is successfully accomplished – as the flag is raised at the end, the sound-track comes in with the Marines' song, *From the Halls of Montezuma*. Each of the four elements depends on the others in a unified structure. Thus, the narrative which brings the sons into successful imitation of the father also shows the variegated differences of American culture being brought together into a social unity, both processes leading towards a victory for America and democracy, a triumph sanctioned by and in its turn sanctioning the view that the enemy are outside culture and civilization. Unity of narrative and theme sit perfectly with the realist mode. *Sands of Iwo Jima* is filmed in black and white with a consistent realism close to that of a documentary (action footage from the battle of Iwo Jima is in fact spliced easily into the narrative).

This inherited structure cannot cope with the Vietnam War. Doubt and uncertainty are encountered on every score – about napalming the enemy, trusting the leadership, unifying the command, the possibility or even value of victory. As the traditional war genre falls into crisis, traditional Hollywood realism fails along with it. What is too often treated as a merely neutral 'form', a 'vehicle' for conveying 'content', in fact intimately affects and limits the kind of meanings that can be produced. To understand this requires some brief, schematic and introductory outline of the nature and effect of realism before testing the argument with five examples.

Realism

Realism aims to naturalize ideology. That is, it seeks to change the effect and force of constructed meanings so that they do not appear constructed but rather as obvious, inevitable and part of how things really are. Strictly, ideology always appears unified, as it must do since it aims to provide a position of imaginary unit for the ego. Realism cooperates with and supports ideology because it tries to turn process into fixity and resolve contradictions in the form of 'common sense'.

The strategy of realism operates on both the level of the means of representation (or signifier) and on that of the represented (or signified). In Western culture, since the Renaissance, realism demands that the signified of the narrative should seem invisible, by being set in the world of the everyday with a contemporary setting and a plot enacted generally by middle- and lower-class people. Accordingly, Cervante's *Don Quixote* is a seminal work of bourgeois realism, for it dismisses both the supernatural and the aristocracy (with its dragons, knights and damsels) in favour of a secular present and ordinary people (the disillusioned Quixote and Sancho Panza). At the same time realism requires that the operation of the signifier should as far as possible be held in the background, that the signified or represented of the narrative – what it's 'about' – should be produced but the fact of that production effaced. How this is attempted will vary greatly from mode to mode, but in the cinema it involves deploying camera, image, sound, the relation of sound and image, and particular codes of editing and narrative so that none of these will be brought to the attention of the spectator.

The two planes of signifier and signified, of course, function together so that disturbance in one will be registered in the other. For example, an implausibility in the plot risks drawing attention to the narrative codes and the fact that it *is* plot. In realism narrative is crucial because it tries to stitch together signifier and signified. The aim will always be to render the sequence of events and their motivation in character as an inevitable unfolding of the story that hides the process of its telling, to lead the spectator from enigma into resolution, from an appearance of truth to its (supposedly) full revelation in a reality which was already there to be known – that of unchanging human nature.

Traditional post-Renaissance ideologies equate this unchanging human nature with the separated and private human individual. Realism reinforces the idea of the individual, whole and undivided, source and origin of action, in two ways at once. By telling stories of individuals as they are seen in the world of everyday, empirical reality, realism will relegate to the background any form of general understanding of reality through such abstract conceptions as empire, nation, society, class, gender, etc. At the same time the very operation of realism, how it works to make sense to the viewer, will make the viewer appear to themselves as simply *there* like the represented reality they watch, single, unconstructed, conscious only of coming to know truth. Within realism individual consciousness will appear to determine being rather than the other way round.

Of course realism can never succeed, and this for an accumulation of reasons. Human nature keeps changing and so the realism of yesterday (in, say, the films of the 1930s) will seem false and artificial today. The invisible will become visible, the apparently natural be revealed as constructed. Then again, you cannot have a signified without a signifier, nor the apparent closure of a plot without the process of narrating which brings it to closure. Such cracks constantly keep appearing in the unified surface of realism which itself is constantly trying to win unity and closure from contradiction and process. Unity is one side of realism but the other is recuperation.[3]

The Vietnam films are not mirrors but lamps. They do not passively reflect historical events; rather they are textual interventions, acts of signifying practice that *rework* on their own terms the ideologies they reproduce. And the effort to anneal ruptures and recuperate contradiction becomes more and more difficult. This can be seen if we take the four features isolated from the traditional war film; victory, leadership, collective unity, the enemy. In a sentence: the leadership is discredited, the local fighting unit (and equally its originating basis in the American community) becomes fraught with antagonisms and dissent, history has made victory impossible and, finally, the enemy, far from staying in place as an inhuman other, constantly threatens to emerge as the real goodie.

Five texts will be examined in detail here. The first brilliantly recuperates contradictions around Vietnam by reworking realism. In the second and third, realism is attenuated and undermined in different ways so that contradiction is expressed. Finally, two recent versions of Vietnam seen as combat will be examined. Because there can be no fully unified text, no film can simply hold together as 'conservative' or 'radical'. So attention must always be given to the specific form or economy in which a text simultaneously contains and expresses contradiction. But first some comments on the development of the genre.

Only connect

Just as all films made in Hollywood between 1948 and 1958 allude in some way to McCarthyism and the House Committee, so all Hollywood productions in the war years can be read in relation to the issue of Vietnam. For example, when at one point in Arthur Penn's Western of 1974, *Missouri Breaks*, a ruthless lawman firebombs some outlaws hiding in a shack at night, the incident clearly connotes Vietnam and specifically 'napalm'. (Possibly the way the Western genre is committed to a certain sense of America's national mission explains in part why the genre cannot be successfully made in the decade after 1974, something Cimino didn't know when he made *Heaven's Gate* in 1980.) Or again, consider *Dark Star* directed by John Carpenter in 1976, a science fiction movie in which a group of men wander endlessly in the universe wiping out 'unstable planets', the sophistication of their technology in weird juxtaposition with the filthy and dishevelled state of their bodies (and, for that matter, their minds). Every film of the period, then, contains an implicit, sub-textual reference to the war (how could it not?).

Others are explicit. *The Green Berets* directed by John Wayne in 1968 was the only major film made during the war itself and it entirely fails to engage with contradictions posed by the war. Even a trade journal, *The Hollywood Reporter*, recognized it as 'A cliché-ridden throwback to the battlefield potboilers of World War II, its artifice readily exposed by the nightly actuality of TV news coverage.'[4] Read against other discourses of the time the realism of *The Green Berets* reveals itself as the construction it is ('artifice'), the attempt to reproduce once again the narrative and ideologies of *Sands of Iwo Jima* fails to convince. Why?

An answer may be proposed if we examine Ted Post's *Go Tell the Spartans* (1978) and what, in a very different way, goes wrong with that film. Briefly, this film also tries to be *Sands of Iwo Jima*, with a group of fighting men (including South Vietnamese rangers), a father figure (Burt Lancaster), and a mission (to defend Muc Wa) leading to victory (they succeed in rebuilding the base and fighting off Vietcong attacks). But the father figure gets shot and dies mumbling 'Oh shit', the Americans are ordered to pull out of the base leaving behind the South Vietnamese (so much for collectivity) who are over-run by Charlie (so much for victory). The film trips unwittingly on the reason for its own relative failure: at Muc Wa there is a cemetery for the French who died at Dien Bien Phu and an inscription which gives the film its title. Confronted in this cemetery by a not unsympathetic enemy, the sole survivor of Muc Wa closes the film with the words, 'I'm going home, Charlie.' Rather schematically, my conclusion from the example is this. The unity of *The Green Berets* is too transparent, too close up against ideology, achieves closure too easily to interest or persuade. On the other hand, *Go Tell the Spartans* stumbles on a complex and interesting contradiction but fails to recognize it as such and tries to close it off.

Close to the centre of the contradictions around Vietnam, worked over in dozens of different texts (films, novels, poems, propaganda, prose, polemic, and so on), is the question 'Why are we here?' To this *Sands of Iwo Jima* can answer confidently 'Because we're Americans and we're going to win', showing Americans operating 'over there' without question and so concealing the imperialist basis of their mission. What makes the United States 'the most modern form of bourgeois society'[5] is the radical break with feudalism in 1776 which left mainly the optimistic positivism of the Enlightenment as the founding tradition. Faced with defeat, therefore, American culture does not have available the tragic acceptance of contingency borne by the Australian reply, 'Well everyone's got to be somewhere.' To preserve the Whig inheritance the question has to envisage a happy alternative and so be transformed into, 'Why am I here when I could be at home?', thus *naming the link* and articulating the connection between the United States and South Vietnam, between the two worlds of dream and nightmare, between home – which is wonderful – and over there – which is awful (for Australian, as for European culture, being *anywhere* has at least something awful about it). And, as will be argued in a minute, the immediately related question, when we've got home, is 'What did we leave behind?' But any film that does not confront the link between Dallas and Da Nang, San Francisco and Saigon, cannot begin to work on the contradictions surrounding the war.

The connection is made in many different ways, though often through the figure of a returning vet, sane or mad, e.g. *Taxi Driver* (1976), *Heroes* and *Rolling Thunder* (both 1977), and *Coming Home* (1978).[6] Of course naming the connection confronts the contradictions that ensue only in order to wrap them up in a way which provokes further contradiction. But that film and television constantly recur to the idea of the veteran shows, I think, that the link between Vietnam and home must be made in some way.

'The Deer Hunter'

The link is certainly made in the troubled realism of *The Deer Hunter* as the narrative shifts between Clairton and Vietnam. But it's a troubled realism because this film about Vietnam doesn't show Vietnam until 1 hour and 10 minutes into the action, because the two halves of the film are only tenuously and somewhat enigmatically held together across the story of four shots from a gun – one when Mike kills the deer with 'one shot', a second when the Vietcong force their prisoners to shoot themselves with one bullet in a six-shot revolver, one when Mike sights the deer but decides not to pull the trigger, and one at the end when Nick says 'One shot' and manages to kill himself. In fact, by stretching narrative realism to its limits, *The Deer Hunter* manages to reproduce almost all four of the features in the structure of the traditional war film. The hero, collectivity, the enemy as other – only victory is missing (and is replaced by mourning).

The constraints set by the attempt to reproduce ideology as a unity and so without contradiction are well seen in the way community is portrayed in the text. Why white working class, Ukrainian, Orthodox, Pennsylvania steel town? Mike Westlake speculates:

> Think, for a moment, of the alternatives. A New York Italian community? Too much the special case, not American enough. A mid-West small town? Hard put to convince that such is other than the TV-ridden,

individualistic, socially fragmented world in which all too many Americans live. A Black community? Now *that* would make an interesting film, but it would hardly be this one. A middle class suburb? But all the kids were making sure they got deferred. No, this choice of community allows both the plausibility and the distance necessary for it to function as a representation of the American essence.[7]

So it had to be Clairton and it had to be everyday life, an hour long wedding (with group dancing) and a hunting trip concluded with drunken protestations between buddies: 'You and me, Mike', says Nick, and 'the rest are arseholes'; but, facing the war, 'whatever happens bring me back'. As Andrew Britton points out, the first half of the movie establishes 'two antagonistic forms of ritual – asocial and male (the hunt), and traditional/communal and female (the wedding)'.[8]

Clairton and 'the sublimated homoerotic romance'[9] between the buddies together provide a sufficient sense of collective unity to carry over into the combat scenes. It's not the same active forging of a social democratic collectivity from regional and class differences that went into John Wayne's Iwo Jima marines but, in the circumstances, it will do.

As will its hero, Mike 'this is this', one-shot deer hunter (Robert de Niro), the man with the sharp black beard and narrowed eyes who seems to grow taller as the film progresses (he certainly gets smarter, exchanging hunting clothes for dark uniform with gold braid and a sharp, dark green beret). Mike leads the hunting expedition, saves Nick and Steve from the Cong, learns that killing is not much fun if you're on the end of it, returns to the Delacroix inferno of burning Saigon, finds Nick, loses him, and ends up, with Nick's girl, a sadder and wiser man, a *better* man, a hero, a father figure. Not Sergeant Stryker, but close enough.

The American essence, Clairton, works as a springboard for a sense of the collectivity of the fighting unit since here the unit consists only of the three buddies from the same tight-knit community with other, different Americans marginalized. Luxuriously defined by the first half of the film, this essence enables Mike to become a hero and defines the enemy as unspeakable other. First seen in the first sequence in Vietnam deliberately and motivelessly dropping a grenade into a cellar full of women and children, the Vietcong are portrayed as forcing decent people to kill themselves by playing Russian roulette (an incident, by the way, whose historical accuracy is hotly disputed).[10] While lemon-coloured Iwo Jima Japs can be burned off like waste grass, Charlie can't because he has a higher moral status (not least because his national destiny is to win). There has to be some active process of recuperation. Charlie has to be turned into the Merciless Ming, initially by being recognized as like us (we too, with Mike, want the joy of killing with a single shot), and then by the same token expelled from being like us (since the second time we don't kill the deer). In the logic of *The Deer Hunter*, he who kills people, not animals, that creature must be an animal itself, an inhuman other.

Community, hero, enemy as other: only victory is missing. Its place is taken by loss and mourning, which at least yields a moral victory for experience. *The Deer Hunter* is able to work as it does because, in a convincing fashion but entirely according to the traditional mode of Nixon-Paramount (it is able to transform the social and historical contradictions surrounding Vietnam into a version of personal experience) At the centre is Clairton, the experiencing group and its representatives. It's all there before the war and after, so the war is able to figure only as the pain of growing up that happens to all of us (human nature). Thus the war becomes merely a sensational background to a psychodrama in the foreground, consciousness determines social being. Defeat, the loss incurred in the war, is displaced into the *personal* loss of Nick. That manoeuvre is precisely the strategy of realism, consistent with its commitment to the everyday, to common sense and to reality as it appears to the individual. It only takes a certain degree of narrative strain for *The Deer Hunter* to contain the contradictions it expresses. Unlike *The Green Berets*, *The Deer Hunter* does not evade the connection between home and over there but it does, brilliantly, contrive a way to hold that connection within its more flexible narrative unity, making a surrogate 1970s version of *Sands of Iwo Jima*.

'Who'll Stop the Rain?'

Distributed in Europe as *Dog Soldiers* and directed by Karel Reisz in 1978, this is a Vietnam film in the thriller genre, a story of crime and punishment about heroin smuggling but one which makes the essential connection between home and abroad because the drug is carried from Da Nang to Los Angeles. If read only for its realism and the overt meanings of its genre plot the film appears beautiful but banal, as Gilbert Adair says, 'a risibly lightweight indictment of a society's decline which develops into a fairly conventional chase movie'.[11]

But this reading ignores the fact that the closure of realism is impossible, that a narrative can never close off its connotations as the mode seeks to do. Realism aims to treat characters as particular and events as singular, but in fact they are always characters and events for us, for an audience making sense of them, and so they will always accrue meanings the people in the represented narrative can't know about. Out of this inevitable excess of signification left over from the film's apparent project, *Who'll Stop the Rain?* creates another, consistent set of meanings not acknowledged by its central narrative. Just as the firebomb incident in *Missouri Breaks* connoted Vietnam, so *Who'll Stop the Rain?* makes allegorical reference precisely to the causes of crisis and 'a society's decline'.

Unlike other Vietnam films, in which the connection between first and third world is merely personal, made through the experience of characters who move between both countries, in this text the two are linked by a very literal connection, the bag of heroin. What functions in the narrative as an object of desire (2 kg of meaningless white powder) is thus available to the allegory as a signifier for more general relations between the place of colonial war and the nation of imperialist aggression. Crossing the Pacific concealed underneath a military helicopter (an icon for the American presence in the war), the drug, highly valued in Saigon, takes on even greater value in California, though value of the same kind, and the same shadowy organization which sold it in Saigon regards it as still theirs in the United States.

A relation between home and abroad, Los Angeles domesticity and Vietnamese horror, is brought out through the whole text. It is as though South-East Asia has come to America. John Converse (Mick Moriarty) arranges the shipment of the drug and then arrives home on the West Coast to find two heavies looking for the stuff. They torture him to get him to tell them where it is and, as they do, sitting him for example on the red-hot ring of an electric stove, a television set in the adjoining room shows newsreel of the war, the bombing and strafing of villages.

The climax of the plot consists of a raid on a hill top. The commander, Antheuil (Anthony Zorbe), arrives by helicopter and organizes the raid by radio telephone. His men are shown the way up to the top by one of the local peasantry under duress, a Mexican farmer, who deserts them as soon as he can and gets shot at for it. Everything suggests a search and destroy mission – 'get in position', 'take cover'. Antheuil warns his men that the group on the hill top 'may be actively hostile' and later his men negotiate with the defenders in Pentagonese: the exchange of John Converse for the heroin is concluded with the words 'It is agreeable'. Such images and verbal details strongly connote Vietnam.

At the level of allegory the text may be read as asserting that American involvement in South-East Asia is motivated by capital in a system of relations stretching out to Vietnam from its source in the United States. Disillusioned with the war John Converse discards his previous liberal ideals as a writer and photographer and decides to smuggle the heroin. What Converse thinks of as a Nietzscheian act of authentic individualism ('this is the first real thing I've ever done') at once implicates others – his friend Ray Hicks (Nick Nolte) who is forced to transport the drug, his wife Marge (Tuesday Weld) when she picks up the gun to defend Hicks when they are attacked by Antheuil's two brutal agents. Converse thinks the heroin belongs to him by right of purchase but finds in fact that it is controlled by an undefined organization in America for whom he and the others are merely unwitting supports.

A man of ideas, John Converse can be seen as representing the ruling American liberal tradition, which mixes idealism with committed individualist entrepreneurship. Charmian, who sells him the white stuff, remarks on his puritanism, calling him 'a dedicated non-swinger'. His decision 'to follow the advice of the Founding Fathers to serve God and grow rich' rapidly fails in a way which satisfies both his underlying sense of guilt (he tells Marge's father, 'I've been waiting all my life to fuck-up like this') and a masochistic drive which leaves him an ineffective and even serene victim to the atrocities of Antheuil and his agents.

The figure of his wife, Marge, offers the feminine side of American liberalism. A golden girl in the tradition of Henry James and Scott Fitzgerald, Marge is pretty and kindly, shown to us first in her affectionate relation with her child Janie. But driven to confront something of the nature of the world she lives in by her husband's attempt to do 'something real', she escapes into narcissism, withdrawing first from her child into the paternal affection of Ray Hicks and then into addiction.

Hicks (Nick Nolte) is initially barbaric as, in our first view of him, he rises from the mud of a football field. Then he intrudes into Marge's apparently peaceful home and batters the two thugs who try to take the heroin. But soon he moves to the centre of the film and attracts a complex range of connotations. Partly he represents the counter-culture, practising Chinese boxing, heading for New Mexico and the valley there with the faded relics of the 1960s – grass, strobe lights, music, the hippy commune, the Asian Indian bells, Red Indian tepees. Hence his interest in Nietzsche which he has learned from Converse (the director himself regards this as one of the most important aspects of the film[12]).

In addition, Hicks also is the country boy, as he says. His name is *Hicks* and at one point he does country dancing with Marge. He is always sleeveless, often wearing a vest (undershirt), so that his appearance is all arms and shoulders surmounted by a pug nose. But he is also the man who works with his hands as a deckhand, a hard hat, digging for his gun or servicing the Range Rover, cleaning his rifle, fixing electronics on the mountain. In these terms Hicks represents that rare figure, the American working-class hero. He is finally seen as a common soldier, the grunt, singing soldiers' songs as he marches along the railroad at the end, representative of that class on the American side whose sons and brothers died in the war.

In realism we do not expect sympathetic identification with a main character to move from them to someone else in the middle of the narrative. Such a shift is just what takes place in *Who'll Stop the Rain?*, as attention moves from Converse to Hicks. Unprepared and insufficiently motivated at the level of realism, the change of direction makes fine sense in the allegory: possession of the heroin (capital) passes from a liberal representative of the ruling class to a representative of the working class. Of the heroin Hicks says, 'It belongs to whoever controls it', and he fights actively and aggressively to retain it. Yet if this reading is pressed we also have to recognize Hicks as tied emotionally and subserviently to Marge and her class. Hicks' final words about her are as idiomatic as they are passionate: 'She's the love of my life, man – no shit.'

If Converse represents the state as liberal democracy and consent, Antheuil signifies it as the necessity for force. Like the FBI agent in *Dog Day Afternoon* (whom Jameson argues stands for 'multinational capitalism'[13]), Antheuil is the man in the dark suit with a police badge who knows all the answers. He may work for the local police or the FBI or the Mafia or 'the Agency'. He certainly has connections 'in Washington', though it is never clear who he's really working for. He represents the State, seen as a sinister and ambivalent force.

The final sequence of the film is set in the New Mexico desert, a scene which recalls the famous ending of Von Stroheim's *Greed* (1923), when two men lost in Death Valley and dying of thirst fight over the gold they've stolen. Here Converse, having regained the heroin (at the cost of Hicks' life), spills the white powder into the sand. Antheuil, trying desperately to scoop it up after him, is killed, shot by another unidentified authority figure who appears behind him. Outside the social relations within which alone it takes on value, the heroin, like capital or gold, has no more inherent worth than desert sand.

If the film is read as having a worked out connotation, as allegory – and there is of course no guarantee this will happen – we are left with two questions. In *The Deer Hunter* Mike grows up in Vietnam and learns from it. At the end of *Who'll Stop the Rain?* what has Converse, representing white middle-class America, learned as he drives off into the empty desert with Miss America, now a junkie? On the soundtrack, Credence Clearwater Revival sing *Who'll stop the rain*. Who will now Hicks is dead?

'Apocalypse Now'

After completing this film in 1979 Coppola dropped 'Ford' as his middle name, presumably because his claim to make the American epic was now no longer merely nominal. *Apocalypse Now, the* Vietnam film, presents the war as a tissue of contradictions. Its first hero, Captain Benjamin Willard (named after the chief rat of the 1974 teenage cult movie), a neurotic, war traumatized, drunken wreck, is called from the disarray of his Saigon hotel room to perform a very special, secret mission. Surrounded by the accoutrements of haute cuisine and high culture at luncheon with a general and two sycophantic aides-de-camp, he is given orders 'to terminate with extreme prejudice' a fellow American officer, the renegade Green Beret Colonel Walter E. Kurtz, who is somewhere up country, up river and out to lunch. Aided by Colonel Kilgore, whose battalion launches a helicopter attack on a peaceful seaside Vietcong village to the sound of 'The Ride of the Valkyries' so one of his men can try out the surf there, Willard's riverboat reaches the upper waters carried underneath a helicopter. Arriving at Do Lung bridge, built every day by the Americans and blown up every night by the Vietcong, Willard seeks out the Commanding Officer, only to find his question finally answered by the question from one of the men there, 'I thought you were?' Reaching Kurtz's sanctuary Willard kills him before the whole area is devastated by B52s (Operation Arclight).

Apocalypse Now is able to express contradiction because it is a work of fantasy and avowed fiction rather than realism. Its genre is essentially that of the art movie but it is able to draw other 'lower' genres into itself – from the thriller and film noir as well as the traditional war film – which are then mixed with satire, surrealism and absurd comedy. Leaving their boat ('Never leave the boat') in search of mangoes, Willard and a crew member are attacked in the jungle not by a Vietcong patrol but by the beast you'd least expect in a Vietnamese jungle, a tiger. Later the captain of the boat, a handsome, kindly and responsible older black, is killed by tribesmen and looking down at the weapon sticking out through his dark chest exclaims in mortal surprise, 'A spear!' Mixing the tragic and the comic together, its tone and effect is well suggested by Beckett's definition of the three laughs, the bitter 'at that which is not good', the hollow 'at that which is not true', and the mirthless laugh, 'the dianoetic laugh . . . the laugh of laughs, the *risus purus* . . . at that which is unhappy'.[14] Realism requires a careful discrimination between genres – *Apocalypse Now* collapses serious and funny into this third, 'the mirthless laugh'.

The narrative of *Apocalypse Now* never gives up a concatenated representation of what happens – it does not, for example, show two contradictory versions of the same event as in some avantgarde films. But though the story of Willard and Kurtz is sustained, it increasingly loses its basis in the representation of an external, everyday reality. From its start in the hotel room when Willard, punching his image in a mirror, tries to break out of a close dyadic world of self on self, the man is always in search of a symbolic position outside himself with whom he can identify, the father figure whose promise seems to be fulfilled in Colonel Kurtz, perfect American, perfect soldier. Thus the progress up river becomes also an inward journey, a psychological progress.

At each stage, a new degree of surrealism is entered, from Saigon to the river, from the raid on the village to arrival at the bridge. After the bridge the boat floats upstream amid clouds of coloured smoke, between walls of silk inscribed with foreign writing, into showers of arrows and tracer bullets, through a phantasmagoric landscape (recalling that in Herzog's *Aguirre Wrath of God*), past at one point the gigantic tailplane of a B52 caught in some trees above the fires and corpses of the river. When the boat finally pierces the mist and smoke in the cul de sac of Kurtz's stronghold at the head of the river it appears more like a symbol of uterine closure than a real place. Willard hoped for the hero to imitate, but in Kurtz discovers instead a figure surrounded by severed heads – the castrating father (or mother). In this *paysage interieur*, external and internal have merged in a mode entirely surpassing realism.

With realism subverted, the contradictions of Vietnam can be articulated with a sharp juxtaposition more explicit than in any comparable text. At every point Willard's fascination with the person and life of Kurtz, recorded in the secret folder he pores over obsessively, marks the connection between Vietnam and the heartlands of the American military. The younger hero, then, is an obsessed neurotic and his mission is to assassinate an American Colonel; and the older hero, the ideal West Point graduate and career soldier, is insane, a killer who kills for the sake of it. The mission contradicts itself – it is to destroy one of your own side. The collectivity of the fighting unit is imaged in the members of the boat crew – Lance, who paints his face and drops acid, the boy who is out of control with fear, Chef who is hysterical. But it is imaged also by the Montagnard warriors surrounding Kurtz, manifestly 'them' not 'us', an image of what 'we' have become. Only the enemy retains something of its traditional presentation as the other, an issue that brings the argument towards the film's limitations, its ending.

The meretricious portentousness, archetypal symbolizing and literary flim-flam of the conclusion to *Apocalypse Now*, which has so exercised critics of the film, can be best understood as the necessity to keep the text at last just about within the confines of being the same film Hollywood has always made. Having broken with realism in its exploration of contradiction, the film struggles to resolve the contradictions it has opened up in a logic which runs something like this. The Vietcong are, as ever, the unspeakable other, this being the drift of the parable Kurtz tells of how they cut off the arms of all the children who had been inoculated by American doctors and piled them in a heap.[15] This is the 'moral terror' Kurtz as anti-humanist, existentialist hero says we must make into our own weapon. But the narrative has shown that our side have little to learn already in the exercise of 'moral terror' – 'we' are as bad as any 'them'.

At this point one option would have been to show the nexus of historical and social forces, militarism, capitalism and imperialism, which issued in the American intervention in South-East Asia. *Apocalypse Now* escapes this only by choosing the only other option it has made possible for itself. It evacuates the domain of the historical entirely, transcending it by moving into the terrain of myth. In this respect, for all its muddle, the film follows Coppola's intention of giving the audience:

> a sense of the horror, the madness, the sensuousness and the moral dilemma of the Vietnam war . . . to illustrate as many of its different faces as possible. And yet I wanted to go further, to the moral issues that are behind all wars.[16]

Archetypal, universalizing and entirely ahistorical, the narrative closure of *Apocalypse Now* aims to recover once again a dimension in which 'Man' has an unchanging nature in the necessary eternal recurrence of the Golden Bough ritual in which the son kills the father and the terrible but necessary sacrifice must be made through the death of the bull (and the symbolic king). These supposedly are 'the moral issues behind all wars'. Swopping history for myth, the film has nowhere else to go if it is not to step finally outside the limits of that same realist film Hollywood has been making for 50 years. But they are extreme limits. American cinema rapidly withdrew to safer territory.

The return to realism: 'Platoon', 'Full Metal Jacket'

No contradiction in ideology is beyond recuperation. In 12 hours on the night of 13 February 1945, with only the most tenuous strategic justification ('helping the advance of our Soviet allies'), Bomber Command of the Royal Air Force killed over 125,000 women and children at Dresden, a war crime equal if not surpassing any of the Second World War (and noted as such by Kurt Vonnegut's *Slaughterhouse Five*). Yet film seemed able to make good any consequent ideological damage in *Dambusters* (1954), by showing skilled pilots in their Lancasters destroying Nazi dams with pinpoint accuracy and a minimum loss of (civilian) lives. An American President sponsors dirty tricks against the Democratic Party and brings himself to the verge of an impeachment he only escaped by resigning. In *All the President's Men* Hollywood shows indefatigable reporters uncovering Nixon's guilt in a way which contains

corruption by balancing it against the Free Speech provisions of the Consti-
tution. *Platoon* (directed by Oliver Stone in 1986) and Stanley Kubrick's *Full
Metal Jacket* (1987) are similar enough to be discussed together [and
Hamburger Hill (1987) is part of the same sub-genre]. They seem to confront
the worst aspects of the war by presenting it with fully restored realism as
combat, by placing everyday empirical experience directly at the forefront of
attention. As Chris Taylor, the main figure in *Platoon*, says at one point,
'Counting the days, and the six inches in front of my face, not much else.'

The effect is achieved by severing any clear emotional, ideological or
narrative connection between here and over there so that Vietnam and
American military engagement is presented hermetically, cut off from the
previously felt necessity to show and explore a link between political decisions
in the United States and the experience of American soldiers fighting in the
jungle. Already in Vietnam, *Platoon* opens with new guys coming out of the
belly of a transport aircraft at base camp, *Full Metal Jacket* with recruits on the
first day of military training. Instead of connecting 'We're here' because 'we're
not at home' via the inescapable 'Why?', the second wave affirms, in the words
of the First World War trench song, 'We're here because we're here because
we're here', encapsulated in the war experience, and America is an unreal
dream, as the slang termed it, 'the world'.

Two factors help make the effect persuasive in the revised ideological
situation of Reagan's declining years, post-Irangate. One is that since the films
of the late 1970s the war had been familiarized as pastiche. After the dextrous
and partial working through of the war in such films as *Apocalypse Now*, by the
early 1980s the figure of the vet had become a cliché, both in television (with
the *A-Team*, *Airwolf*, even *Miami Vice*, for Crockett turns out to have been
there) and in the cinema with the Superman-like excesses of *Missing in Action*
and the Rambo cycle. The ground was thus prepared for Hollywood to move
from manifest exaggeration back to its traditional claim to show the real. Just as
the fantasy conflicts of *Star Wars* (1977) made way for realistic, contemporary
combat in *Top Gun* (1986), so *Rambo* leads on to *Platoon*.

Secondly, in the mid-1980s it becomes possible to present American combat
experience as history, mere history. It is one of the most entrenched forms of
ideological recuperation to keep the archive secret for a generation and open
the books only when the contemporary participants – and the issues – are safely
dead or at least forgotten. During the war Hollywood hardly touched Vietnam
directly but now it can be revisited in a kind of documentary, as historical fact,
actually as costume drama. So these two texts scrupulously mark a distance
between now and then, stressing the stylistic difference of the 1960s (hippie
dress and manners), 1960s vernacular ('You can talk the talk but can you walk
the walk?'), and, especially in *Full Metal Jacket*, unrepentantly, 1960s pop
music. Plausibly now, part can stand for whole, American involvement for the
total war, combat for that whole political and historical engagement, one man
and his platoon for the general war effort and, in final sequences filmed with
the full deployment of post-*Star Wars* film technology[17], a spectacular single
engagement for the agony of a whole decade. This juncture reached,

traditional Hollywood stands ready to do again what it has always done best: the male Oedipal transition, how a boy becomes 'a man' by doing what he has to do.

Within a merely empiricist dramatization of the individual and his particular experience an attenuated, flattened but nevertheless partly rejuvenated version of *Sands of Iwo Jima* can now be made. Though not able to realize fully all the features of the traditional 1950s war genre, *Platoon* manages a passable reproduction. As in older examples, the hero is young and sensitive, the command is led by a weak 2nd lieutenant. Sergeant Barnes, the bad-ass veteran, resuscitates such figures as that played by Jack Palance in Robert Aldrich's *Attack* (1956) or Steve McQueen in Don Siegel's *Hell is for Heroes* (1962). And like its predecessors, *Platoon* offers suspense, excitement, spectacle and the pleasures of realism.

Because the commitment is to American combat involvement in these two films the enemy continues to be effectively invisible while something like unification of the command once again occupies the foreground. Leadership is again crucial, and though victory remains impossible, its place is taken by individual survival. Even so, in different ways each feature continues to be problematic. Acquiring a human face – and, moreover, a woman's face – the dying sniper who prays and speaks English at the end of *Full Metal Jacket* becomes disturbingly sympathetic. While Kubrick's film spends its first half showing, however ambivalently, the moulding of a group of diverse teenage individuals into a military unit, Stone's *Platoon* begins to explore unannealed divisons within its representative American sample – white versus black, lifer versus draftee, gung ho versus hippie, country boy versus urbanite (as the hero says, 'we didn't fight the enemy, we fought ourselves, and the enemy was within us').

Both films show leadership as uncertain, if not corrupt. In *Platoon* Bravo Company is used as expendable bait to draw out the NVA and when their position is over-run, an air-strike has to destroy it in order to save it; in *Full Metal Jacket* the final engagement with a single sniper in bombed-out Hue during the Tet offensive shows lives wasted because of an incompetent command. Both make leadership problematical, one in the figure of the drill instructor, Sergeant Hartman, shot by Pile at the end of training, the other in the opposition between Sergeants Barnes and Elias. But, crucially, both texts work by showing – and vindicating – their hero's survival.

A young man survives by growing up:

> For the son this task (i.e. of becoming a member of the social community) consists in detaching his libidinal wishes from his mother and employing them for the choice of a real outside love-object, and in reconciling himself with his father if he has remained in opposition to him, or in freeing himself from his pressure if, as a reaction to his infantile rebelliousness, he has become subservient to him.[18]

The Oedipal transition Freud describes (remarking drily how seldom it is carried through 'in an ideal manner') requires the son to avoid both excessive rebellion and excessive submission to the father. In the face of the father's castrating threat the son must oppose him in order to take his place, but opposes only finally to submit to him by accepting his threat as general, not merely personal. In the son's fantasy the father can thus appear polarized as the Bad Father, menacing him, and as the Good Father, enabling him to grow up, white hat versus black hat in the western.

In *Star Wars* this opposition is almost comically explicit in the figures of Darth Vader (= Death Father?) and Obi-Wan Kenobe (= 'You can be what you want to be'). In *Platoon* it forms the substance of the plot as Sergeant Barnes ('I don't need this shit, I am reality'), who wants to kill everyone, and Sergeant Elias, who wants to save them. Taylor, the young man, sides with Elias and shoots Barnes, an action in which he both *becomes* like Barnes, a killer, but unlike him, in that he kills for the general good. In *Full Metal Jacket* Pile, the fat boy, obsessed like an infant with eating, takes his suffering merely personally, shoots Hartman and destroys himself, while Joker, on the other hand, opposes his teacher but finally takes his place, killing the sniper (and with her the feminine side of himself?). Unlike Pile, he accepts castration, and his final words are, 'I'm alive and I am not afraid.' All this is familiar Hollywood, all too familiar. As has been argued, it has as its necessary condition the realist mode, operating to present everything as personal experience.

These texts of the second wave work (and it's not that easy) because they integrate effects worked out and made plausible in the earlier movies. Vietnam combat as the necessary pain of growing up was anticipated in *The Deer Hunter*; combat was successfully portrayed in the Rambo movies; and ideological contradiction superseded on the non-contradictory plane of universal human experience was the final achievement of *Apocalypse Now*. This last is the explicit meaning of both films. Chris Taylor speaks of the two sergeants as 'fighting for possession of my soul', like the Good and Evil Angel which address Faustus in Marlowe's play; and Joker, when asked why he both wears a peace badge and has writing on his helmet 'BORN TO KILL', replies they stand for 'the duality of man – in a Jungian sense'. Ideological contradiction has been plausibly reworked as experiential conflict, a rite of passage, growing pains. This is the narrative basis for a careful ambivalence in each film's diffuse connotations.

In the United States both *Platoon* and *Full Metal Jacket* were hailed by conservatives and liberals as their film (*Platoon* won Academy awards and a cover story in *Time* magazine while Stone's much more radical *Salvador* did not). The right, responding to the exhibition of courage and the hero's achievement of manhood, could celebrate in each the demonstration of American fighting spirit, while more liberal spirits, attending to the hero's loss and the suffering of those around him, read each film as a vague assertion that the war was wrong.

In Kubrick's movie, to pursue the argument, the drill instructor could be seen as both fascistic, turning the recruits from individuals into killing machines fused together into the Marine Corps *and*, at the same time, as the voice of the Reality Principle, making boys into men. He is killed for his cruelty, but at the same time he is killed by Pile, obviously crazy and a loser from the outset. Joker kills the female sniper but in so doing he loses his fear and learns to survive. Detailed empiricist realism is the condition for these and other multiplying ambivalences, for it enables each text to advance its narrative as brute, unmediated and uninterpreted fact – 'this is this', 'six inches in front of my face'. Both films rely on the apparent objectivity of documentary technique; in fact, in *Full Metal Jacket* there is a sequence in which a platoon individually speaks its varying views on the rights and wrongs of the war in direct address to the camera, reactions which cancel each other out except for the viewer who is free to single out the interpretation of their choice.

Epic can be defined as any genre aiming to encompass some general statement of the meanings central to a culture, from Homer to 'Paradise Lost'. In their different ways, by confronting the connection between America and South-East Asia *The Deer Hunter, Who'll Stop the Rain?* and *Apocalypse Now* inevitably took on epic significance and connotation by expressing contradictions arising from a historical situation and the historical forces at work in it. By contrast, the new sub-genre reduces history to biography in historical dress; a restored realism, inviting the viewer into identification with the hero, operates to make their experience of the personal into no more than a personal experience. Even so, these two films circle around a sense of loss, even if it is merely personal, as is frequently said, 'the loss of innocence'. In the now famous scene from *Platoon*, as the soldiers move down and away from the burning village they have sacked, the music on the sound-track is sombrely elegiac.

Mourning and melancholia

These Vietnam films have had an important function for American culture. This was well recognized when *The Deer Hunter* was first shown, in a review from *Esquire*:

> The politicians announced that the war was over, and it was – for them and most people. But it wasn't over for those guys in the Chelsea Naval Hospital, it wasn't over for my family. . . . Then came the Vietnam books . . . next came the television shows. . . . I saw them all. . . . And then I saw *The Deer Hunter*. Michael Cimino got it right. . . . *The Deer Hunter* is telling us that finally we can grieve.[19]

With the cycle of Vietnam films Hollywood, always closer to the centre of American culture than its European (or Australian) equivalents, finally told people that they could grieve. They performed an act of public mourning.

Surfacing alongside the motif of the connection between home and abroad in the Vietnam genre is the theme of the lost object. In *The Deer Hunter* it is a person, the dead Nick, who got left behind over there, while in another cycle – *Missing in Action* (1982) and *Rambo* (1985) – the lost object is figured as American prisoners of war still held in camps in Vietnam. *Apocalypse Now* records a quest for the lost hero, the Good Father, *Who'll Stop the Rain?*

mourns the loss of Hicks, *Platoon* and *Full Metal Jacket* regret a loss of innocence. Concerning a lost object psychoanalysis would make two suggestions. One is that the manifest meaning of what is lost differs from what is really lost. And so one might wonder then what was really lost by the Whig culture in facing its first defeat; the American war record from the War of Independence through the 'Mexican' War and two World Wars being, as they put it in sporting terms, six played (or more), one drawn (the Civil War), one lost. 'We won't lose – 'cause we're Americans.'

Secondly, psychoanalysis distinguishes between mourning and melancholy. Mourning is a process in which, for example, the death of a loved one is faced and satisfactorily worked through; melancholy does not know what it is mourning for and so cannot properly end. For Jean Vallely many American films such as *The Deer Hunter* effected a mourning for Vietnam and all that was lost there. So everything's all right. Or is it? There's another possibility, as suggested by this passage by Ron Faust in which he explains that the problem for vets is that, though living in America, they still cannot come home:

> not as long as the rest of the country refuses to *let* us come home; that is, not until it faces up to what *we* did as a nation in Vietnam. We will 'finally come home' on the day we can look at other Americans in their eyes and see there the confession: 'Yes, we did this terrible thing *together*.'[20]

Much more is at stake than the loss of comrades or even the loss of a war, for the proposal is that what was lost was something like the moral and social centre of a whole culture. If this were truly the lost object, then no working through can take place until the historical realities of the war are confronted and worked through. Until then, acts of retrieval and burial, like that which ends *The Deer Hunter*, consist only of melancholy passing itself off as mourning. If so, the American melancholy will persist, the rain won't stop.

Notes

1. Peter Pierce, 'The Australian Literature of the Viet Nam War', *Meanjin*, 1980, **39**, (October), pp. 290–303.
2. Phillip Caputo, *A Rumor of War*, New York: Ballantine Books, 1977, p. 255.
3. Besides the work of Brecht collected as *Brecht on Theatre* (translated by J. Willett), London: Methuen, 1964, this account of realism draws on G. Genette, *Narrative Discourse* (Oxford: Basil Blackwell, 1980), Stephen Heath, *Questions of Cinema* (London: Macmillan, 1981) and the essays on realism collected in Colin MacCabe, *Theoretical Essays* (Manchester: Manchester University Press, 1985). What we have now is an all but 'canonical' account of textual unity and contradiction originating mainly in Pierre Macherey's 1966 book, *A Theory of Literary Production* (London: RKP, 1978), and developed by, for example, Fredric Jameson in *The Political Unconscious* (London: Methuen, 1981).
4. Cited by Lawrence H. Suid, *Guts and Glory, Great American War Movies*, Reading, Mass.: Addison-Wesley, 1978, p. 232.
5. Karl Marx and Frederick Engels, *The German Ideology* (translated by C. J. Arthur), London: Lawrence and Wishart, 1974, p. 144.

6. See, for example, Richard Berg, 'Coming Home: The Veteran on Television and in Film', *Cultural Critique*, 1986, No. 3 (Spring).
7. Mike Westlake, 'The Deer Hunter 1', *North by North West*, 1979, No. 8 (Autumn), p. 15.
8. Andrew Britton, 'Hollywood in Vietnam', *Movie*, 1980, 27/28, pp. 2–23.
9. Ibid. Elsewhere I have discussed 'The Deer Hunter' in terms of masculinity and the male bond. See *What a Man's Gotta Do: The Masculine Myth in Popular Culture*, London: Paladin, 1986.
10. See Martha Gellhorn, John Pilger and *Time* magazine as cited by Phil Braithwaite in the *Guardian*, 3 April 1985.
11. Gilbert Adair, *Hollywood's Vietnam*, London: Proteus, 1981, p. 99.
12. In an interview Reisz said that Hicks feels 'that there is a possibility of a heroic life, and he lives that out at the end'. See *Framework*, 1978–9, No. 9 (Winter), pp. 35–8.
13. Fredric Jameson, '*Dog Day Afternoon* as a Political Film', *Screen Education*, 1979, No. 30 (Spring) pp. 75–92 (reprinted from *College English* **38** (8)), p. 88.
14. Samuel Beckett, *Watt*, London: Calder, 1963, pp. 46–7.
15. On this issue Nguyen Khac Vien in an article on the film remarks that 'Mass vaccination always was the first preoccupation of Indochinese revolutionaries, even during the hardest stages of the war' ('*Apocalypse Now* viewed by a Vietnamese', reprinted from *The Vietnam Courier* 1980, No. 7, Hanoi in *Framework*, 1981, No. 14, pp. 42–3. And this is perhaps the appropriate place to make the obvious point that *Apocalypse Now* conforms precisely to the dictates of the genre in presenting the Vietnamese as an Oriental Other that makes no sense until it has been worked by the Western mind. (Edward Said specifically refers to Conrad's Kurtz in this connection. See *Orientalism*, Harmondsworth: Penguin, 1985, p. 216.)
16. Coppola, cited in 'Apocalypse Now Press Booklet', the promotional brochure for the film's premier.
17. See Steve Neale, 'Hollywood Strikes Back: Special Effects in Recent American Cinema', *Screen*, 1980, **21** (3), pp. 101–109.
18. Sigmund Freud, *Introductory Lectures*, Harmondsworth: Penguin, 1973, p. 380.
19. Jean Vallely, *Esquire*, 2 February 1979.
20. Ron Faust, letter to *The Nation*, 18 December 1982, p. 642 [cited in 'Vietnam and the Media', *Wide Angle*, 1985, **7** (4) (Winter)].

Further reading

Adair, Gilbert, *Hollywood's Vietnam*, London: Proteus, 1981.
Berg, Rick, 'Coming Home: The Veteran on Television and in Film', *Cultural Critique*, 1986, No. 3 (Spring).
Brecht, Bertolt, *Brecht on Theatre* (translated by J. Willett), London: Methuen, 1964.
Britton, Andrew, 'Hollywood in Vietnam', *Movie*, 1980, 27/28, pp. 2–23.
Caputo, Phillip, *A Rumor of War*, New York: Ballantine Books, 1977.
Combs, Richard, 'Beating God to the Draw – *Salvador* and *Platoon*', *Sight and Sound*, 1987, **56** (2) (Spring), pp. 136–8.
Easthope, Antony, *What a Man's Gotta Do: The Masculine Myth in Popular Culture*, London: Paladin, 1986.
Genette, Gerard, *Narrative Discourse*, Oxford: Basil Blackwell, 1980.
Heath, Stephen, *Questions of Cinema*, London: Macmillan, 1981.
Jameson, Fredric, *The Political Unconscious*, London: Methuen, 1981.

Jameson, Fredric, '*Dog Day Afternoon* as a Political Film', *Screen Education*, 1979, No. 30 (Spring), pp. 75–92 [reprinted from *College English* **38** (8)].

MacCabe, Colin, *Theoretical Essays*, Manchester: Manchester University Press, 1985.

Macherey, Pierre, *A Theory of Literary Production*, London: RKP, 1978.

Pierce, Peter, 'The Australian Literature of the Viet Nam War', *Meanjin*, 1980, **39** (October), pp. 290–303.

Said, Edward, *Orientalism*, Harmondsworth: Penguin, 1985.

Suid, Lawrence H., *Guts and Glory, Great American War Movies*, Reading, Mass.: Addison-Wesley, 1978.

Time Magazine, 'PLATOON – Vietnam as it Really was', *Time*, 26 January 1987.

Vien, Nguyen Khac, '*Apocalypse Now* viewed by a Vietnamese', reprinted from *The Vietnam Courier*, 1980, No. 7, Hanoi in *Framework*, 1981, No. 14, pp. 42–3.

Westlake, Michael, 'The Deer Hunter 1', *North by North West*, 1979, No. 8 (Autumn).

Jeffrey Walsh

2

First Blood to Rambo:
A Textual Analysis

This essay, based on the premise that hugely successful popular works like the *First Blood* series are ideologically significant, examines the four texts that create and sustain the image of Rambo in popular fiction, film and other media. My objectives are three-fold – to discuss the two novels and two films as a continuing cultural practice (*First Blood III* will soon be released as a film); to compare and contrast their formal qualities; and, in conclusion, to attempt a brief historical overview of their social and political meanings. For my argument a strictly chronological awareness of the texts is needed: *First Blood*, the novel, translates to the film of the same name, and then the process reverses, *Rambo* the movie spawns a book of the film based closely on the screenplay. The four works comprise a kind of discourse or extended articulation rather like the James Bond novels and films. I hope to show that the works exhibit transference, interchange and circulation and yet have clear individual identities relating to and constituted by different phases of post-Vietnam American culture.

It is helpful to start by analysing David Morrell's 1972 best-selling novel *First Blood*[1] and to focus on how its protagonist – called simply Rambo (significantly a man without a Christian name) – is represented as a returned veteran. The novel replicates the first widespread stereotype of the vet as a man in a state of post-traumatic shock who is quickly provoked into acts of excessive violence. Rambo is presented before the action of the novel begins as extremely violent; he has killed almost casually in self-defence during a brawl. It is clear then that any undue pressure will cause him to erupt equally savagely.

What is especially distinctive and interesting in this primary novel of the series is how Rambo acquires his characteristic features of style and appearance. A transformation takes place when he escapes naked from the police station into the woods, of course, but he is initially portrayed as one of the bedroll brigade, a hippie who will not cut his hair. He therefore signals early on his opposition to the war through such unmilitary attire, unlikely dress for the decorated hero that he turns out to be. Rambo at this stage of his development displays affinity with those veterans who threw away their medals in disgust at the conduct of the war. In narrative terms Rambo's unconventionality of clothing and manner suggests trouble to Wilf Teasle, sheriff of the seedy town of Madison, Kentucky: such rebellious grammar of dress he believes defies civic authority and pride. In the later works we tend to identify Rambo by his alternative clothing: he retains vestiges of his counter-cultural insignia yet, as this essay argues, these signifiers take on different ideological meanings according to their context. The counter-cultural rituals, of protest and a semantics of rebellion, are later appropriated: the folk devil finally changes to militarist cult hero in *Rambo* (1985).

The other key distinguishing feature of the first set of the *First Blood* works is their unsatisfactory vision of family life or love: running through them is a pattern of defunct or flawed parental and marital relationships. Women are entirely absent in the movie *First Blood* (1982), and in the earlier novel they are shown as frigid, like Teasle's wife, asexual and maternal, as is Orval's wife, or dead, as is Rambo's mother. Interestingly, too, Rambo is seen as a loner; his buddies are dead and he is the only survivor from the 'A' Team at Bragg; Huck and Jim are dead in Vietnam.

In the novel *First Blood* there are only two fully explored relationships; one between Teasle and his stepfather Orval, which is fraught yet affectionate, and a more central conflictual one, between the two rival putative heroes, Teasle and Rambo. Perhaps in accord with the crisis in sanctioning traditional male values in the aftermath of Vietnam, both Teasle and Rambo fall some way short of being virile John Wayne models of heroism; they are potentially, though, the stuff of heroes, having both endured the rites of combat. Teasle matches Rambo in professionalism, having been decorated with the marines in Korea and is similarly an expert tracker and woodsman.

Morrell's novel concentrates less upon traditional formulations of heroism than upon Oedipal collisions. The tropes of sibling rivalry are replayed in startling fashion; Korea–Vietnam, old veteran–young veteran, pillar of the community–vagrant, respected sheriff–criminal, metaphors which explore aspects of 'the masculine' and 'the father'. Teasle, who is abandoned by his wife and is significantly childless, refers to Rambo throughout the novel as 'the kid', perhaps compensating in some arcane way for his wife's refusal to bear him a child. Fulfilling heterosexual relations do not seem possible in the ethos of the novel and are replaced by problematical man to man relationships. Such absences of women, as Leslie Fiedler has shown, are found widely throughout classic American literature.

Because Rambo has no living father he lacks, like his country, a positive sense of his own identity; he has not come to terms with his absent history. Some attempt at mending this fracture of consciousness is imaged in the narrative through another version of father–son interplay, that between Rambo and Colonel Sam Trautman, his former training instructor in the Green

Berets who makes his entrance with the deathless lines 'Well I'm Sam Trautman . . . I've come about my boy.'[2] Trautman, showing some potential for redemptive action, is the state's surrogate father who dignifies the values of militarism and presents the acceptable face of the Pentagon. The only authority Rambo recognizes is that invested in this élite Green Beret commander, the father to whom he finally submits.

A reading of *First Blood* the novel leaves the reader with two overwhelming impressions which, I believe, are closely connected. First, is the aura of what has been called a primal warrior mythos, Rambo's Samurai image and, secondly, Rambo's search for fatherly authority. If we take the historical context of *First Blood* in 1972 to be that of a nation in shock after losing its first war then both of these narrative patterns are ideologically significant. The episteme novel, *First Blood*, suggests that Rambo is an unwanted child of Vietnam, the alienated throwback to an unpopular war – he is the detritus of history. When he loses his former beliefs, is goaded by the police and acts violently to take revenge against them, his confused and negative actions become symbolic. He changes into a pure fighting machine, an autonomous warrior, yet his values are confused; he has no clear sense of purpose. Male courage at this point in history has no positive iconography, just as the bravery formerly shown by Vietnam veterans also seems pointless.

First Blood (1972) allows its reader to construct a parable of the search for leadership in a country where institutional and moral breakdown are rife. This is the point of the relentless search for authority narrated in the text. My argument here is that the narrative patterns suggest that there is no settled place for a generation of young men who experienced both the explosion of 1960s youth culture and war in Indo-China. This is how we may understand the three potential fathers of sons in the novel – Orval the stepfather, the fatherless Teasle who relates paternally to his surrogate son, Rambo, and Trautman (who is a father of daughters it turns out later in the sequence), the military father. In an interesting way *First Blood* by means of an open-ended play of signification dramatizes social and legal authority and also the institutional authority of the family in the form of patriarchal repression commingled with love, regret and filial confusion. A sense of family and community is missing from the novel and instead men without women connote through their fighting and their wounded psyches wider cultural disorder. No catharsis is yet possible it seems in presenting a vision of the Vietnam veteran.

Whereas the novel *First Blood* images Rambo as an assailant-victim stained with the blood of over 20 men, its film version more clearly expresses sympathy for his suffering by more explicitly exonerating his deeds. Its closing song, written by Hal Shafer and Jerry Goldsmith, overtly situates the Vietnam War as back in the world: it is a war omnipresently 'outside your front door' and for the veteran there is no alternative but to fight 'to keep alive'.[3] The movie likewise portrays Rambo in justifiable action against those who call him babykiller and psycho, a man driven into an easily comprehensible, defensive stance.

The film *First Blood* (1982) was released after a 10-year interval, and the time gap is marked by a difference in context. Following a plethora of representations of demented ex-Vietnam killers such as Travis Bickle in *Taxi Driver*, the public's taste for savagely metamorphosed vets has understandably diminished. Our first impressions of the film confirm this difference in consciousness. Immediately the director, Ted Kotcheff, places emphasis upon the veteran as victim. Compared with the novel that initiated the Rambo submyth, the most profound change in the feature film *First Blood* is its concentration upon the situation and character of Rambo to the exclusion of the subtle Teasle–Rambo equilibrium. In the movie attention has shifted almost exclusively to Rambo, Teasle being a more stereotyped intolerant cop. Throughout the film Rambo is massively provoked by officers of the state; unlike the novel, where he kills early on without much hesitation, he is depicted as very reluctant to kill.

In the opening shots Rambo is shown in a concerned sensitive light; he visits an old war comrade but is told by the boy's negro mother that her son has died from the effects of Agent Orange. An explanation and exoneration is thus supplied for Rambo's (now called by his Christian name John) frustration and anger. The prelude shots, especially in their ironic framing of the small town 'Welcome to Hope', linger on Rambo's patriotic insignia. In appearance he is far less of a hippie than the description of him suggests in the novel. Although he has longish hair, what matters most is that his khaki army surplus jacket has the American flag sewn on it. The audience senses that this portrayal will be more sympathetic than the earlier one – the drifter has become a patriotic vet.

As in the novel *First Blood*, the movie of the same name challenges myths of consensus through symbolic violations of the social order. Pursued by Teasle's men in the forest, who through a subtle interchange of symbolism now wear the white hats of virtue, Rambo's self-definition is that of a victim: 'They drew first blood not me.' A major departure from the text of Morrell's novel is the much larger part of the film devoted to Rambo's revenge upon Teasle's town. This is spectacularly visual and clearly alludes to the burning and torching of hamlets in Vietnam. Rambo incinerates the town's trading store which is resonantly titled *The Outpost*, and brings the war home. Old western values are done away with as he atavistically destroys every building in sight and fatally wounds their custodian, Teasle. Interestingly, the screenplay and montage do not show Rambo murdering people but stress instead that his fury is vented against property. His private battle is waged in the mode of the New York vandal, the subway sprayer and demolition man. He is now executing vengeance on American culture which has betrayed him, an avenger with a confused cause.

The film's narrative of cruel policemen and man-hunting dobermans greatly emphasizes Rambo's post-traumatic stress. Trautman (Trauma or Trout-man, whose name symbolizes his deadly and slippery nature) creates sympathy for his warrior stepson. He explains that Rambo has learned to live off the land: 'God didn't make him: I did.' The audience perceives Rambo from three perspectives; from his own viewpoint as hunted victim, from Teasle's as 'hard ass' psycho, and from Trautman's as élite guerrilla fighter whose prowess is such that, when cornered, 'a good supply of bodybags is needed'.[4]

Fugitive, potential psychopathic killer, Samurai, Rambo unites all three roles, and is consistently represented sympathetically. When Trautman persuades him to cease firing the film offers a coda in the mood of elegy as Rambo reiterates his dutiful patriotism. In the novel, of course, he dies in a stylized shoot out with Teasle, but here he is exhumed and reinvented, a protagonist with an urgent message that Vietnam cannot be evaded: it is right outside everyone's front door. That old war, the source of his troubles, was fought decently: 'I did as you asked. I did what I had to but you wouldn't let me win.' Rambo's lament speaks of his nation's collective abnegation of responsibility, of economic and moral neglect: 'I was in charge of a million dollar gunship but here I can't hold a job.' His weeping is a token for America's defeat and its sporadic guilt over the way it treated its veterans.

First Blood is a thoughtful film and, like the novel that generated it, worthy of critical attention as a sophisticated and well-directed action movie: the artistic quality of these two popular works, as I shall try to demonstrate, far exceeds that of their two more lucrative successors which borrow their cadences and repertoire of styles.

The thesis of my essay is that the Vietnam War for Americans can only be recuperated through such mythic narratives as films and novels. As US foreign policy shifts and political perceptions change, media revisionism and popular television series accommodate what was a serious defeat by reinventing history. A major thrust of my argument is that the *First Blood* texts deploy certain recognizable signifiers (for example, Rambo's partially clad body or his headband), but that the *meaning* of these signs changes in evolving context. The characterization of Rambo continues to develop as does that of other mass cultural heroes such as James Bond. Rambo is an adaptable commodity, a man without lineage, a fatherless ex-soldier in quest of authority. Because he has no family, close ties or constricting environment he is capable of being a vehicle of values and ideological inflections. His evolving masculinity, for example, continues to be a focal point. In the movie *Rambo – First Blood II* (1985) previous signifiers – of courage, military prowess, male purity, latent homosexuality, rebelliousness – become factors in the making of political statements. The film's huge success testifies to the power of popular works to make influential ideological interventions. Rambo is transported back to Vietnam infused with the strength of not only the two previous *First Blood* texts but a host of other films, television series and popular novels. It is his mission to make the definitive ideological statement of cultural revisionism.

Turning now to the recently released *Rambo: First Blood Part II* movie (1985),[5] directed not by Ted Kotcheff but by George P. Cosmatos with screenplay by Sylvester Stallone and James Cameron, who wrote *The Terminator*, it is necessary to note as a preface to any discussion the fact that the film coincided opportunistically with the tenth anniversary of the end of American direct involvement in Vietnam. American newspapers, television screens, magazines and radio programmes were flooded with reminiscences, memoirs and flashbacks to the evacuation of Saigon. At least three books a week were published in 1985 devoted to the Vietnam War, in marked contrast to the immediate post-Vietnam years when it was virtually impossible to find a publisher willing to take on war books. If we recognize Rambo mark three as the son of a previous Rambo father and grandfather then it is important to heed the new public context. The perception of the once-vilified and forgotten war has again changed. Some of the previous political perceptions – of My Lai, Tet, Khe Sanh, the fall of Saigon – are incorporated into new cultural configur-ations. From a detailed study of cultural productions during 1985 the retroactive vision appears much softened.[6] The culture has re-educated itself, evolved new symbolic codes to articulate an understanding of Vietnam; it has undone or deconstructed previous 'readings' of the war. As signifying 'text' the Vietnam monument is instructive: the Veterans' wall in Washington has become one of the capital's three most popular tourist attractions and often draws over 10,000 visitors a day. The aporia of Vietnam is over, the impasse resolved. A collective response of cathartic release now seems possible.

Rambo II is the most famous example of the new ideological dispositions. It is a film which draws upon many influences and, in particular, upon three contemporary filmic genres: the neo-cold war movie as represented by such films as *Red Dawn, White Knights, Firefox* and *Rocky 4*; the missing in action sequence of films including *Uncommon Valor* and *Missing in Action I and II*; and a series of one-man army films such as *Lone Wolf McQuade, Invasion USA* and Arnold Swarzenegger's *Commando*.

Making the feature film *Rambo* involved its producers in a complex logistical exercise. In one sequence, the destruction of Camp 3, over 300 gallons of gasoline, 200 pounds of black powder, 1500 feet of cord and 400 car tyres were used to simulate the reality of bombing. Filmic art imitates, in grotesquely ironic ways, the reality of life. In the film the Vietnamese woman, Co, who works for the CIA desires to live in California – the actress playing her, Julia Nickson, a half Chinese girl and Hawaii's top model, actually resides in Los Angeles; the danger of combat is simulated by a team of daring stunt men, one of whom, Cliff Wenger Jr, tragically dies – he is memorialized through a special credit line in the film, becoming a dead warrior in the continuing war to win audiences.[7]

Rambo II is witness to more absurd ironies even than these. The principal encoding of America's involvement in Vietnam, the use of napalm from helicopters such as the famous Huey U.H.I.B., is parodied in the film when Rambo is initially attacked from the air. The film's narrative would have us believe that he is strafed and napalmed from a gunship left behind by the Americans and renovated by the Russians, and so any vestiges of historical truth are sanitized. After the scene when Rambo captures the Huey he is pursued by a massive mocked-up soviet MIL M124 Hind Assault gunship (actually a French Puma), notoriously emblematic of Russian presence in Afghanistan and Nicaragua. The comic strip turns out after all to deliver a message.

Rambo, probably the most successful film ever worldwide, is a movie of its time, capturing a worldwide mood if its box office success in Arab countries such as the Lebanon, in South Africa, the Philippines and China is recognized.

One may theorize that the revenge theme of the movie appeals because virtually all of the world's peoples' inhabit a terrorist culture either as producers or consumers of terrorism. As the potential for internecine struggle and armed anarchy increases so the movie *Rambo*, a cult film for the young, seems to be attuned to the pulse of future history.

The audience for Rambo products signifies how marketing is geared to the young consumer – colouring books, computer games and bubble gum for pre-adolescents, and annuals, magazines, records and the lucrative video cassettes for teenagers. Since the advent of computer games the West's high-technology market has inflicted psychic damage on its young people through the popularization of militarist culture. The multiplication of weaponry in children's TV programmes and the exaltation of the human being who borrows the supernatural qualities of the assault weapon, like the jargon of accompanying violence, is a deeply worrying cultural trend. A recent teenage magazine which features a major article on Sylvester Stallone, and may therefore be aimed at both sexes, capitalizes on the Rambo cult by including a summary of the film peppered with words such as 'garrotte', 'lobotomised', 'severed vocal chords'.[8] Insidiously this account of the *Rambo* movie also incorporates a garbled history of the Vietnam War comprised of half-truths and 'disinformation'.

Rambo, a technically sophisticated movie, is heavily dependent upon what Stallone has called 'pure technique' and 'brooding lighting effects'. It also draws heavily on Jerry Goldsmith's noisy musical score which points up the film's tendency towards the non-verbal. Stallone's body through its movements and gestures creates a kind of language and becomes the principal site of enunciation. According to one critic the camera lingers over his muscles 'with an abandon not seen on the screen since Joseph Von Sternberg made movies with Marlene Dietrich'.[9] The mode of the film is also anti-realistic in its implausible borrowing from the techniques of cartoon and comic strip. While posturing as caring for a generation of lost young men, *Rambo* falsifies its premises by narcissistically flaunting Stallone's sexuality. The subject of the film is essentially the male body. Probably the only words that matter are those which prefigure the action, 'Do we get to win this time?', and those that end it: 'We want for our country to love us the way that we love it.' John Rambo's patriotism, expressed in restricted utterance is undiminished,[10] the former criminal is metamorphosed into second time around hero.

The projection of the body is one of the film's central ideologies – a sexist assertion of male dominance – while its other stereotypes are found in its unpleasant fusion of racism and gratuitous violence. *Rambo* has attracted widespread criticism for its exploitation of violence: it has been argued that there are more deaths shown in the film than in the actual Tet offensive. Some critics have taken the opposite viewpoint and have defended the film on the grounds that the violence is, like that of the comic strip, distanced and therefore not harmful. It is difficult to mobilize this defence against the frequent aestheticizing of wounding and killing where camera shots of horrific death are lingering and graphic. The film clearly puts a low premium on the worth of human life, and it is no mitigation to say that other films such as *Nightmare on Elm Street* or *Halloween Part 4* are much more violent.

A particular example of racism will have to suffice, how it portrays the puritanical North Vietnamese Army (NVAS) who purged Saigon of prostitutes, as sexual degenerates; the image is of Vietnamese Communist soldiers so sexually permissive that their security is nightly breached by a visiting whore. Their competence and discipline are also represented as grossly inadequate as Rambo is seen to out-manoeuvre them easily. Racism is insidiously fostered in a traditional vision of oriental soldiers as vicious, callous, effeminate and genetically inferior. The élite Russian corps of Spetsnaz treat the Vietnamese condescendingly. Podovsk and Yashin are pros in the same league as supervet Rambo, whereas Captain Vinh and Sergeant Tay, the leading Vietnamese adversaries, are caricatured as corrupt and inefficient.

Rambo II is an adventure film according to its initiator, David Morrell, in the tradition of comic book and fantasy. He expressed the opinion in a recent interview that the movie always reminds him of 'Star Wars in Vietnam'.[11] Rambo is, then, back in the Badlands, visually reminding us of the vanished American. As well as the 'grace' of Stallone's performance, the thrill of action and occasional moments of vision, the movie acts out another ideological fantasy. The film tells us that Rambo, the lone frontiersman, is opposed by vastly superior forces. As his creator theorizes, not only is he 'put upon by the Establishment, twisted and perverted by a system that was', but he is also frustrated by the Communist forces of Vietnam. Their superior technology and well-equipped army put him paradoxically in the position formerly constructed for the Vietcong, of underdog; America has again become David not Goliath. Rambo, like the United States is released from spiritual captivity. (Rambo is literally set free from gaol and is free at last from his angst. Now he can be a man again, a reluctant superhero confronting overwhelming odds, as free from the contamination of ideology as older heroes.) He points to America's links with Nature, an entrepreneur of the frontier rather than a colonizer of culture. Rambo's ontological significance is thus considerable – he has lost the war only to win it. America's manhood is intact – the veteran, formerly calumniated as a babykiller, is restored through new rites of passage. A new cultural historiography is apparent, firmly established here through the restoration of the male filmic hero. *Top Gun*, a film released in 1986, also reinforces the traditional consolidation of male dominance and competitive power, and is an heir to *Rambo*.

The *Rambo* sequence, then, dramatizes a cultural history. Morrell, the novelist, killed off his protagonist at the end of the first novel, *First Blood*; however, consumer culture exhumes him. He is literally brought back to life in a process of cultural deracination: the psychopath is deconstructed, put together again in redeemed form. When he tears a strip off his dead woman Co's dress and wears her metonymically in a sweatband, the woman semiologically adorns the man, her intrinsic reality as a human being appropriated. In synecdoche the 'message' is coded thus: a macho man such as Rambo will carry a devoted woman's favour in the old fashioned way. The

Vietnam War is here represented through such sanctioned ideological signifiers. Rambo, the decoy of the sinister CIA, is expendable and yet, facing the torture of the Indo-China jungle, comes through unscathed. The film suggests that there is truth of a simple 'moral' kind kept from the public by agents such as Murdoch – it implies that we should not trust governments of either complexion because it is only the patriotic, selfless, unexpendable individual who can ultimately impose control. What Rambo wants is for America to be healed through the movies: 'What every guy who ever came over here and spilled his guts and gave everything he had wants . . . for his country to love us as much as we love it. That's what we want.'

David Morrell, the academic with a Ph.D. in the novels of Barth, has explained that the massively popular novel based on the screenplay of the film, *Rambo – First Blood Part II*,[12] offered him an opportunity to expand the film's script and flesh out its narrative and characterization. The poor literary quality of the later novel compared with its initiator suggests that Morrell perceived his task in the same spirit as one of his characters perceives Rambo: 'Your boy's a helluva guy. I mean Flash Gordon. Good Old Nam', Doyle said, 'The gift that keeps on giving.'[13] The body count of readers who have read the novel proves that the formula is commercially right and the Vietnam rematch has the approved result: Rambo, from Bowie, Arizona, son of an Italian Catholic and Navaho mother 200, People's Republic of Vietnam 0. Rambo also outwits the Russian pros from Denver who have seen Eliot Gould and Donald Sutherland in M.A.S.H. American individualism in-country drawing upon spears, rocks and catapults defeats CIA mercenaries, Russians and trained Vietnamese military personnel. Rambo's sexual purity and abstinence, endorsed in the novel, also contribute to his invincibility.

The subtext of the second novel is a set of conservative assumptions and myths about personal conduct in society. By proclaiming that 'the country's different' and, although it was a 'bad war' the soldiers 'weren't bad',[14] the narrative places emphasis upon the foregrounded subject. In an influential account of the poet W. B. Yeats's proto-fascism, George Orwell drew attention to the anti-democratic nature of Yeats's mysticism and interest in the occult.[15] Terry Eagleton has made a similar charge against T. S. Eliot's *Four Quartets*.[16] Interestingly, there is a strong streak of mysticism, too, in the novel *First Blood II* which is associated both with the novel's discourses on weaponry and its assertion that 'what people wanted wasn't politics but to be left alone'.[17] My point here is that Rambo's litanies over his serrated hunting knife and explosive arrows clearly reflect a *laissez-faire* mystification of the individual's rights (such a conservative strain is a coping stone of United States hunting culture). What the novel celebrates is the pure vigilante right to commit violence and love the commital and its instruments. Textual evidence for this abounds in the novel: the opening advertisement for weapons, the essays on the longbow, the many instances where Rambo, priest-like, exalts weapons and 'treats them with respect – indeed, with almost religious reverence'.[18] The essay on the bow and arrow, redolent with technical detail and philosophical phoniness, is not merely a commercial plug but also a distasteful celebration of the right to wield offensive arms.

Trautman deplores the lax leisure culture and calls for discipline: what America needs is not 'super surfers. Not hot doggers. You're still machinery. We base our operations on precision.'[19] The individual should emulate the functional serrated bowie knife with its box-of-tricks handle. Towards the conclusion of the second novel, and rounding off nicely the *First Blood* series of texts, Ronald Reagan is mentioned affectionately by Rambo when filling the recaptured POWs in on what has happened to America. The States have a new president: 'Despite his agony Rambo had to chuckle, Death Valley Days himself. . . . Yeah John Wayne, Ronald Reagan and the Movies.'[20] (There is also an important reference here to Vietnam changing to Nicaragua, which suggests the continuing need for a John Wayne style president.) The wounds of Vietnam are now, the text implies, being healed despite Nicaragua and other problems of communism because we have an authentic American hero at the nation's helm. Rambo has no real father but he has two surrogate authority figures – Trautman, the Pentagon's purest embodiment, and a humorous grandfather, Ronald Reagan. The nation is, as in the days of Ike, led by a glamorous patriarch. It is no accident that Ronald Reagan is often satirized as 'Ronbo', and called for a Rambo to aid America after the Beirut hostage crisis.

To conclude my discussion I will try briefly to construct an overview of how the *Rambo* texts have evolved. They broadly follow – if we understand them as both process and representation – a trajectory that correlates with certain aspects of America's recent consciousness of itself. For example, David Morrell's originating novel, written in 1972, equates with early post-war attitudes of disillusionment and cultural amnesia. The novel, through its metaphors of excessive violence, castigates the insensitivity and corruption of those who 'didn't get over' and Rambo's multiple killings are presented as not entirely without justification; significantly, Rambo is killed off like a dangerous animal.

When Rambo re-emerges in the first movie, after an interval of 10 years, there has clearly been a significant shift in perception and expectation. The signifiers of art and popular culture have been modified, both responding to a new complex of sensibility and indeed acting as agent in its formation and dissemination. Rambo is now differently textured, a more sympathetic hero of the new mood. His filmic presentation allows the audience to identify with a persecuted veteran who has merely done his duty. Rambo, no longer inherently violent, is now a broken hero whose final weeping symbolizes the United States' unconscious guilt at neglecting its veterans. John Rambo, in this film, is not entirely expendable: his portrayal is transitionally attuned to impending recuperation. When the box office success *Rambo*, the movie, is released in 1985, it seems that previous missing-in-action films, together with the 10-year anniversary of the evacuation of Saigon, have again shifted popular assumptions and values. Buoyancy and, in the popular mind, a new metaphor encoding Vietnam as a dignified struggle are now apparent, the sense of a war that could and should have been won if only incompetent politicians had not interfered. The Asian conflict is re-mythologized through the narrative of the avenging super vet.

To verify this tracing out of connections we need to examine not only the texts of fiction and movies but also the conditions, events and processes of politics and economics, an investigation only marginally touched upon in this paper. Without the support of this more substantive analysis any conclusions are likely to be provisional, and yet it is probably accurate to suggest that the later *Rambo* works exemplify the notion of 'conservative optimism', thereby demonstrating a populist sense that America has restored itself after the Nixon and Carter presidencies. It is no accident that John Rambo's favourite films are said to be *Star Wars* and *Flash Gordon*: he is a regenerative hero of the satellite era of Space Defense Initiative (SDI) technology and advanced weaponry. The later novel of course, and the film *Rambo II*, unashamedly spiritualize the weapon. This excessive reverencing of the gun, the fetishistic adoration of the M16 or the AK47, celebrates through metaphor the invincible and unstoppable American arms industry and culture of death. The film is thus an example of what William Gibson has termed 'paramilitary culture'.[21]

My analysis of the *Rambo* productions ignores such easy targets as the rampant commercialism of the cult and how its themes reinforce this orientation. Yet it is nevertheless interesting finally to note how representation and style have altered over the 13-year span separating the various artefacts discussed. The bunker mentality and defeatism that inform the original *First Blood* novel are expressed through the quirky figure of a bearded hippie, unwashed and rebellious. The first Rambo is initially presented as a deviant offshoot akin to the radical counter-cultural protesters of the late 1960s. By the time we reach *Rambo II*, the target audience encounters a more stylized, macho figure, a commodity-star marketed towards box office success. Stallone's Rambo is the heir to Rocky Balboa.

The *Sunday Times* film critic has succinctly described the metamorphosis:

> The male cinema heroes of yesteryear – Gary Cooper, Jimmy Stewart, John Wayne, were strong silent and would themselves have laughed at a preening lout like Rambo wearing his machismo on his sleeve. In an earlier day he would have been the heavy – now he's the hero. What's gone wrong?
>
> Twenty three years old Jack Merslek has seen *Rambo* three times and says he's the perfect symbol of the 1980s. He's sensitive *and* macho. He can kick the hell out of you and then cry at your funeral.[22]

It has been the purpose of this essay to argue that the *First Blood* series expresses through its denouement these new modes of taste, sensibility and concepts of the heroic. The later *Rambo* characters open out towards an ethos of demeaning lowest-denominator populism. From 1982 a new cultural trend is visible: the blend is one of lauding super-élitism (the super vet), of recurrent and displaced racism, of narcissistic masculinity, of feting and aestheticizing violence, and of backward-looking anarchism (Rambo at the end of the film blows up the new technology). If ideology is the relation between discourse and power then it is no surprise that Rambo has become synonymous with jingoism, sexism, racial prejudice and a certain kind of machismo style, seemingly an irresistible combination if box office figures are to be taken seriously.

Notes

1. All page references are to David Morrell, *First Blood*, London: Pan Books, 1973. First published in 1972.
2. Op. cit., p. 146.
3. *First Blood* (1982) is adapted from David Morrell's novel of 1972 and is directed by Ted Kotcheff. It stars Sylvester Stallone as Rambo and Richard Crenna as Trautman.
4. Quotations are from the film *First Blood*.
5. *Rambo: First Blood II* is directed by George P. Cosmatos with screenplay by Sylvester Stallone and James Cameron. It stars Sylvester Stallone with supporting actors, Richard Crenna as Trautman, Charles Napier as Murdoch and Julia Nickson as Co.
6. See R. A. Berman, 'Rambo: From Counter Culture to Contra', *Teleos*, 1984, No. 64 (Summer), and Rick Berg, 'Losing Vietnam. Covering the War in an Age of Technology', in *Cultural Critique*, 1986, No. 3 (Spring), a special edition on Vietnam, for a discussion of the new cultural context of revisionism.
7. For the background to the making of the film, see *Action Screen*, 1985, No. 1, which discusses *Rambo II*, pp. 3–19 and *Miami Vice*.
8. *Action Screen*, pp. 12–19.
9. D. Gram, 'The Politics of Machismo', the *Sunday Times*, 7 July 1985.
10. See earlier filmed heroes who eschewed too much talk and created the strong, silent machismo image such as Marlon Brando in *On the Waterfront*, James Dean in *Rebel Without A Cause* and Gary Cooper in *High Noon*. These characterizations suggest variations of the theme of the quiet but tough male character.
11. See William Alland, *Knave*, 1986, **18** (6), pp. 60–4.
12. David Morrell, *Rambo – First Blood Part II*, London: Arrow Books, 1985.
13. Ibid., p. 113.
14. Ibid., pp. 33–4.
15. George Orwell, 'W. B. Yeats', in *Critical Essays*, London: Secker and Warburg, 1961.
16. Terry Eagleton, *Literary Theory: An Introduction*, London: Blackwell 1983.
17. *Rambo* (the novel), p. 79.
18. Ibid., p. 75.
19. Ibid., p. 101.
20. Ibid., p. 235.
21. James William Gibson, 'Paramilitary Culture and the Reconstruction of Vietnam', in *Vietnam Images: War and Representation* (eds Jeffrey Walsh and James Aulich), forthcoming.
22. D. Gram, op. cit.

Alan Fair

3

The Beast in the Jungle: Mailer, Eastlake and the Narrating of Vietnam

experience is never limited, and it is never complete.

Henry James

Julia Kristeva begins an essay on the work of Roland Barthes by typifying the contemporary moment as one of exhaustion: 'As capitalist society is being economically and politically choked to death', she writes, 'distance is wearing thin and heading for collapse at a more rapid rate than ever before.'[1] This pronouncement, though a little optimistic about the decline of capitalism, is nevertheless emblematic of a contemporary sensibility. In the past 40 years we have witnessed an explosion of information; everywhere we turn we are confronted with the sounds and images of late capitalism; our consumer society has produced an effect of plentitude in a world where scarcity is the major day-to-day problem faced by most people on the planet – a society where consuming and being consumed is the difference between freedom and paranoic phantasy of freedom. Everywhere we look we are bombarded with images, images of ourselves consuming, images to be consumed. It is, as the situationists of the mid-1960s had it, a society of spectacle, a spectacular society where the gaze holds and is held in a constant oscillation between subject and object.

Death and destruction, the burning of babies and of old people, is nothing new in human society, but what is new and profoundly affective is the need to look. The victims of Buchenwald, Hiroshima and My Lai are now double victims; they suffer the outrages of rampant militarism, but alone this is not enough, for they have to be seen to suffer them. The ubiquitous camera lingers over the emaciated, over the burnt, over the slaughtered. The mushroom cloud has become an object of contemplation; it is reproduced in poster form and hangs on kitchen walls and undergraduates' studies, transformed into an aesthetic object. Popular memory has given way to television histories and bi-weekly collectables. The struggle for hegemony is marked by the ability to reproduce a Utopia of individual consumption, a place where forgetting takes the place of memory and pleasure becomes the dominant principle.

History, it seems, has become a surface and a superficiality, endlessly reproduced in our living rooms, a product of a society in which, as the American scholar Frederick Jameson[2] reminds us, the bourgeois instructs us to convert things into ideas, ideas into images and images into names . . ., and when this surface ruptures the people either cry for revolution, for insanity, or for authority: they demand new forms, exploded forms or a return to old forms once and for all fixed. It is this moment that has recently (in literary circles at least) been given the name, the post-modern. This new name attaches itself to a new aesthetic caught in a configuration largely determined by an intellectual atmosphere that seems to be removed from any idea of social action. I wish to address myself to this configuration in the following pages by looking at two texts produced at what, in retrospect, can be seen as a turning point in contemporary society: the mid-1960s, a time of disruption and innovation. Both novels are tied implicitly to the social, and are texts within a context of national and international struggle – two novels concerned with the production of aesthetic codes, both liberated and constrained by the new paradigmatic forms of narrative.

First there is the past, then there is history, history the grand narrative of our coming into being. What is at stake when we narrate our past, especially when the past event is something as monumental as war, is not the facts but the truth. The two constructors of narrative I have chosen to discuss both seek this seemingly ahistorical, transcendental construct, the truth; even if, as we shall see later, the 'God-given' will by her actions deny that we can ever get to the truth, we can nevertheless honestly speculate that the facts of the Vietnam War will not concern these fabulators, rather the profound penumbration of that which seems to lie beneath the symbolic world it signifies. Nothing is denoted, save jungle and confusion, and yet everything is connoted, everything that is, that is named as the truth of America in Vietnam.

The novelist has lost her/his naivety: no longer does the writer work within the purity of a formalized tradition, but within the disruptions of the volatile velocity of the space age, an age paradoxically where there no longer seems to be any space, filled as it is with the babble of contemporary consumer capitalism. One has only to walk down the lower east side of Manhattan Island, that shock city *par excellence*, a shrine to the post-modern, to see that almost every available space is taken up with the pathetic inscriptions of the lost, of the forgotten, where identity is marked by the spray-can flourish, the tag, a name derived from the GI's dog-tag, the indelible mark of the self, a palimpsest of the unnamed, named and then obscured. This phenomenon is something that Norman Mailer will address himself to after his Vietnam novel, as though the initial question posed, 'Why Are We In Vietnam?', found its most emblematic answer on the crumbling walls of Fifth Street and Second Avenue. In this environment the act of writing is challenged to make sense, to once more concern itself with the act of making new a world spinning in a whirlwind of language. If the initial question was 'why?', the second and more important question seems to be 'how?' or, more properly, how does the writer present this 'why'. Mailer implies that in order to understand America's involvement in South-East Asia we need to look to the post-modern cluster, the plethora of image constellations, the soap opera, the pornography industry, advertising and the intellectuals' name-bag emptied onto the hi-gloss surface coffee table of the TV chat-show. The novel *Why Are We In Vietnam?* opens with the all too familiar background noise of the chirpy D.J., the radio voice as narrator of the modern psychosis:

> Hip hole and humpmobile, Braunschweiger you didn't invite Geiger and his counter for nothing, here is D.J. and friendlee voice at your service-hold tight young America – introductions come. Let go of my dong: Shakespeare, I have gone too long, it is too late to tell my tale, may Batman tell it, let him declare there's blood on my dick and D.J. Dicktor Doc Dick and Jek has got the bloods, and has done animal murder, out out damn fart and murder of the soldierest sort, cold was my hand and hot.[3]

Here we have the violent multiplicity of discourse: science, technology, culture (both élite and mass), sexuality and death, the psycho-babble of American nihilism cavorting in a painful gesture of teenage defiance. From this opening paragraph we are dealt the whole pack, a tarot of indifference: the novel is condensed, a microcosm of Mailer's vision of the lost, from the plate-glass reflective city of Dallas to the Wagnerian heroics of Alaska and on, finally, to Vietnam, a place that rhymes with 'Hot-Damn'. The first two chapters of the novel are an agglomeration of names and images denoting a cultural hot-pot, full of significance and yet bereft of meaning, a textual world that produces its own context, a mass cultural steam-bath, sweating male sexuality in the guise of a desired mother in the ultimate Oedipal Russian roulette, where the name of the father spells out the initiation into pre-cultural death rites. This lexicon of lasciviousness seems to leave us – the readers – out, and yet we are constantly called upon to respond to the narrator's repeated affirmative gesticulation – 'Yeah! Yeah!'.

Mailer produces a pastiche of style, where all cultural intonation is levelled by the surface of pure language. The novel plays with the Beats' gambit, the stream of unconsciousness of William Burroughs, a dense verdant lexical jungle whose literary lions are the father figures of this textual adolescent (T. S. Eliot thrown in to throw us off balance), and the book becomes self-consciously writerly, treading a fine line of supposed schizophrenic discourse while nudging us in the ribs with authorial asides.

> There's not a colon in captivity which manufactures a home product that is transparency proof to Dr. Jekyll's X-ray insight. He sees right into the claypots below the duodenum of his father, and any son does that is fit candidate for a maniac, right T.S.? the point here, Eliot, is that D.J. will never know if Rusty dropped points in the early stages of his contest with

Luke because he was dying inside for not being down at the Canaveral table where big power space decisions were being made . . .[4]

This novel then is the story of what, by all accounts, is the universal preamble to male adulthood, the adolescent's trial by combat. The story of Ronald Jethroe (otherwise known as D.J.), the son of a Dallas tycoon, and his pals going to the wilderness, is an orgy of blood and male sexuality. They are finding positions for themselves, fixed American subjects just waiting to take on the 'gooks'. Told through flash-back from the point of imminent departure, we follow the travels of D.J., Tex and Rusty as the question 'why are we in Vietnam?' is answered, with the invocation of the American male mythos, the frontier spirit of Leatherstocking, John Glenn and General Westmoreland.

While these textual rich kids strut their sexual sadism on the penultimate frontier the *real* poor kids of the ghetto do the same in Indo-China, but somehow the allegory is lost in the confusions of the pleasure principle. D.J. is the perennial 'white negro', all pose and artifice without having to deal with the material conditions of black urban life. This is a world of life-styles and personalities rather than people and lives, and yet one feels the force of a certain accuracy in Mailer's work. If modernism articulates the plight of the alienated subject then post-modernism articulates the multiple cry of the fragmented subject. In this sense D.J. moves beyond the existential angst of the white negro; he is both Harlem nigger, a jitterbug Jehovah taunting white morality *and* spoilt rich kid, a hedonist of linguistic stupefaction. The narrative follows structures but, like the subject, is broken by a confusion of time. Mailer acts as narrator. Or is it interrupter? Or is it explainer, like the voice-over at the beginning of Flash Gordon serials? The difference being that it is narrative not plot that attention is drawn to; narrativity problematizes ideas of time (relativity for the lay-man), where memory and a projected future collide in the textual weft and warp.

> This is after labor day, early September in Alaska, two years (to remind you) before the period of D.J.'s consciousness running through his head, hence form is more narrative, memory being always more narrative than the tohu-bohu of the present, which is old testament Hebrew, cock-sucker, for chaos and void.[5]

It is this subject, then, that Mailer implies is at the centre of the reasons for the United States' adventure in Vietnam, a paranoid who is assailed on all sides by mythic memories of America, but yet is lost in the 'chaos and void' of the present, the powerless subject retrieving meaning from the past for a future that may be the end of meaning. The w.a.s.p. paranoiac whose racist, sexist ravings remind one of Judge Schrieber with the light of God emanating from his backside. The fragmented society drawn to the chosen one, the single w.a.s.p. centre, God's chosen people attacked by twentieth-century anomie:

Yeah sighs Rusty, the twentieth century is breaking up the ball game and
Rusty thinks large common thoughts such as these.

There follows a list of demented white male fears about women, about
blacks, about Jews, about the 'yellow-races', about Communism. When the list
is finished the conclusion is that:

He, Rusty is fucked unless he gets that bear, for if he don't white men are
fucked more and they can take no more. Rusty's secret is that he sees
himself as one of the pillars of the firmament, yeah, man – he reads the
world's doom in his own fuckup.[6]

Shades here of that 1970s w.a.s.p. psychotic Travis Bickle (*Taxi Driver*,
directed by M. Scorcese, 1976), driven to the limits of delirium, sensing that the
only way out is to destroy what seems to threaten, and in the ideology of
cold-war America that is everything, everything that is apart from the
Marlboro Man and the gingham dress housewife who stays in the kitchen while
the men have homo-erotic phantasies that disgust their received self-image to
such a degree that they beat up 'queens' and gooks and Communists, which
amount to the same thing. Rusty must kill the bear, the untamed nature that
threatens culture, the unconscious that looms too close to the surface for
comfort. These people can't trust anything anymore – not even the American
eagle – and in a moment of questioning in the high mountains of Alaska, D.J.'s
father says to his son:

But I think it's a secret crime that America, which is the greatest nation
ever lived, better read a lot of history to see how shit and sure a
proposition that is (E. Pluribus Unum) is nonetheless represented,
indeed even symbolised by an eagle, the most miserable of the
scavengers, worse than a crow.[7]

It is here in the loss of this certainty that war seems to offer a return to
nationhood, one nation out of many bound together by battle. If in the
wilderness the senses of the hunter are heightened, it is a sensuality of violence
and death; while the signifiers remain, their ability is stripped bare and then
transformed. The context, a vortex of violence and struggle, never allows
meaning to settle; each character struggles for a fixity which can only be found
in facile slogans ('Vietnam hot-damn'), but these are textual actants, meaningful only at the level of utterance, dissolved in the play of narrative only to
reappear at the privileged moment of address, a political moment where the
triad of novel, reader and society combine to make sense – political sense – of
meanings constructed. Mailer recognizes the efficacy of fiction but never
allows our imaginations to run away with our intellect, reminding us constantly
through his shifts in modes of address that a job of work needs to be done. It is
in this sense that *Why Are We In Vietnam?* operates as didactic fiction yet never
falls into the trap of the hector.

Mailer, then, sees the reasons for the American involvement in Vietnam as
explainable not only at the level of capitalist economics (can we say here that
war is the continuation of accumulation by other means?), but also at the level

of deep structural cultural forces. In *The Bamboo Bed* (a novel set in Vietnam), William Eastlake explores not so much the reasons for engagement as the capacities of the text itself to comprehend/represent the American psyche. For Eastlake these problems of representation – of the relations of text and world – derive from the difficulty of depicting the inner truth of the quotidian, rather than the veracities of grand scale analyses of class struggle, expansionism and cultural imperialism. This, of course, does not mean that an enquiry into this struggle for representation cannot lead us to conclusions about the activities of capital, activities which, for Marxists at least, are always already inscribed within the domain of conflict.

It is in the first three paragraphs of *Bamboo Bed* that Eastlake articulates his task of representing truth:

> Madame Dieudonné arose, stark and stripped, in her underground villa at 0600 hours as was her wont, turned on the shortwave radio and heard the report from Laos that Captain Clancy was dead, then she walked, still naked to her jewel box, removed a small black, heavy object, raised it to her head and blew her pretty French brains out. Pas vrai. Not true. That's the way the papers had it, but they did not get it right. They never do. The newspapers seldom get anything right because they are not creative. Life is an art.
>
> It was true – c'etait vrai – that Madame Dieudonné went to the jewel box, removed the gun, but nothing more. Another death did not follow fast upon. The newspapers made a good story. But there is a better one. The truth.[8]

There is what the newspapers say, the story, and there is the truth. A fictive truth but, the narrator implies, a truth closer to the idea of a truth which in itself is merely a tetxual position. The truth is rendered as architrace of the movement of glyphs across the page, a rendering of history as narrative of what might have *really* happened in Vietnam.

This is the story of what 'really happened to Clancy', marooned on hill 904 in a vain quest for land and glory, the dizzy heights of self-esteem, state and honour in the thinned air of the Indo-Chinese mountains. From Alaska to the borders of Cambodia is just a hop, skip and a text away. But while in the wild North American landscape the truth is revealed to be a mythic past and a sense of national belonging, a congruence of personal desire and public aspiration, in the chaotic jungles of South-East Asia the truth is a more difficult thing to figure; and so if we, stranded here in the late 1980s, cannot tread over rain-soaked vines to read the bloody hieroglyphs in order to examine this imaged real, then trapped in the textual symbolic we become like Clancy, mesmerized by the absurdity of war.

For at the level of cultural discourse what war represents is the explosion of the semiotic. The conventional meanings anchored in the sign are subverted by the absurdist moment of carnage. How, for example, can a tree be simply vegetation when death in the shape of a sniper may lurk there? Hence, the unconscious of the text articulates the surrealists' dictum, 'the fortuitous juxtaposition of incongruous objects'. Everything in war is made strange, and the text makes strange this strangeness. It doubles our distance in a struggle for proximity and in so doing ruptures our perception, allowing the fissures exposed to articulate the truth of its effects:

> 'That's right. Not one fucking Iota!' Janine wondered what Iota meant. She wondered what fucking meant. She wondered what anything meant. In a jungle where words become meaningless you wonder what every-thing means.[9]

This is Janine, nurse Bliss and Knightsbridge – Jane and Tarzan – who, above the green canopy in a helicopter – the bamboo bed – make love striving for the 'highest screw' ever while on their mission to locate Clancy. In contact with the ground by radio they get a message from Alpha Company, Clancy's outfit: 'Meaningless. You said you picked up something that was meaningless. What was meaningless?', Jane asks Knightsbridge. 'They', Knightsbridge answers.[10] The truth here is meaninglessness. There are only versions of the real. 'They' are the 'unfriendlies', the soft soap slang of official turning away. Tarzan and Jane in their mythic bliss, together with Lavender and Elgar and the others, are on search and rescue. A search and rescue for Clancy, Clancy the almighty protofascist warrior whose solitary jungle reverie reveals a truth, a truth like the inarticulable truth of Marlow's jungle – a horror – Clancy's individual version of the real, his subjective response to authority, sexuality and war, set as it is against the collective authority of the state and the unfriendlies' all-knowing certitude. A kind of existential perception that loses out to the history of Indo-China and the time of the jungle's steady engulfing. Whereas Mailer deconstructs his narrative with temporal dislocation, Eastlake uses space. All episodes seem to happen simultaneously but in different parts of the war – in the air, in the jungle, in the field headquarters – each place mapping out its own version of what happened on hill 904. This fragmented text mirrors a war without a front line. This is indeed, from the point of view of the European mind, what creates the anxiety of knowing. The boundaries of position are transformed into the limits of knowledge, the arbitrariness of the friendlies and the unfriendlies. What is the difference between Yvor, the man with no arms who is commander-in-chief – 'God', as Billy Boy his aide remarks – and those other controllers who lurk behind the jungle's cover? This is Yvor's war, he is god, he makes it happen, but so too do the unfriendlies. Clancy is caught in Catch 22, they *are* all out to kill him: the Vietnamese because he is an imperialist aggressor, the industrial/military complex because he is an embar-rassment to them. For Clancy the war can never end:

> No not for Clancy. There would always be dreams. The dark shadow on the wall, the myriad dead. The unfriendlies had become the friendlies and the war would never end.[11]

Clancy is caught in the heraclitian flux, the minute grades of differences where there is no fixed identity to carry him through his self-analytical quest. If we can talk about the realist discourse as precisely the gambit of fixing the subject, producing for us a place of recognition, then the post-modern text seems to remove this possibility, producing an effect of pure surface and difference resembling nothing other than the super enlargements of newsprint images that Lichtenstein turned into 'high pop' icons. It is this moment that Freud recognizes in the child's game, 'Fort-da', and which Lacan so success-fully analyses as the transition from the imaginary into the symbolic.[12] The imaginary coming into being of the subject, splitting from its mother, transformed by language as the symbolic articulation of absence and presence, finds its clear definition in the post-modern moment. Here in the textual jungles of Vietnam we are in the realm of the pure symbolic – the imaginary oppositions so useful to understanding in European culture are lost, and all that can be identified is difference and deferment (differrance?). Everything is put off only to reappear in another place; things are recognized, but in a world of pure relativity nothing has the certainty of fixed being. Clancy has conversa-tions with snakes, with tigers, with elephants, all symbolic representations of his own fragmented psyche, all forms of that most radical other – death. The absolute certainty of the imaginary gives way to the differential experience of the symbolic. If, at the end of *Why Are We In Vietnam?* there is, at least, the paranoiac America left in the whirl of discourse, in *The Bamboo Bed* all we have is death, the 'Captain's Bride'. If, as the name implies, Clancy's is a gift from God, then the deferred moment of their coupling re-emerges at the end of the narrative in the awful metaphor. Here is the figure *par excellence* of the post-modern condition, the figure of death as an absent presence. For it is this moment that has become the space for the ultimate transgression on the obverse side of bourgeois individualism – anarchy. It is cheating death, or at the very least having some power over it that produces the intoxicating sense of self. Witness the Russian roulette scenes in *The Deerhunter*, producing in its audience an orgiastic moment of release as the hammer clicks against the empty chamber, a chamber of space reserved specifically for death. As Rosetta Brookes has pointed out in a different context:

> The taboo of death in advertising practices is everywhere being trans-gressed. The anti-ads and the horror ads of health and safety campaigns reveal the power of negative advertising and of the fascination with the image of death. Now cars, life insurance, even tobacco companies are flirting with the sacred space of death.[13]

Caught, as it were between technology and nature, the helicopter is often likened to a butterfly in *The Bamboo Bed* and to a 'giant overgrown hog' in *Why Are We In Vietnam?* The characters are forced into a new idolatry, a religion of the death machine capitalism:

> For God was a beast, not a man and God said, 'Go out and kill – fulfil my will, Go and Kill.'[14]

To avoid the void, the space that is reserved for death is filled in by everyone's death except our own. What these novels represent is the obsessional fear of the death of Capitalism, taken to its logical conclusions. The paranoia of the American state reveals itself in the mass-bombings of Vietnam. I have chosen these two novels, for nowhere in them do we find the rhetoric of the Reagan doctrine of a just and honourable war. What we discover is that these texts articulate what was to become an inability to talk of the real, to turn everything into mere discourse, what is now termed the post-modern. They, it seems to me, prophesy the production of a new aesthetic, an aesthetic that refuses history and thereby refuses culpability. Both novels are uncannily perceptive about the future condition of America. Not prophetic so much in the detail of the conduct of the war, but rather in the representation of that war. Both contain scenes reminiscent of two major American feature films about the war, *Apocalypse Now* and *The Deerhunter*. Both express the cultural underpinnings of American Imperialism at the level of representational forms. For it seems to me that it is at the level of the cultural (and by this I don't mean some epiphenomenon – the base-superstructure model is only workable when seen as a dialectic of relation not opposition) that America is most powerful. It is the flagships of 'Coca-Cola' and *Dallas* that colonize our unconscious long before the Trident rips up the road surfaces of Europe. It might be worth quoting at some length here some passages from Walter Benjamin's thesis on the Philosophy of History.

VI

To articulate the past historically does not mean to recognise it 'the way it really was' (Ranke). It means to seize hold of a memory as it flashes up at a moment of danger . . . only the historian will have the gift of fanning the spark of hope in the past who is firmly convinced that *even the dead* will not be safe from the enemy if he wins. And this enemy has not ceased to be victorious.

VII

Whoever has emerged victorious participates to this day in the triumphal procession in which the present rulers step over those who are lying prostrate. According to traditional practice, the spoils are carried along in the procession. They are called cultural treasures, and an historical materialist views them with cautious detachment. For without exception the cultural treasures he surveys have an origin which he cannot contemplate without horror. They owe their existence not only to the efforts of the great minds and talents who have created them, but also to the unconscious toils of their contemporaries. There is no document of civilization which is not at the same time a document of barbarism. And just as such a document is not free of barbarism, barbarism taints also the manner in which it was transmitted from the owner to another. An historical materialist therefore disassociates himself from it as far as possible. He regards it as his task to brush history against the grain.[15]

The paradox of course is that the US lost the war in Vietnam; the liberation of Saigon marked a heavy defeat for US foreign policy and prestige. But if we measure victory in numbers we see that many, many more Vietnamese than

Americans lost their lives. The Vietnamese infrastructure as well as its eco-
logy was destroyed, so what was the loss for the Americans? Of course we all
mourn the useless death of 58,000 American men and women, but what else?
Was it precisely those images so graphically described by Mailer that were the
real victims – machismo, national identity and mythic history? Well if it was,
what is happening now is disturbing, for it is precisely at the level of the cultural that those wounds, so deeply felt, are being sewn together. A suture
whose only scar is a fading memory. Through the crowded images of TV, the
newspaper and the cinema, the national identity, indivisible, is being reconsti-
tuted at the cost of history. The struggle for hegemony, the production of a
Utopian collective known only by signs, is once again being assembled. And
in the subways and in the living rooms the freedom to 'switch off' is always
undermined by the duty to 'stay tuned'. It is because of this that a properly
exhaustive analysis of that struggle must be carried out. We locate power not
just in the one-dimensional representations of power (although these themselves are awesome discourses), but also at their roots in the capitalist war-
machine; the quest for ever more exciting pictures of reality will produce for
us the spectacle of war. For we need to be aware that what we deduce from
the history books is not reality but meaning, and that this meaning will always
be dependent upon the position we find ourselves in during the process of that
reading.[16] We need, in short, when we approach the past either through 'history' or 'fiction', to be aware of our critical responsibilities.

What Mailer and Eastlake offer us in these novels is two distinct figurations
in their attempts to render both the war and the psyche that produces and is
produced by it. Mailer's critical fiction develops a meaningful analysis which
produces a sense of the national dependency on myth, whereas Eastlake explores the personal effects of those myths. Both in their own way provide us
with a historical sense, that is yet more than just facts.

Notes

1. Julie Kristeva, *Desire In Language*. Oxford: Basil Blackwell, 1980, p. 92.
2. For more on this, see Jameson's essay, 'Postmodernism, or the Cultural Logic of
   Late Capitalism', *New Left Review*, 1984, **146**.
3. Norman Mailer, *Why Are We In Vietnam?*, London: Panther Books, 1970, p. 7.
4. Ibid., p. 35.
5. Ibid., pp. 42–3.
6. Ibid., p. 77.
7. Ibid., p. 91.
8. William Eastlake, *The Bamboo Bed*, London: Michael Joseph, 1970, p. 7.
9. Ibid., p. 95.
10. Ibid., p. 95.
11. Ibid., p. 95.
12. See S. Freud, *On Metapsychology: the theory of psychoanalysis* (transl., James
    Strachey) Harmondsworth: Penguin, 1984, pp. 269–338 and J. Lacon, *Ecrits: a
    selection* (transl., Alan Sheridan). London: Tavistock, 1977, pp. 1–7.

13. Rosetta Brookes, 'Advertising Death's Space', in *ZG*, New York: Fall, 1984, p. 11.
14. William Eastlake, op. cit., p. 140.
15. Walter Benjamin, *Illuminations*, Glasgow: Fontana, 1979, pp. 257–9.
16. For further discussion of these concepts, see Houston A. Baker, *Blues, Ideology and American Literature,* Chicago: University of Illinois Press, 1987, Ch. 1 passim.

A note for readers

There are a number of books written about post-modernism: two that are useful because they cover both literature and the general social milieu are Ihab Hassan's *Paracriticisms* (1975) and *The Right Promethean Fire* (1980), both published by the University of Illinois Press, Chicago.

Recently, a number of journals have appeared dealing with the post-modern. *Semiotext(e)* concerns itself with contemporary philosophy and social theory and is published by Columbia University Press. *Boundary 2* is a journal of post-modern literature, mostly North American, but not exclusively, and is published by the State University of New York at Binghamton.

Three recent novels that deal with the American Vietnam experience through the use of imaginative literary techniques are:

Jerome Charyn, *War Cries over Avenue C.*, London: Sphere Books, 1986.

William Gaddis, *Carpenter's Gothic*, London: Andre Deutsch, 1986.

Stephen Wright, *Meditations In Green*, London: Hamish Hamilton, 1984.

Alf Louvre

4

The Reluctant Historians: Mailer and Sontag as Culture Critics

When the Chairman of the Writers' Union, Dang Thai Mai, said in his speech of welcome to Bob, Andy and myself, 'You are the very picture of the genuine American', why should I have slightly flinched? If what I feel is that flag-waving Legionnaires and Irish cops and small-town car salesmen who will vote for George Wallace are the genuine Americans, not I – which I fear part of me does feel – isn't that cowardly, shallow and simply untrue?

Susan Sontag, 'Trip to Hanoi'[1]

Like *Armies of the Night*, 'Trip to Hanoi' was published in 1968 at the height of the domestic and international protest against the war in Vietnam. Yet reading both texts, we are struck by something very different from the visionary radical confidence popularly associated with that year. Indeed, the isolation and self-doubt of American literary radicals at that moment are recurrently in evidence. In response to perhaps the most crippling paradox that perceived isolation produced – how to square commitment to consolidating and extending the Anti-War movement with their own recurrent contempt for the masses and for many of their fellow intellectuals – Susan Sontag and Norman Mailer adopt the confessional strategy; they speak in the voice of conscience and they talk at first of and to themselves. The movement of 'Trip to Hanoi' and *The Armies of the Night* is remarkably similar: from assurance or arrogance to modesty. The hope is that by stripping away the accoutrements of exceptional status and singular ability, by the honest admission of all that makes them indeed untypical (not least their intellectual loquacity, their taste for irony and metaphor) they will reach and reveal a bedrock – elements of their personality that are rooted in and shaped by the common American 'experience'. The strategy is not to offer political and social commentary to a popular audience who can 'follow their line' (for the gap between them and such an audience is profound), but to engage in self-examination and analysis, to offer their personality, their psyche, their instinctive reflexes as an index of the culture as a whole. The reader does not derive a 'line' but, as father confessor, shares an experience. Or, more accurately, investigates the nature of 'experience'.

If this is a conventional cliché in defence of novels as against tracts and, equally, echoes a truism about the American novel itself, as romance or gothic rather than socially dense,[2] we should remember and mobilize, too, the tradition of American culture criticism where the confessional mode is so recurrently evident that it could be considered as dominant (from Adams' *Education* to Agee's *Let Us Now Praise Famous Men*).

Conjunctural as well as traditional determinants are also in evidence. Asserting the significance of 'the self as index', tracing the links between personal instinct and the structure of power is, of course, the contemporaneous project of Marcuse (*Essay on Liberation* considers alternatives to the psychic repression of capitalism), and of Cohn-Bendit who shares the common antipathy to Stalinist reductionism and the common assertion that 'c'est pour toi que tu fais la révolution').[3] Sontag and Mailer recognize these connections and affirm the counter-cultural politics of what Sontag calls America's 'subtlest minority generation of the decent and the sensitive'.[4] With the growing analysis of the extent to which the State and its ideologies have penetrated – indeed to some, constituted – the individual (fuelled in one direction by Marcuse and shortly afterward in a very different direction by Althusser), and hence of the need to revolutionize our existing 'psychic geography', Mailer's old interest in 'remaking the nervous circuits'[5] takes on new life. Existentialism, in an era of situationist politics and symbolic confrontation, seems less of an arcane indulgence.

The confessional project is carried out, in both cases, with impressive integrity. The temptation is to rest with easy relativism. For Sontag, the Vietnamese 'other' could be presented in the usual reassuringly exotic fashion as simply different: in fact, it is convincingly depicted as superior. For Mailer, his own adventures in the novelistic section of *The Armies of the Night* could be equated with the actions of other participants described in the 'historical' account that ends the book: in fact the courage of those enduring 'the Battle of the Wedge' emerges as qualitatively different.

***

My first reaction to the didactically positive way the Vietnamese have of recounting their history is to find it simple-minded. . . . I have to remind myself that historical understanding can have other purposes than the ones I take for granted: objectivity and completeness. *This* is history for use – for survival to be precise – and it is entirely a *felt* history, not the preserve of detached intellectual concern.

Sontag, *Trip to Hanoi*[6]

. . . an explanation of the mystery of the events at the Pentagon cannot be developed by the methods of history – only by the instincts of the novelist . . . the novel must replace history at precisely that point where experience is sufficiently emotional, spiritual, psychical, moral, existential and supernatural to expose the fact that the historian in pursuing the experience would be obliged to quit the clearly demarcated lines of historical enquiry.

Mailer, The Armies of the Night[7]

These comments on historical discourse might be chickenfeed to a competent historiographer but they are significant in further defining the project of Mailer and Sontag. Conventional historical discourse is for them discredited: partly (due to the incorporation of historian/intellectuals) because it legitimates American power; partly (concerned for 'objectivity and completeness') because it sails too close to technocratic thinking and brickwork logic;[8] mostly, the reaction is to a discourse that intends to describe patterns of determination, to explain eventuation only in terms of what can be quantified and documented. Mailer attacks conventional 'history', Sontag affirms the (Vietnamese) alternative to it, their common stress is upon a subjective dimension: the felt and common history Sontag values, the experiential dimensions Mailer implies are traditionally neglected. At root, the reaction is to history as, they suggest, innately a deterministic and reductive discourse: what they affirm is human agency.

According to Sontag, 'in Vietnam what was ostensibly a somewhat passive experience of historical education became, as I think it now had to, an active confrontation with the limits of my thinking'.[9] According to Mailer, 'you created the revolution first and learned from it, learned of what your revolution might consist and where it might go out of the ultimate truth of the way it presented itself to your experience'.[10] Mailer's comments here – about the 'Cuban' sympathies of the New Left – might stand as an epitaph for the marchers on the Pentagon. In both assertions, the unstated premise is precisely the capacity to *transcend* determinations, to remake the self, whatever the depth of social and cultural conditioning. They turn to imagination.

We might expect them, then, to adopt the discourse of the novel – more particularly, perhaps, the historical novel (imaginative recreation giving due weight to 'subjective experience') – but we get, in each case, something more and less than this. In Mailer there is an expansive, inflationary self-engendering rhetoric, in Sontag minimal, deflationary self-interrogating notes: an advertisement and a diary. In terms of sexual economies, Mailer is the unabashed masturbator (spend, spend, spend with his asides – yes! – recalling Molly Bloom); Sontag, the celibate in the nunnery of North Vietnam. One parodies phallocratic realism, exploding its linear historicist certainties, the other gently undermines it with ruminative essayistic circularities.[11] Both texts, significantly, feature decentred and occasionally schizophrenic narrators – which is perhaps where the claim to representativeness comes to rest. For the hegemonic crisis then evident in America threatened not only the stability of the State, but of discourse and the self.[12]

Mailer's advertisement

Part I of *The Armies of the Night* is called 'History as a Novel', part II 'Novel as History'. This opens floodgates for literary doctoral students, but how telling are the distinctions?

> The novelist in passing his baton to the historian has a happy smile. He has been faster than you think. As a working craftsman, a journeyman artist, he is not without his guile; he has come to decide that if you would see the horizon from a forest, you must first build a tower . . . [History as Novel, part I, is 'the tower']. Of course the tower is crooked, and the telescopes warped, but the instruments of all sciences – history so much as physics – are always constructed in small or large error: what supports our use of them now, is that our intimacy with the master-builder of the tower . . . has given some advantage for correcting the error of his instruments and the imbalance of his tower. May that be claimed of many historians?[13]

The claim that intimacy with the historical narrator will allow us to redress his 'bias' seems implicitly to voice a commitment to 'objectivity'. But we've already seen how this distinction between historical and literary discourse is effectively collapsed – that the events at the Pentagon in the end can only be explained by the 'instincts of the novelist'. If the novel – and its tower – is initially subordinate to the demands of history, it seems that history eventually has to make way for the novel.

One response to this conundrum would be a cheerful assertion of the dialectic relationship of discourses, rather than a dependency of one upon the other. Parallels might usefully be made with the techniques of Steinbeck's *The Grapes of Wrath*, where the interchapters heroize the fictive story of the Joads (preventing merely a cathartic reaction to their tragedy), *but* where the Joads' story also acts on interchapters to reveal subjective dimensions of the historical process – the 'figurin'' – conventionally neglected.

But in *The Armies of the Night* the weight of each element and their sequence – the novelistic is first and by far the larger of the two – together with Mailer's final explicit assertion of its primacy, suggest something other than supportive equivalency. My reading of the text is that it works to depict a *contradiction*, to assert and *yet, despite itself, to challenge* the primacy of the novelistic. It is precisely in pushing his symbolic and subjective aesthetic to its limits – and realizing its limits – that the confessional mode of the text is constituted.

The aim of *The Armies of the Night* is to produce an alternative reading of the events in Washington to those offered by the dominant journalism of *Time, Newsweek, The Washington Post* and *The New York Times*. It begins with *Time's* account of Mailer's part in the march and – the pun is crucial – Mailer says: 'Now we may leave *Time* in order to find out what happened.'[14] Leaving *Time* (the magazine) and time (conventional narrative history) means leaving behind what Mailer calls the 'brickwork logic', the resolutely syntagmatic and historicist axis of 'this happened, then that'. To assert the imaginative, the paradigmatic axis means, too, challenging the confident *singular* fixing of signifier to signified, the regimenting of connotation that consolidates and extends hegemonic power. This challenge, as we might anticipate, is strenuously resisted. *The Washington Post's* account of Mailer's impassioned speech on his release from custody (a speech self-consciously taking up the Christian language of commitment and inspiration) punctures his imaginative self-inflation. Its closing sentence, 'Mailer is a Jew' devastatingly mobilizes and re-affirms orthodox connotations while (disingenuously) merely denoting the 'historical' fact.[15]

The text manipulates a tension between a closely detailed chronology of the events as they unfold and a recurrent focus upon intense, experiential moments. These moments are not given a singular meaning, pushed into place in a relentless narrative chain of cause and effect but, rather, subjected to a paradigmatic expansion that records not 'facts' but metaphors, guesses, suppositions, imaginary dialogues and speculations. Faced with 'new experience' the response is not to describe it with worn conventions, but multiple accelerated labels jostling and contradicting each other. The predominating feature of the discourse is the sustained 'aside', so sustained that the 'aside' is actually at the centre. The account and the argument rest upon the pyrotechnic capacity for metaphor: new nervous circuits mean new stylistic circuits too.

Just about the time Mailer had decided he was romanticizing these young men in tribute for his English vest and suit, his avoirdupois, his hangover, his endless blendings of virtue and corruption – Harris did something which nailed down the case. A few loaves of bread, a jar of peanut butter, and a couple of quarts of milk were being passed around. No one took very much – numerous subtle manifestations were present of a collective philosophy, which for many of them might even have included a casual abstemiousness about food – at any rate, the meagre rations seemed more than enough for the group. The neat remains came back eventually to Harris' feet. Since he had just finished asking if everything was clear about the actions at the Department of Justice in the afternoon and the meeting to discuss further action at night, he now stared out at the listening onlookers, picked up the bread and said 'Anyone like some food? It's . . . uh . . .' he pretended to look at it, 'it's . . . uh . . . white bread.' The sliced loaf half-collapsed in its wax wrapper was the comic embodiment now of a dozen little ideas, of corporation-land which took the taste and crust out of bread and wrapped the remains in wax paper, and was, at the far extension of this same process, the same mentality which was out in Asia escalating, defoliating; yeah; and the white bread was also television, the fun of situation comedy shows with commercials, the humor they had shared as adolescents when pop art was being birthed; the white bread was the infiltrated enemy who had a grip on them everywhere, forced them to collaborate if only by imbibing the bread (and substance) of that enemy with his food processing, enriched flours, vitamin supplements, added nutrients; finally, and this probably was why Harris chuckled when he said it, the bread was *white* bread, not black bread – a way to remind them all that he was one of the very few Negroes here. Who knew what it might have cost him in wonder about his own allegiances not to be out there somewhere now agitating for Black Power. Here he was instead with White bread – White money, White methods, even White illegalities. It was exorbitant, Mailer decided glumly, to watch such virtuosity with a hangover.[16]

Mailer's virtuoso performance is at its height in reconstituting American history, in comparing the demonstrators at the closing vigil of the march with other American rites of passage – the original settlements, Valley Forge, Gettysburg, the Alamo. . . . Here what Mailer creates through metaphor (not least the metaphor borrowed from Lowell of the 'chinook salmon') is the felt and common history, the history for survival Sontag sees in Vietnam.

All of which suggests our (novelistic) narrator is less idiosyncratic than heroic, the literary performance in the text on the march legitimizing his act on the day: the master-builder of metaphor uniquely suited to the politics of symbolic confrontation.

Yet during his discussion of the final rite of passage, Mailer relies upon, rather than giving alternatives to, more sober and fixed accounts. He quotes the press (albeit the *Free Press*) for its insight not its idiocy. And the quotations are devastating to the aesthetic he has promoted. Thorne Dreyer's article is particularly relevant:

People have to come to terms with what violence means. It's not something to groove on and cleanse your soul with. Using violence in a situation where you do not have the institutions of violence or an equal strategic position, is insane.[17]

The limits of symbolic politics and Mailer's own symbolic countertruths are in the closing stages laid bare. Dominant versions of the truth in the last resort persuade by repressive violence. There is something beyond ideological apparatuses and effusive verbal gymnastics on them. The brickwork logic of hard-headed revolutionary strategists at this point is revealed in a new light. And it is the courage of 'naked Quakers on the cold floor of a dark isolation cell in a D.C. jail' that we salute as exemplary. No hipsters these.

The contradictory twist in the closing pages of the text effectively signals the re-emergence of the historical: the recognition of material determinations that constrain even Mailer's egoistic flights.

With this in mind we might recall the passage theorizing the connections between history and the novel and what we've mentioned of the sexual economy of his writing:

Of course the tower is crooked, and the telescopes warped, but the instruments of all sciences – history so much as physics – are always constructed in small or large error: what supports our use of them now, is that our intimacy with the master-builder of the tower, and the lens-grinder of the telescopes (yes even the machinist of the barrels) has given some advantage for correcting the error of his instruments and the imbalance of his tower.

Towers that are crooked, telescopes, instruments, the master-builder, the machinist of the barrels: the nature of our 'corrections' is less to take the novelist to the history, Part I to Part II, than the history to the novelist – whose grinding of lenses, machining of the barrels, whose masturbatory macho individual self-projection is, in the end, insufficient. Not the victorious climax, then, but anti-climax, the tower not just crooked but, in a courageous act of self-exposure, limp.[18]

Sontag's diary

In *The Armies of the Night* history returns with a vengeance: in 'Trip to Hanoi' its claims are never forgotten. Mailer's denouement exposes the limits of sophistication; Sontag's entire essay is preoccupied with that theme. Mailer confronts the dominant American discourse and attempts a *Time*-less alternative of paradigmatic expansion. Sontag approaches an alien orthodoxy: the dominant Vietnamese discourse (in her account the *only* Vietnamese discourse) is her alternative. The radicalism of her intervention is a function of her long struggle to embrace rather than escape the 'world of history' (albeit as the Vietnamese conceive it).

While she tells us that 'direct experience is . . . something that one repudiates at one's peril',[19] the universality of personal experience, the liberal commitment to individualism and the experiential are under threat from the outset. For she recognizes that experience is culturally constructed and the profound cultural differences between urban America and Vietnam haunt her account and structure her assessment. The differences amount to a series of interrelated polarities which we might characterize as:

Vietnam	*America*
Ethics	Aesthetics
Public role	Private self
Politeness	Authenticity
Directness	Irony
Shame	Guilt
Formality	Expressivity
Feelings	Articulation
Will	Talk
Decorum	Gluttony
Organic community	Alienated self
Actor	Spectator
Singular discourse	Multiple discourses
History	Psychology, sociology, philosophy, metaphysics . . .

Sontag simultaneously describes her different reactions to the disjunctions these polarities create (reactions ranging from condescension, to detachment, to sentimentality and, finally, to an affirmation of the Vietnamese other) *and* explores the reasons for them. In the diary entry for 8 May she says:

While I don't think I'm lacking in moral seriousness, I shrink from having my seriousness ironed out; I know I'd feel reduced if there were no place for its contradictions and paradoxes, not to mention its diversions and distractions. Thus the gluttonous habits of my consciousness prevent me from being at home with what I most admire. . . . I live in an unethical society that coarsens the sensibilities and thwarts the capacities for goodness of most people but makes available for minority consumption an astonishing array of intellectual and aesthetic pleasures.[20]

The initial inadequacies of her reactions to Vietnam are the product of her being Western, being American and (the guilt is pervasive and over-determined) being an intellectual, an artist, a gluttonous consciousness. We are reminded of a long line of American culture critics similarly disposed to confess their extravagant and indulgent sensibilities – most immediately of Mailer, but also of Agee and Adams. Internal exiles all, their guilt could be expunged by an interior pilgrimage – to Washington, or Arkansas or St Louis. For the corrupt theorist of camp who had once collapsed the very distinction between irony and morality, the voyage of discovery is longer, the confrontation with a victimized majority more blunt, dramatic and final.

                                        * * *

I have shown myself as I was; contemptible and vile when I was so; good, generous, sublime when I was so; I have unveiled my interior such as thou thyself has seen it, Eternal Father. . . .
           Rousseau, quoted in the preface to *The Education of Henry Adams*[21]

The diary is arguably the most directly confessional literary mode: the private, the personal, the secretive . . . the closest equivalent to 'inner speech', whose problematic nature as discourse causes even semioticians to draw breath.[22] Recurrently in American cultural criticism this 'private' record has come to public light reluctantly, unintentionally, in the unwilled accident that is the guarantee of its authenticity. Adams' *Education* was privately circulated, regarded as 'unfinished' and published after his death. Agee's *Let Us Now Praise Famous Men* grew, uncontrollably, out of a commissioned article (for *Fortune* magazine – the discrepancy between presumed editorial intention and final result *its* mark of sincerity). Sontag went to Hanoi with no intentions to write about it. Indeed, inevitably, the lack of professional purpose in her trip was, she later tells us, the necessary condition for her receptiveness to the experience.[23] The structure of the diary is present directly or residually in all these texts. Most evidently in 'Trip to Hanoi' where daily jottings are given verbatim and occupy large sections of the essay; but also in *The Education* where each chapter has a suffix indicating the year of its concern; and in *Let Us Now Praise Famous Men* where an ambitiously symphonic form begins its main movement with 'observations on the porch, July 1936'. Typically, in Mailer, the diary conventions are present and parodied: the authority of the chronological sequence (the major and relatively weak determinant of this discursive form) is corroded by the repetition of events and responses in the two sections. What price the authenticity of the personal record if each day's meaning can be reinterpreted at will? Moreover, at perhaps the most significant moment of personal crisis, the moment of arrest, we learn (some confession this) that Mailer's private and tortured decisions are in fact being filmed; that his participation on the march (like the text in which we read of it) has been, from the outset, *commissioned*. The interior is unveiled not before the Eternal Father, but made up for the cameras of a BBC documentary team.

Mailer reveals and revels in some of the latent contradictions of this private-cum-public mode. In Sontag the contradictions take other shapes.

On one hand the diary seems a discourse particularly fitted to her project – recognizing the superiority of the public, ethical and essentially historical consciousness of the Vietnamese. Like the Vietnamese it puts 'all information into a historical narrative'.[24] In many respects the essay echoes their linguistic temperament: 'Trip to Hanoi' enacts as well as describes their (inherited), her (learned) predilection for directness, for simplicity of statement, for an economic, 'verbally and conceptually meagre style',[25] for intellectual re-cycling. As they return to notions of 'piracy', 'henchmen' and 'sacrifice', so she time and time again takes up three or four themes – the relations between public and private roles, the simplicity of their discourse, the 'moral' society and the nature of her own reflexes. Irony is present as a topic rather than in her style, which veers toward the disingenuous. The narrative is sparse: strung between the happy sleep of her first night in Hanoi and her wakeful night on her return to Vientiane are the plainly-described itineraries of her stay, peopled by small groups of quickly-familiar names and punctuated by three or four intensely moving moments.

But there are too, of course, her reflections. And while these follow a progression – she is first disappointed, then patronizing, then quizzical and detached, then affirmative about her hosts – the reflexive mode itself stands between Sontag and her goal. For it rests precisely upon notions of interiority, authenticity, the revealed, but private self, that are essentially at odds with the Vietnamese ethos she would embrace. The confessional impact of Mailer derives from his eventual failure to transcend the historical: in Sontag from the failure wholly to rejoin it. A residue of the personal, the psychological interest remains doggedly inscribed in the very mode of the diary.

The difficulties of self-effacement (or transcendence) preoccupy the final sections of the essay. Her own failures are there presented, as ever in the confessional strategy, as representative. Talking about the difficulties common to us all she offers implicit commentary on the personal dilemma described in the text:

Increasing numbers of people do realise that we must have a more generous, more humane way of being with each other; and great, probably convulsive, social changes are needed to create these psychic changes. To prepare intelligently for radical change requires not only lucid and truthful social analysis. . . . An equally relevant weapon is the analysis of psychic geography and history: for instance getting more perspective on the human type that gradually became ascendent in the west from the time of the Reformation to the industrial revolution to modern post-industrial society. Almost everyone would agree that this isn't the only way human beings could have evolved, but very few people in Europe and America really, organically *believe* that there is any other way for a person to be or can *imagine* what they might be like. How can they when, after all, that's what they are more or less? It's hard to step over one's own feet.[26]

The difficulties Sontag faces – one foot planted in the 'adult', 'psychological', 'aesthetic', 'gluttonous', 'violent' and 'various' world of the post-Reformation west, the other stepping toward the idealistic, historical, moral and assiduous world of Vietnam – are focussed sharply in the act of writing. As she finally becomes sympathetic to the historical discourse of the Vietnamese (who 'lack both time and incentive for symbolic controversy',[27] whose 'psychic types have not yet reached a high degree of articulation'[28] and who need less words because they are 'without irony'[29]) so, in equal measure she sets herself against the verbal effusiveness that blights the West, and its revolutionaries:

One can indeed 'talk' revolutions away, by a disproportion between consciousness and verbalisation on the one hand, and the amount of practical *will* on the other. Hence the failure of the recent revolution in France. The French students talked – and very beautifully too – instead of reorganising the administration of the captured universities. Their staging of street demonstrations and confrontations with the police was conceived of as a rhetorical or symbolic rather than a practical act: it too was a kind of talking.[30]

Like Mailer before her, Sontag is finally driven to consider the legitimized violence of the state, and the immense explanatory power given in this passage to a casual 'hence' signals a similar disillusion about symbolic reactions to it . . . about words. That such an observation is delivered in a footnote (as this is) is significant: such a position is suicidal for a writer. However minimalist her chosen mode, what else can it be – with this set of categories – but 'rhetorical', 'symbolic', merely a kind of 'talking'?

One way beyond this seemingly terminal double-bind is occasionally broached in the essay. Sontag's speculations about Vietnamese discourse seem to propose, in ways reminiscent of Barthes' *Mythologies*, the notion of a 'transitive' language, where meaning is guaranteed by history, in direct and practical connection with event and activity rather than in promiscuous and mystifying dissociation.[31] Her early negative reactions to an abstract, bland and repetitive Vietnamese mode are subjected to critical examinations:

All the words belong to the same vocabulary: struggle, bombings, friend, aggressor, imperialist, patriot, victory, brother, freedom, unity, peace. . . . It's not that I judge their words to be false. For once, I think the political and moral reality is as simple as the communist rhetoric would have it. The French were 'the French colonialists'; the Americans are 'imperialist aggressors'; the Thieu-Ky regime *is* a 'puppet govern-ment'.[32]

None the less, such language disturbs Sontag, thinking about which she draws what is surely the pertinent moral:

> I both assent to the unreserved moral judgement and shy away from it, too. I believe they are right. At the same time nothing can make me forget that events are much more complicated than the Vietnamese represent them. But exactly what complexities would I have them acknowledge? Isn't it enough that their struggle is, objectively, just? Can they ever afford subtleties when they need to mobilise every bit of energy to continue standing up to the American goliath? Whatever I conclude, it seems to me I end up patronising them.
>
>   Perhaps all I'm expressing is the difference between being an actor (them) and being a spectator (me).[33]

The Vietnamese cannot afford subtleties (of nuance, ambivalence, of signifiers without anchor), but what is first perceived as a necessity eventually emerges as a virtue:

> Vietnam is a culture in which people have not got the final devastating point about talking, have not gauged the subtle ambivalent resources of language – because they don't experience as we do the isolation of a 'private self'. Talk is still rather a plain instrumentality to them, a less important means of being connected with their environment than direct feeling, love.[34]

Talk (and language) is conceived of here as in a potentially subordinate relationship to history, 'direct feelings' and revolutionary will. Sontag's own essay, constructed out of the discourse of the diary, attempts to exemplify this relationship – legitimizing the discursive by the extra-discursive, language by feeling, feeling by event. Her attempt to transcend the 'isolation of the private self' (intensified by her role as American *intellectual*) necessarily insists upon the possibility, indeed inevitability, of change in our 'psychic geography and history', in 'the human type'. Her plea that *we* should accelerate 'the process of recasting the particular historical form of our human nature' is charged by the confessional disclosures of her *own* transformation in Hanoi:

> An event that makes new feelings conscious is always the most important experience a person can have. . . . (Though the new feelings that were revealed to me are undoubtedly quite old in an historical sense, I personally had never experienced them before, or been able to name them, or hitherto had been capable of believing in them.)[35]

The distinctions between 'reality' and 'rhetoric', between 'practical' and 'symbolic' acts, the causative sequence of events, experience and naming, the idea of talk as 'a plain instrumentality', may seem laughably naive from the high plateaux of structuralist and post-structuralist thought. Occupants of this ground, we have come to reject the primacy of experience as the origin of meaning and the stabilizing guarantee of 'history' (in de Man's classic formulation: 'The bases for historical knowledge are not empirical facts but written texts even if these texts masquerade in the guise of wars or revolutions').[36]

But the qualification evident in Sontag's conclusion works against easy dismissal: 'Though the new feelings that were revealed to me are undoubtedly quite old in an historical sense, I personally had never experienced them before, or been able to name them.' This claims neither the uniqueness of her personal experience nor of her naming; it points instead to their location in history (a remote and alien history that predates 'the type that became ascendant in the West').

In this context it is appropriate to recall that Derrida's assault upon 'presence' intended to deconstruct *Western* metaphysics, *Western* discourses.[37] His problematic, though vast, is not universal. To forget this, to deny the possibility of discourses otherwise constituted, is to replace one kind of transcendentalism (the sign legitimated by God or Nature or the autonomous self) with another (the sign as eternally and ubiquitously arbitrary, meaning always and everywhere plural). The imperial imperative of 'play' replaces the imperial imperative of 'duty' but, equally transhistorical, both buttresses and can be accommodated by the liberalism it purports to subvert.[38] Catherine Belsey incisively points the implications:

> Endlessly to deconstruct the metaphysics of presence, to celebrate the unfixing of meaning as an end in itself, is to settle for a relativism which is political paralysis. . . . The alternative is to lay claim to specified meanings in the name of politics not truth . . . we need to question discourse in order to identify not its deeper meaning, its concealed residue, but what is at stake in this or that interpretation. If knowledge-as-discourse is power, it is the excess of the signifier which is the location of discursive struggle.[39]

Sontag's ruminations on the excesses of crucial signifiers from Western liberal discourse ('honesty', 'truth', 'integrity' and 'experience'), the interior discursive struggle the diary enacts and, most of all, her non-accommodating confrontation with the *other*-ness of Vietnamese discourse make 'Trip to Hanoi' more than another weary pastoral.

Like Mailer, if analytic rather than demonstrative, Sontag there laid claim to 'specified meanings in the name of politics'.

The readings on offer in this essay attempt a similar intervention though, 20 years on, in a very different intellectual and political climate. Now, when distinctions between 'rhetoric' and 'reality', 'symbolic' and 'practical' are scathingly undermined and when the causative sequence more often than not is reversed to read 'naming', 'experience', 'events', the trajectories of Mailer's and Sontag's texts seem to me particularly significant. The force of their confessions is to provide an antidote to a fashionable solipsism. Evident everywhere in the very different strategies adopted in *The Armies of the Night* and 'Trip to Hanoi' is the *gulf* between being an 'actor' and being a 'spectator', between effective intervention and commentary. In concert with the radical philosophers and activists of that era, they both attempt to transcend this alienated duality. Each returns to history, to extra-subjective determinations: Mailer, reluctantly, perversely, bravado egotism in tow; Sontag with a never-quite-convincing self-sacrifice (for the diary insists that the self describe its own effacement). *Yet . . .* Mailer can never forget his comparatively puny role as actor, Sontag cannot but enact her role as commentator. Whether mobilizing expansive or reductive modes the duality is never finally effaced or escaped. The repressed term – 'actor' in Mailer, 'spectator' in Sontag – returns.

Compared to the intellectual self-assurance of 'radical' deconstruction (to privilege 'the text' as de Man does is of course, too, to privilege the reader-critic), this 'failure' provides a salutary contrast, especially in view of ideological shifts in the world beyond the academy. Before we rush to expose the frailties of Sontag's premises concerning language, discourse and history, we might be wise to look where we stand (and try to step over our feet). For sophisticated academic assaults upon historical discourse have been in embarrassed but maybe complicit co-existence with a wilful collective amnesia in American popular consciousness. On one hand, historical discourse undergoes terminal interrogation; on the other, historical traumas are forgotten or reinterpreted in cartoons of nationalist fantasy.[40] Nostalgia, under intellectual attack in one arena, re-surfaces far more poisonously in another. The culture criticism of the 1960s matters now, in an era of reaction, because it acknowledges, sometimes willingly, sometimes despite itself, the forces of historical and material determination, an awareness of which the new right must repress, and because it acts in the name of politics not in the name of anaesthetizingly pluralistic truths.

The tenth anniversary of the retreat from Vietnam was celebrated in the West by an obscene audio-visual montage whose chorus ran 'nuh, nuh, nuh, nuh, nuh, nuh, nuh, nuh, nineteen!'[41] We might respond to this in a semiotic vein by stressing the subversive significance of its syllabic repetition. We stand more chance of exposing its mythic distortions (Vietnam simply another occasion for the 'suffering of Eternal Youth in War') if, following the lead of our reluctant historians, we expose its self-deluding stammer by adding the historical suffix of America's defeat: not just 'nuh, nuh, nuh, nuh, nineteen' – but nineteen seventy five.

Notes

1. Susan Sontag, 'Trip to Hanoi', in *Styles of Radical Will*, New York: Farrar, Straus and Giroux, 1969, pp. 266–7.
2. I have in mind the well-known arguments of Richard Chase's *The American Novel and Its Tradition*, New York: Doubleday, 1957.
3. The title of a chapter in Cohn-Bendit's *Obsolete Communism: A Left-Wing Alternative*, London: Deutsch, 1968.

4. *Styles of Radical Will*, p. 204.
5. The phrase 'psychic geography' occurs in 'Trip to Hanoi', 'remaking the nervous circuits' in 'The White Negro' (in Mailer's *Advertisements for Myself*, New York: Putnam, 1966).
6. *Styles of Radical Will*, p. 220.
7. Norman Mailer, *The Armies of the Night*, London: Weidenfeld and Nicolson, 1968, p. 255.
8. Significantly, for Mailer, the historians of the Left are as guilty of using the 'Sound-as-brickwork logic of the next step' as the apologists of the establishment. See *The Armies of the Night*, p. 85.
9. *Styles of Radical Will*, p. 270.
10. *The Armies of the Night*, p. 87.
11. For a discussion of feminist alternatives to phallocratic discourse, some of which extend such 'Ruminative circularities' to the point of 'refusing the linearity of reading', see the essay of Mary Jacobus in *Writing and Sexual Difference* (ed. E. Abel), Brighton: Harvester Press, 1982.
12. The fragmentation of popular political discourse in the period is perhaps most dramatically suggested by recalling the polarities: on one hand the Pentagonese of Melvin Laird *et al.*, on the other the spontaneous rap of Jerry Rubin's hippies.
13. *The Armies of the Night*, p. 219.
14. Ibid., p. 4.
15. Ibid., p. 215.
16. Ibid., pp. 62–3.
17. Ibid., p. 275.
18. The tendency toward (self) parody is recurrently evident in Mailer's fiction: a point of some significance in assessing the sexism of, say, *An American Dream* (London: Deutsch, 1965).
19. *Styles of Radical Will*, p. 259.
20. Ibid., pp. 223–4.
21. Henry Adams, *The Education of Henry Adams*, Boston: Houghton Mifflin, 1961, p. xxiii.
22. For a discussion of the linguistic and ideological significance of 'inner speech', see Volosinov's *Marxism and the Philosophy of Language*, Ch. 1. This is reprinted in Bennett, Martin, Mercer and Woollacott (eds), *Culture, Ideology and Social Process*, London: Batsford, 1981. His argument is that 'consciousness' (including 'inner speech') 'takes shape and being in the material of signs created by an organised group in the process of its social intercourse'.
23. *Styles of Radical Will*, p. 206.
24. Ibid., p. 221.
25. Ibid., p. 263.
26. Ibid., p. 272.
27. Ibid., p. 256.
28. Ibid., p. 247.
29. Ibid., p. 238.
30. Ibid., pp. 263–4 (footnote).
31. See the essay 'Myth Today' in Roland Barthes' *Mythologies*, London: Paladin, 1973.
32. *Styles of Radical Will*, p. 216.
33. Ibid., p. 218.
34. Ibid., p. 264.
35. Ibid., p. 273.

36. Paul de Man, *Blindness and Insight*, Minneapolis: University of Minnesota Press, 1983, p. 165.
37. See the opening section of Derrida's *Of Grammatology*, Baltimore: The Johns Hopkins University Press, 1977.
38. The best account I know of the accommodation of radical criticism within the liberal orthodoxy is Frank Lentricchia's *After the New Criticism*, London: Athlone Press, 1980.
39. Catherine Belsey, 'The Politics of Meaning', in *Confronting the Crisis* (eds F. Barker *et al.*), Guildford: Essex University, 1984, pp. 28–9. To gloss too condensed an argument: Derrida's project is dehistoricized by taking it as universal in scope. Insisting that we speak in the name of politics, Belsey returns us to (our own) history in another way. For assessing the disruptive power of the signifier's 'excesses' (a power by no means evenly present or realized in all discourses at all times), requires a historical assessment of the hegemonic control – or counter-hegemonic struggle – evident within a given discourse. This is a variable ignored by functionalist readings (of which Althusser and Foucault are sometimes guilty) and by the freewheeling, pluralistic stress upon the arbitrariness of the sign. Deconstructionism can forget that the sign is also conventional, a matter of assent – in Gramsci's sense! – in a linguistic community marked by massive but changing inequalities of access and control.
40. See, for instance, the *Rambo* movies.
41. '19', the multi-national chart-topper recorded by Paul Hardcastle.

David Huxley

5

Naked Aggression: American Comic Books and the Vietnam War

Despite a gradual reassessment of the aesthetic and cultural value of comics (which to an extent parallels the earlier reassessment of film), they are still a neglected and often despised medium. The value of American comic books can be expressed much more simply, if rather inadequately, in dollars.

They are often regarded primarily as collectors' items and, rather like a stamp collectors' guide, the standard reference work on comics *Overstreet* is essentially a price guide. A single 1940s comic can be worth $20,000. Viewed as a financial investment, comics form a distinct hierarchy; near the bottom of the scale in terms both of price and general esteem are war comics. These are collected only infrequently and are, therefore, difficult to find and to catalogue in any systematic way.[1] Equally there is only a minimal amount of literature which provides any background information on or analysis of war comics. Before looking at the ways in which the Vietnam War was portrayed in American comic books it is necessary to look at what constitutes the genre of war comics.

On the face of it the genre of war comics appears to be easily identifiable: possibly by the obvious imagery of warfare, such as soldiers, weapons and tanks, and these images can be from any one of a number of wars. Normally a range of equally obvious key words such as war, fighting, combat, attack and so on are put into the titles of war comics. However, this points to the dangers inherent in taking an over-simplistic view of the genre. The influence of a war can be felt in many other genres, not merely in the most obvious. This is true, particularly of Vietnam. For example, the response to the Vietnam War by Marvel, a major comic company, occurred not in its few war comics but in the large proportion of super-hero titles which formed the major part of the company's output. Equally, there are stories in war comics, set in another war, which appear not to be about Vietnam, but which are nevertheless a comment on the Vietnam conflict.[2]

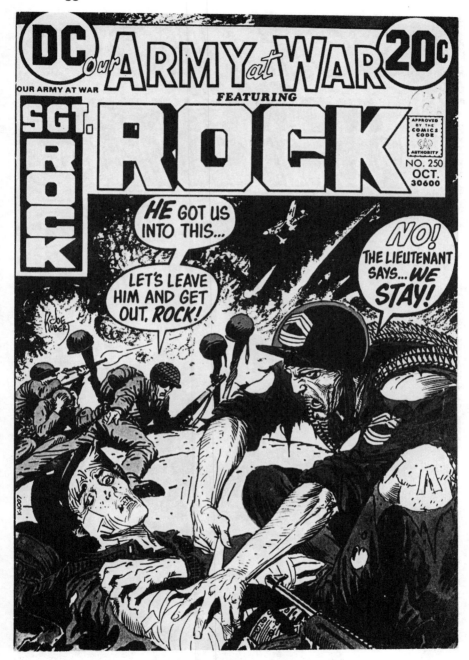

Fig. 1   The body in Battle: Sergeant Rock. © 1972 DC Comics Inc.

Fig. 2   The body in battle: Sergeant Fury. © Marvel Comics.

	Charlton	Dell/Gold Key	D.C.	Marvel	Others	Underground/Warren
Format	Short stories (up to 8 pages) from various periods	Separate titles each set in a separate war, some 'documentary'	Continuing heroes, mainly WW2, combined with shorter one-off stories	Continuing heroes, mainly WW2		
Titles	*Army War Heroes* (1963–70) *War Heroes* (1963–7) *War And Attack* (1964–7) *Fightin' Marines* (1951–76) *Fightin' Army* (1956–84) *U.S. Air Force* (1958–65) *Army Attack* (1964–7) *Marine War Heroes* (1964–7) *Fightin' Air Force* (1956–66) *Marines Attack* (1964–6) *War Wings* (1968)	*Combat* (WW2) (1961–73) *World War Stories* (1965)	*G.I. Combat* (1952–) *Star Spangled War* (1952–77) *Our Fighting Forces* (1954–78) *Our Army At War* – with *Sgt Rock* (1959–)	*Sgt Fury* (1963–81) *Capt. Savage* . . . (1968–70)		

Rock and Fury are the major continuing characters in US war comics. They share some major characteristics:

1. Rank

2. Both lead 'multi-ethnic' squads

3. Virtual invincibility. Only minor wounds possible, but severe damage to uniforms may be sustained

	Charlton	Dell/Gold Key	D.C.	Marvel	Others	Underground/Warren
Response to Vietnam	1–3 short stories per issue given over to Vietnam (1964–)	Whole new titles created on Vietnam, e.g. *Tales of the Green Beret* (1967–9), *Jungle War Stories* (1962–5) becomes *Guerilla War* (1965–6)	Attempt at continuing character: Capt. Hunter in *Fighting Forces* (1966). Then occasional short stories given over to Vietnam in existing titles	No direct reaction, e.g. *War is Hell* 1972: (1973–5) reprints Korean, WW2 stories. 1985: *Savage Tales* featuring occasional Vietnam stories 1986: The *'Nam* developed from *Savage Tales*	Lightning: Tod Holton, *Super Green Beret* (1967)	Warren: *Blazing Combat* (1965): anti-war short stories in various settings, including Vietnam Last Gasp: *The Legion of Charlies* (1972) First: *Jon Sable, Freelance* (1983) adventurer with Vietnam background

Unfortunately it is not possible to include within the scope of this paper all these 'other Vietnam' stories. This study has been limited to the sub-genre of stories in war comics which contain specific images or text which relates to Vietnam, but it is important to recognize that this is an artificial dividing line. Limitation of space has meant, also, that the recent interest in Vietnam which pervades the American media has not been covered, although there have been many contemporary comic stories which would fit into the definition given above.

In order to understand the ways in which the Vietnam war comic differs from its predecessors it is necessary first to know something of the American war comic in the previous decade. In the 1950s the Second World War dominated the genre, despite the outbreak of the Korean War early in the decade. Indeed, the Second World War virtually created the genre, and continues to dominate it today.

The two great continuing characters of American war comics are Sergeant Rock and Sergeant Fury (see Figs 1 and 2). Some of their similarities are shown in Fig. 3 and some of their differences will be discussed later. In effect, both these characters reflect their names accurately: Rock can in reality always be depended upon, and Fury is a human tornado, ever likely to win the war single-handed.

The most obvious similarity between Rock and Fury is their rank. The sergeant is the key rank in this type of comic, just as it is in many American war films. Sergeants Rock and Fury have the total trust of their men because they are both 'the best'. They lead from the front and, perhaps what is most important, they know when to break the rules. Because of this there is frequently the implication that those in the hierarchy immediately above them actually decline in effectiveness in inverse proportion to their increase in rank. Thus lieutenants and captains may be out-of-touch college kids or 'desk men' who have an excessive faith in the rule book. This is partially to do with class, because the sergeants are almost always working class; for example, Fury appears to come from Brooklyn. The exceptions to the officer rule are either sergeants who have been promoted unwillingly or generals who are great individualists. These latter are vaguely based on General Patton. In other words, they are successful because they are generals who again know when to break the rules.

The images of Sergeant Rock and Sergeant Fury are also surprisingly similar. Apart from sharing almost identical formats, they share the strange common

Fig. 4 Drawing styles and the image of the body (in cartoons, comics and film). The four fields of comics, pulp magazines, animation and film have displayed an interrelated view of the human body. In almost every case the idealized drawn version of the body has preceded and influenced the film version (e.g. Tarzan). Although animation has centred on animal figures, their drawing styles have often been closely related to newspaper comic strips, and through them to comic books. *Key:* Straight lines indicate a company or artist who moved from one field to another. Lines with arrows indicate a direct stylistic influence. Dotted lines indicate a working relationship (e.g. Carl Barks worked for the Disney Company).

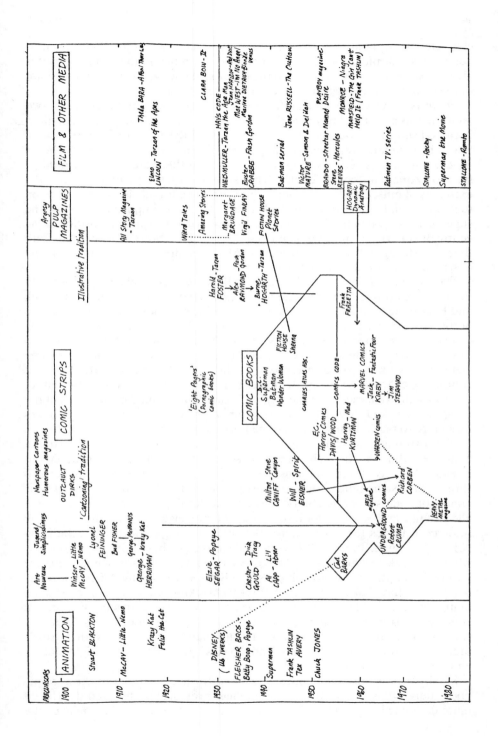

characteristic of being unable to survive an adventure without their uniforms being ripped to pieces. Even if this damage is minimal in the actual story it is always extensive on the cover; and the cover is of course the main selling point of the comic. This is especially true with Sergeant Fury.

There is, however, a radical difference between the physiques of the two men and this is tantalizingly revealed to the reader through the jagged openings in ripped shirt and trousers. Rock, as drawn by Joe Kubert or Russ Heath is a fine, but comparatively realistic specimen of American manhood. Kubert's style is a unique pared-down, gestural version of the more usual 'cartooning' style of American comic books. This style is not suited to rendering the extremes of muscular development which are to be found elsewhere. Fury, on the other hand, was drawn by Jack Kirby, the most important artist of the super-hero revival of the 1960s. Figure 4 shows Kirby in a pivotal position at the centre of American comic book drawing style. In his rendition of Sergeant Fury there are strong stylistic similarities with Marvel's super-hero characters, many of whom were also drawn by Kirby.

The meaning of the semi-naked flesh in the drawings is open to question. On the most obvious level it is evident that the ripped clothes of Sergeants Rock and Fury indicate the dangerous life-threatening situations into which the two heroes are regularly plunged. By comparison, however, the 'one-off' characters on the covers of most Vietnam War comics suffer little or no flesh-revealing clothing damage: and the lives of these 'one-off' characters were just as likely to be in jeopardy. This possibly points to the fact that continuing characters such as Rock and Fury need to operate on a different set of criteria than characters of the 'one-off' sort. Thus it could be argued that the glimpses of naked flesh which are so commonplace in the continuing comics owe more to market forces than to the horrors of war.[3]

The torn uniforms of Fury and Rock provide an interesting visual parallel with the nature of their characters as sergeants, which has been described already. Usually, their uniforms, the very symbol of authority, are torn to shreds at the same time as they are performing their duty to the utmost of their almost boundless, heroic ability. The ripped clothing is a visual device which allows Fury and Rock to look romantic and powerful, though still obviously soldiers: it leaves them unencumbered by restricting uniforms and the fussy detail of insignia. In short it becomes *obvious* that these are men who know when to break the rules. There are other possible reasons which make these covers so ubiquitous, one of which is purely technical. Many American comic book artists have learned to draw figures by blocking muscle masses of a naked figure and then adding clothing afterwards. Burne Hogarth's book *Dynamic Anatomy* has been a seminal influence in this method.[4] It is ideal for super-heroes, but it does mean that in many other genres the artist's predilection for this type of body leads to cowboy heroes in skin-tight clothes and shirt-less war heroes.

Finally, sex is another important element in the portrayal of these comic book heroes. As this study has implied previously, the well-developed muscular male body is a standard figure in most of the genres that make up the field of American comic books. At the same time the most common advertisement in these books is for body building courses – the most famous of these advertisements is that of the legendary Charles Atlas. It is possible to view comic books as a vast advertising medium for the body building business. For instance, it can be argued that the stories of an unbelievably heroic, muscular figure end, not on the last page of the text, but on the inside back cover of the comic which is embellished with a bodybuilding advertisement ('You too can have a body like mine . . .'). All this is more true of Sergeant Fury than Sergeant Rock. And although the heroes in the advertisements often have diminutive bikini-clad girls admiring them, it must be acknowledged that the appeal of Sergeant Fury's semi-naked body is partly homosexual. The readership of war comics is obviously male in the main, and while many of these males may simply see Fury as a role model whose emulation, through a body building course, would provide many female admirers the reaction of others may not be on heterosexual lines. Bodybuilding culture has always had a strong homosexual element and the drawings of Fury provide a more direct gratification as a kind of homosexual pin up.

Before we leave this subject to look at Korean War comics it should be noted that this image of the male body in comics has had another indirect effect on the image of Vietnam in popular culture. Illustrations in pulp magazines or comic strips have usually preceded cinema adaptations of works like Edgar Rice Burrough's 'Tarzan'. Thus Almo Lincoln's *Tarzan* (1918) follows the image of Tarzan in *All Story Magazine* (1911) and Johnny Weismuller (1932) follows the slimmer more muscular version of Harold Foster's newspaper strip (1929). This reaches its height with the comic book version of *Conan* (1970) and its re-creation by Arnold Schwarzenegger (1982). It is life imitating art, or rather comics, to the point where Schwarzenegger has in reality more extreme muscular development than the type visualized by Jack Kirby in 1962. The Vietnam connection here is that of Sylvester Stallone's *Rambo* films, as David Willson's research in this area indicates; although 'Rambo's' image does not have specific antecedents in comics, it does have paperback cover imagery to draw upon.[5]

John Berger has commented on the wealth of female nudes in Western art and by comparison the dearth of male nudes. Berger wrote: 'A man's presence is dependent upon the promise of the power which he embodies.'[6] The costume historian James Laver demonstrated that much of this power is indicated by clothing, and that men's clothing has traditionally indicated their place in society. It is Laver's argument that the clothes a man wears are themselves based on an 'hierarchical system'.[7] Therefore, this revealing of the male torso, which can be traced through comics to Rambo, might now imply a classless view of society by comparison to the traditional readings of class hegemony and power in the Western world. In any case we have already seen that most of the heroes are working class. However, class appears to be a minor element; the major element is still sexual. As Laver has also argued, 'Complete nudity is anti-erotic, our characteristic permanent eroticism is kept alive by clothes.'[8] Thus, according to James Laver, all clothing is partially erotic, but the most erotic of all is that which partially reveals and yet partially conceals: the two sergeants in their ripped clothes could hardly be more sexily dressed.

Rambo is more directly a descendant of Tarzan the Ape Man. Rambo's muscles mean that, like Tarzan, he can kill a man with his bare hands. For Tarzan, these victims are usually black, for Rambo they are often yellow. It is apparent that even if Rambo loses his weapons he can practically hold down a helicopter with his hand in an association of muscles with sheer power which runs back to Superman. The implication is that if Rambo's muscles are as big as Superman's, then perhaps he is also as strong. The irony of this is that the muscular development of a bodybuilder such as Schwarzenegger is not the best build to generate sheer strength and stamina: the physiques of heavyweight boxers are in fact unfashionably fat. The baroque muscles of Fury, Conan and Rambo are, therefore, largely non-functional decoration.

The Korean War led to an avalanche of thousands of stories by comparison to the hundreds of Vietnam stories in the following years. It could be argued that this is due to the fact that the Korean conflict was both a more popular United Nations war and also much more conventional in its implementation, at least in its early stages.[9] It had the drama of the Inchon landings, and in the figure of General McArthur it had the advantage of a real old-fashioned hero cast in the Patton mould. The Korean War is distinguished in most comics by the level of violence which was permissible both because of the lack of censorship in comics at the time, and the way in which, during an actual war, the enemy are reduced to subhuman and thus easily slaughterable status. The range of material produced in the war is nevertheless very wide including the E.C. war stories of Harvey Kurtzman, which are among the finest American comic books yet produced in any genre.[10]

Martin Barker has said of the portrayal of American soldiers in Korean War comics:

> The biggest effort is being made to make them a centre of ordina-riness . . . *only* an ordinary person could do this job. The price of this is that he is human, he makes mistakes. He is ordinary in a superordinary way.[11]

Indeed the story of the ordinary soldier is one of the standard formula short stories in American war comics. It appears in the Second World War, in the Civil War and in the Korean and Vietnam wars. In other words, the actual setting is irrelevant. Although capable of incredible variety in setting and detail its basic formula is very simple, as follows:

1. Its central character is a private.
2. He is wary of action because of
    (a) an understandable fear (it is often his first time in combat),
    (b) a character defect (bad upbringing, undue pacifist leanings, etc.).
3. He overcomes his fear, and usually undertakes an act of great heroism. The narrative resolution of these stories (in which the character may even be killed) is not vitally important, nor is the way in which he overcomes his fear.

This may be due to an accident, the help of his comrades or to a friendly sergeant. The key factor is that he does overcome his fear.[12]

There are other standard stories which occur set in most wars. One of the most common is the 'technological' story in which superior American know-how or technology (weapons, communications) are displayed as the things which will help the ordinary soldier to win the war. This certainly still occurs in relation to Vietnam, where it really should have been redundant. If the Vietnam War proved anything militarily, it was that a massive commitment of troops supported by high-technology weapons can be totally frustrated by the superior tactics of a less well-equipped army. However, the main point is that there are certain stories which are set in Vietnam which are not actually about Vietnam, despite their settings, the names used, weapons and all other details. These stories are simply a thoughtless reworking of this formula and can tell us nothing about the conflict except to display some of its surface minutiae.

Before considering Vietnam War comics in more detail it is worth mentioning an archetypical figure who appears in Korean War comics. It is an archetype which also appears in innumerable Second World War stories: the evil oriental officer. This figure was equally popular in war films and has a basis even further back in nineteenth-century fiction as part of the 'yellow peril'. In comics the Korean model is simply transposed from the Japanese version and a typical example occurs in *War Adventure* (No. 12, Atlas) of January 1953. In the six-page story 'One More Means Death' we are introduced to North Korean general Sohu Ninn by a drawing of a close up of his evil, obese, bearded face. Ninn shoots innocent South Korean villagers and, before his inevitable demise, he is succinctly summed up as 'cruel . . . to him life is cheap!' The general only differs from some more extreme examples in that he does not actually resort to torturing his victims. The strange thing about this figure, as we shall see later, is that he does not appear in Vietnam stories.

In order to indicate the range of comics produced during the Vietnam War it is necessary to look at specific stories in more detail. The three following stories are not representative of the actual *balance* of stories produced during the war – but they do indicate something of their technical and ideological range. The first story was produced by Charlton comics. They were a comparatively minor company who published the largest number of war comics and thus also produced the most stories about Vietnam (see Fig. 3). Charlton were a kind of bargain basement company who paid low rates to contributors and were particularly badly printed in a field not noted for its excellence of production.

Stories which fit into one of the 'any-war-will-do' formulas have not been considered for inclusion so that the stories examined here each relate to Vietnam in a specific way. Vietnam was a war which produced an unprece-dented amount of press coverage with comparatively little censorship. This led, among other things, to a remarkable series of revelations about atrocities by American troops which culminated in the trial of Lieutenant Calley for the massacre at My Lai. These revelations in turn fuelled the vociferous protest

Fig. 5 From Bill Montes' (artist) 'The War Criminals' (*Fightin' Marines*, No. 77, November 1967, Charlton Publications).

ovement in America. These three related Vietnam issues – the press,
rocities and opposition to the war – are dealt with in 'The War Criminals'
m Charlton's *Fightin' Marines* (No. 77) of November 1967. It is drawn by
ie of Charlton's more effective artists, Bill Montes. His style is very much in
ie mainstream of American 'cartooning', which enables him to overcome
ccasional shaky drawing by a sureness of touch and boldness of design.
 The opening page (see Fig. 5) has the banner title 'The War Criminals'
illowed by three panels packed with visual information. The impression given
that we are watching US marines shooting down an unarmed Vietnamese.
iere is a wealth of other visual information, particularly in the first panel.
ire we see two marines opening fire with another figure between them. The
irines wear helmets, are clean-shaven and well built, carry guns and appear
dynamic poses of action. By contrast, the central figure wears a forage cap
l glasses, has a beard and is very thin. He carries a camera and is in repose.

The text on the page explains and emphasizes the differences between the
physical appearance of the men, but totally negates the initial, fleeting
impression that we might be watching American troops acting as 'war
criminals'. The caption describes the bearded figure in the following way: 'He
is Talbot Cleeves and he's trouble . . . the kind of writer who thinks Americans
have no business in Vietnam . . .' So Cleeves is identified as part of the
'counter-culture', both visually and in the text. He is 'a kind of writer' who is
automatically opposed to the war. Soon, it also becomes evident that the
'unarmed' Vietnamese was in fact carrying a grenade. Cleeves remains
unconvinced by this and several other incidents, including an ambush and a
treacherous attempt by a Vietcong to kill him, despite the fact that Cleeves has
saved the Vietcong's life. Only on the final page of the story does Cleeves
realize 'the truth' and this after he sees that the Vietcong have imprisoned and
threatened to execute a whole village. Cleeves changes sides abruptly, kicking
a gun from the hand of a Cong ('The writers' gettin' a piece of the action') and
identifying himself with this new group by adopting their slang – the enemy are
now 'Charlies' (Fig. 6).

At the point of his final change – his apotheosis – Talbot Cleeves as we knew
him formerly virtually disappears altogether. As he disarms the Cong he is in
silhouette; after this Cleeves is only seen twice from the rear view. Perhaps the
vision of the evil, bearded Cleeves is too much at odds with his new found
status, so it is simply not shown. Thus in the penultimate frame an arm is placed
round Cleeves' shoulder, and he is made fun of in a spirit of camaraderie. Seen
from the back all the visual signifiers of the first page are as minimized as
continuity will allow. Cleeves' bag, camera, beard and glasses have gone. He is
no longer an outsider. But there is one final humiliation, one final expunction
of guilt: Cleeves must apologize to Eglund and the squad, 'I was a gullible fool,
Lieutenant'. Eglund, however, wants just one thing; he says: 'Just write the
truth about what you saw today.' This truth is, of course, the internal truth of
the Charlton comic story which has been spelt out already to the reader.

The position of Charlton comics *vis-à-vis* the American media's attacks on
the war is quite clear: 'The War Criminals' explains to the reader how false

Fig. 6 From Bill Montes' (artist) 'The War Criminals' (*Fightin' Marines*, No. 77, November 1967, Charlton Publications).

atrocity stories might start. The strange thing is that anybody should feel that such a story was necessary in 1967. Atrocities do not seem to become front page news in America until 1969 with the Song My massacre. The story is therefore a 'pre-emptive' first denial which lends some credence to Jules Feiffer's comment about war comics in the late 1960s, that they were 'harmful, distorted and *Pentagon manipulated*' (my italics).[13]

The second story indicates the way in which comic books responded, albeit slowly, to changing public attitudes towards the war. It is '22 hours to San Francisco' (from *Our Army At War*, No. 236, September 1971, published by D.C. Comics).[14]

Originally, in 1966, D.C.'s policy towards Vietnam was not significantly different from Charlton's. They tried a series of stories starring 'Captain Hunter', searching super-hero-like for his missing brother in Vietnam, which lasted for only eight issues. The attitude of D.C. Comics had changed by 1971 when they published '22 hours to San Francisco', drawn by veteran comic artist John Severin.

It is important to consider Severin's drawing style at this point, particularly as its associations for English viewers may well be different to those for Americans. Severin's style contrasts quite dramatically to the drawing of the Charlton story which has been discussed already and, indeed, Severin's style is similar to the drawing frequently found in British war comics. However, the Charlton style, a type loosely known as 'cartooning', is the one which is far more typical of American comics in general. Severin's style is more illustrative: it is inked mainly in pen rather than brush, which is unusual for American comic artists. Most importantly Severin's is a style associated with a documentary approach, and indeed Severin often drew factual stories for E.C. in the 1950s. Equally it is a style that is not really applicable to super-heroes and Severin hardly ever draws them. Super-heroes tend to be drawn stylistically at the most dramatic end of the 'cartooning' mode where the force of the brushstroke is much more fitted to the task of rendering the full extent of muscular development required for that genre.

Immediately upon examining '22 hours to San Francisco', it is evident that Severin's drawing style precludes a wide range of story types. This is evident particularly with the opening three frames which are in a grainy black and white (an effect produced by special 'duotone' drawing card). Severin's drawing style, particularly in black and white, also has overtones of documentary photography. The title, which takes up the central third of the page, is followed by three frames in colour of a bag on a baggage-handling machine. In terms of the narrative, the black and white sequences appear to be operating as a 'flashback' mechanism. The device of black and white (or tinted, or out of focus) film is often used in this way in the cinema to indicate an incomplete (remembered) reality. The colour frames then relate to the immediacy of that part of the story taking place in the present. Alternatively, and perhaps less likely, the black and white sequences could be read as a dream, or nightmare of Vietnam.

On the second page the narrative moves from black and white action to single colour frames of the bag moving on the machine. Two things are now evident. First, the setting is definitely Vietnam. This is obvious because of the equipment (M16 rifles, Huey helicopters) which most people would recognize as contemporary, even if they did not know the precise make and model. The figures who now attack the central character of the story, Tomasz, are also recognizable as Vietcong wearing black pyjamas.

Secondly, it is evident that the narrative is being conducted without recourse to word balloons or even text panels of any kind. There are only eight words which appear in the images in the story and these have the aim of helping to locate the story more specifically and to provide further information such as Tomasz having his name inscribed on his helmet. Both the use of black and white and this 'Silent' narrative method are extremely rare in mainstream American comics. There are several possible reasons for their use in this instance. First, the E.C. tradition, to which Severin belongs, is one of experimentation. Their best work in the 1950s abounds with innovation of all kinds. Secondly, this singular method of story telling allows for a fair degree of ambiguity. When dealing specifically with Vietnam D.C. may appear to be anti-war, but they are also careful not to appear anti-patriotic. Many of D.C.'s other, perhaps more outspoken anti-war stories of the period are set in wars other than Vietnam, although as discussed in the introduction, they may be *about* Vietnam.

The story begins to lose its documentary feel on its third page when 'Tomasz' has to shoot at some Vietcong at incredibly short range as a shot glances off his helmet. What follows in three black and white frames is the key sequence of the strip. The fight over, it appears that everyone else may be dead. Tomasz looks at his gun, and then he throws it away (Fig. 7). This is a specific gesture which is open to only a limited range of interpretations. At its mildest level it can be taken that Tomasz is sickened by the killing and weapons; nauseated by this final violence as he is about to leave Vietnam. Perhaps Tomasz is sick of war or, perhaps, more specifically, sick of the Vietnam War, and wishes it could be thrown away like the rifle. Possibly Tomasz even wants 'peace with honour'. The sequence does not allow for wider interpretations that might have been possible; for example, if he had tried to break or damage the gun or continued to shoot at the dead men or machinery. The gun has served him well formerly; it has just saved his life but, like many American citizens by this date, Tomasz has had enough of violence.

On the final page Tomasz arrives back in America. He takes his bag from the baggage handling machine. 'Arrive home and everything will be O.K.' appears to be the moral of the last frame where Tomasz is embraced by a female who is obviously significant in his life. The happy couple are watched by smiling passers-by. It is interesting that these surrounding figures are dressed as if they come from the 1950s or early 1960s and are, perhaps unconsciously, evocative of a halcyon America, unchanged and untouched by the war. Unfortunately, Severin's drawing style is not at home in this scene of happy reunion. His chunky figures look much more concordant when in action: they tend to look wooden in repose.

Fig. 7 From John Severin's (artist) '22 hours to San Francisco' (*Our Army At War*, No. 236, September 1971, D.C. Comics). © 1971 DC Comics Inc.

The last page of '22 hours to San Francisco' is finished with the 'badge' which adorned all D.C. stories at this time: 'Make war no more.' Even at the time D.C. received much criticism for this device. It was, of course, heresy to those who still supported the war, and to those who did not it suggested hypocrisy for a company to be making a profit from a war comic even if, at the same time, it was making liberal, anti-war noises. Once more the badge illustrates the tightrope which D.C. was trying to walk at this time. It does not say, for example, that there should be no more war in Vietnam. Rather like the discarding of Tomasz's gun, the badge is an ambiguous gesture.

Vietnam stories are comparatively few in number in mainstream American comic books for the simple reason that they did not sell. Why there was this lack of commercial success is open to question. Reitberger and Fuchs, writing in 1971, argued that 'the Vietnam War is much too controversial for an allout engagement'.[15] And this seems to be a major factor in the lack of appeal to readers. However, there is not the space in this paper to follow up this line of enquiry, because it leads into the whole question of the war's unpopularity (or otherwise) in America.

As far as comics were concerned, the war also lacked the drama of great, historical set-piece battles and it had no distinctive visual impact. Although the visual density of jungle warfare can be put to good effect, it takes a lot of work and, more significantly, much talent to do it justice.[16] The real (later defoliated) landscape of Vietnam is hardly represented in comics but is instead depicted in a hybrid of visual clichés derived from earlier comics set in the war in the Pacific. Thus Vietnam was not only a controversial war but it was one which also lacked drama and visual interest. In a medium hardly renowned for its daring, it is not surprising that there are comparatively few contemporary stories about the war.

When the stories which were published about Vietnam are examined, a further question arises, and this concerns the Vietcong: in almost every case the enemy either does not exist or he is a shadowy figure, hiding in bushes. Often he is seen from the back or in the distance. When a Vietcong does appear he is a racial stereotype, adapted from the earlier Japanese model. Yet the wily oriental officer, so common in the comics of the Second World War and Korea, hardly ever appears in Vietnam stories.[17] A possible explanation for this lies in the nature of the war itself. Vietnam was a major guerrilla war, very different from America's previous wars. Yet it was clearly not being won easily. The question that some Americans were asking was how these little yellow men could be defying the might of America's war machine. And the most obvious answer lay in the conduct of the guerrilla war itself. A contemporary right-wing argument was that if only the enemy would stand up and fight properly, then America could win the war. The visual equivalent of this is that the enemy is literally hiding, pushed to the periphery of the comic frame, not even given the dignity of appearing as a wily oriental officer figure. It is as if the presentation of such officers might suggest that the Vietcong had a strategy wider than the continual small-scale ambushes which dominate many comic stories.[18] It is easier to see the enemy as a coward who hides in tunnels and refuses to fight.

These first two stories are both examples of the product of mainstream commercial comic book publishers of the period. The final story is a radical departure in that it is the product of the 'underground' or 'counter-culture' and is thus aimed at a very different audience. Yet it still draws on some of the same traditions which inform 'mainstream' comics because its artist/author, Greg Irons, works in a style and idiom owing much to E.C. horror comics of the 1950s. Irons' drawings are rather like a brutalized, simplified version of one of E.C.'s major horror artists, Graham Ingels. In 1971 Irons produced the comic book 'Legion of Charlies'. The section under consideration here is perhaps the most startling part of this story – a six-page prologue which precedes the title page of the comic.

The prologue has two potentially separate horizontal narratives. The figures in the narratives echo each other visually, often very closely, and they frequently speak almost the same lines. The frames are supported by solid black borders and, after the first page, they separate into two clear lines of narrative. The black has the effect of helping to separate the two parallel narratives and to stress the linear quality. This still leaves two alternative pathways or routes to read the story as the pages are still more easily read in a traditional vertical progression (Fig. 8). The effect of this layout is similar to the cinema code of parallel narrative, sometimes called 'split screen', which was fashionable at this time.

However, there are important differences. In the cinema it is rarely used and rapidly became regarded as a gimmick. In documentaries it may be indicative of a director who has shot too much footage and is unwilling to edit it rigorously. In a fictional cinema narrative its use is limited due to the fact that two or more parallel pieces of action are distracting and very difficult to follow. By comparison, in comics or other graphic forms such as posters, a parallel layout allows the possibility of making a telling direct comparison between two or more static forms. In the cinema such comparisons are made much more successfully in montage, which is therefore the method usually employed.

The top section of the prologue to 'Legion of Charlies' is labelled 'My Lai, Mar. 16, 1968' and the bottom section 'Hollywood, Aug. 9, 1969'. The top shows a 'Calley' figure and his troops preparing to wipe out a village in Vietnam. Below, in almost 'carbon-copy' parallel, a 'Manson' figure and his hippies are preparing to murder 'piggies'. On the second page one of the soldiers asks (in a direct quote from the Calley trial): 'Even women and children, lieutenant?' Both groups declare that their victims do not deserve to live. There follows a double page spread of two scenes of explicit, graphic violence. The murder of the two sets of helpless victims is more gruesome and immediate than anything that appeared in the much vilified E.C. horror comics of the 1950s.

The final page of the prologue exaggerates the denouement of the two real-life stories: Calley is decorated by a grotesque pock-marked judge 'for bravery above and beyond and below'; Manson is executed in the electric chair, muttering 'Father, forgive them. . . .' Calley is likened to the deity of a different religion as the name tag on his uniform is spelt 'Kali'. Irons rams home

Fig. 8   From Greg Irons' (artist) 'The Legion of Charlies' (*Nasty Tales*, No. 5, 1971, Last Gasp Press).

his point about the differing treatment meted out to the two men by the use of these exaggerations. Yet his most telling point has already been made in the previous five pages – despite the public's and the government's different perceptions of the two events, they share a remarkable similarity.

Perhaps the strangest thing about 'The Legion of Charlies' is that it is extremely rare within the underground field. Despite the fact that the very fabric of the underground was anti-establishment, anti-violence, mainly pro-drug and thus implicitly opposed to the war, there is minimal reaction to it in its comics. Such an omission cannot be purely accidental.

There are several possible reasons why the war appears to have been a difficult subject for underground comics. First, these comics were, in a formal sense, quite traditional. Underground comic strips grew as the humorous relief in underground newspapers, just as their traditional counterparts had done at the start of the century. In terms of form rather than content, they were in the main quite unadventurous; only a handful of artists (notably Rick Griffin and Victor Moscosco) experimented with the breaking down of traditional narrative forms. Even then their surrealism and experimentation with the structure, form and meaning of comic strip language went no further than the innovative work of early twentieth-century comic artists like Winsor McCay and George Herriman.[19]

This also meant that the underground strips were rather like their mainstream counterparts in that they were predominantly humorous. Although they often embodied satirical intent, the strips were the underground's 'funny papers', a relief from the more direct and serious political message emanating from the newspapers themselves. This role, combined with a natural inclination towards the imagery of 'love not war', might have made the war a difficult subject in the first instance.

However, as underground comics matured and grew away from the newspapers that spawned them there was a wider range of subject matter, including explicit sexual material – this is especially the case in the work of Robert Crumb and S. Clay Wilson. Wilson is particularly important in this respect, because his strips were normally a mixture of unbridled sex and violence. His stories of lesbian pirates or the 'Checkered Demon', which mixed orgasms with amputations in almost equal measure, do not equate with the notion that underground comics were wary of portraying violence.

But the violence of Wilson and his counterparts is nearly always the violence of fantasy (often sexual) or nostalgia. The nostalgia is for the E.C. horror comics of the 1950s, which were lovingly parodied or alluded to in countless underground comics. Indeed, underground comic artists seem on the surface to have been more concerned about the ban on horror comics in their childhood than with the Vietnam War. The extent to which nostalgia underpins the underground comic is sometimes underestimated. Robert Crumb, the underground's pre-eminent artist is stylistically a direct descendant of early twentieth-century comic strip artists like Rube Goldberg.

So the reasons for this omission seem to be two-fold. First, the undergrounds were wary of looking too much like violent mainstream comics. Thus their violence, although much more explicit, was removed from a contemporary setting into fantasy or nostalgia. Secondly, the expectation that comics should be essentially humorous or satirical dominates the heyday of the underground comic. It could be argued that this flourish ends with the conclusion of American involvement in the war and Nixon's subsequent resignation after the Watergate scandal. These two events may have helped to dissolve the comparatively cohesive counter-culture which constituted the main part of the market for underground comics.

Comics, then, despite certain similarities to film, are in many ways more formal, and they allow their creators greater control over their images. The comic artist/author has control not just of the reader's point of view, but also presents precise moments frozen in time, and even controls the visual means by which this image is expressed. These three methods of control converge at a specific point – the comic frame. Without the additional elements of movement and sound comics remain like a film storyboard and have little potential to imitate the power of transparent narrative cinema and the realistic illusion which mainstream American cinema creates. But the greater control available does make the comic very open to the expression of specific ideological points of view – or, in other words, ideal for propaganda. So 'War Criminals' and 'The Legion of Charlies' represent strong and quite clearly expressed ideological positions. In order to maintain its ambiguity '22 Hours to San Francisco' uses an artist with a comparatively non-committal or documentary drawing style and actually drops one of its usual constituent elements (word panels and balloons) altogether.

Finally, it may be true that Vietnam and Watergate had a lasting effect on the sophistication and attitudes of a wide spectrum of popular media in America. To establish a theory about the extent of this effect, even merely in relation to comics would, however, be a massive undertaking. But it is possible to say that war comics in particular reverted to an almost staple diet of Second World War stories after the end of the Vietnam War. The commercial imperatives of comic book production mean that publishers are unwilling to tamper with generic formulae. Thus comics return, in the main, to a traditional and much safer course after America's disengagement from Vietnam. It is only in 1985, when the war is distant enough to accept reinterpretation, that American comics return to it with Marvel comic's *The Nam*.

Again, they are not unique within the field of popular culture in that they ignored the war almost as soon as American troops withdrew from Vietnam. In Arnold Wesker's *Roots* the intellectual says 'There's nothing wrong with reading comics as long as that isn't all you read.' The fact remains that anyone foolish enough to read only American war comics in the 8 years after the war would not have known that the Vietnam War had taken place.

Notes

1. A survey and bibliography of Vietnam War comics is being prepared by David Willson of Green River Community College. From my own estimates I suspect that

this will prove that comic books were the major contemporary fictional response to the war.

2. A striking example occurs in D.C. comics' 'Our Army at War' (No. 233, 1971) in which the story 'Head Count' is set in France in the Second World War, but concerns American troops killing civilians in a village called 'Alimy' (an anagram of My Lai).

3. Vietnam was the first war not to produce a successful continuing character comparable to Rock and Fury. Of three major attempts, *Capt. Hunter* (D.C.), *Tod Holton Super Green Beret* (Lightening) and Shotgun Harker (in Charlton's *Fightin' Marines*), only the latter lasted any length of time. It is very difficult to tell how successful Harker actually was because Charlton were the least responsive of the comic companies, and did not even run letter columns.

4. Burne Hogarth, *Dynamic Anatomy*, New York: Watson-Guptill, 1958.

5. David Willson, *Themes and Motifs in Cover Design for Vietnam War Fiction*, Paper given at the E.V.A.C. Conference, Manchester, 1986.

6. John Berger, *Ways of Seeing*, Harmondsworth: Penguin, 1972, p. 45.

7. James Laver, *Modesty in Dress*, London: Heinemann, 1969, p. 78.

8. Ibid., p. 79.

9. This is a complicated issue because the Korean War was certainly less popular than is sometimes supposed. Nevertheless, vociferous public protest was much less common than during the Vietnam War.

10. E.C. (initially 'Educational', later 'Entertaining Comics'), published by William Gaines, were a comparatively small company but their influence has been seminal. Ironically their ground-breaking comics were partially responsible for the comics code of 1954 which disastrously set back the standards and aims of the American comic book industry.

11. Martin Barker, *A Haunt of Fears*, London: Pluto, 1985, p. 191.

12. Charlton comics used this formula of the 'superordinary private' in 'The Misfit' (*Fightin' Marines*, No. 76, 1967), 'Terror in a Vietcong Tunnel' (*Army War Heroes*, No. 20, 1967) and 'The Terrible Fears of P.F.C. Bolton' (*Fightin' Army*, No. 83, 1969) among many others.

13. Quoted in R. Reitberger and W. Fuchs, *Comics: Anatomy of a Mass Medium*, London: Studio Vista, 1971, p. 93.

14. D.C. (or National Periodicals), named after their first title, Detective Comics, in 1937 were the first major comic company. They dominated the comic book field with their super-heroes (including Superman and Batman), although they arguably lost their pre-eminent position to Marvel comics in the 1960s.

15. R. Reitberger and W. Fuchs, op. cit., p. 93.

16. Alex Toth, 'White Devil Yellow Devil', in *Star Spangled War*, No. 164, September 1972, is an example of how effective a jungle setting can be. The narrative of 'White Devil Yellow Devil', which shows the human side of a Japanese soldier, is also another example of a story set in the Second World War which may be attempting to make a comment on Vietnam.

17. I have only traced one example, in a very early story, before the specifics of Vietnam War stories were developed, and like some other early stories it retains elements of the earlier Korean stories.

18. The other figure missing from Vietnam War comics is the black American soldier. I have only traced two black characters in all the stories I have seen – a paltry token recognition of the actual percentage of black American troops in Vietnam. In fairness to D.C. comics, however, they did use some of their Second World War stories to make explicit anti-racist statements at this time.

19. Both artists produced 'surreal' images in the first two decades of the century. Herriman's background changed continuously for no reason; his characters address their artist and on occasion use the comic frame lines as a solid part of their universe. McCay's characters bend and transmute, as do the objects and landscapes they inhabit. The visual drama of McCay's world dominates the dream-like narrative relegating it to a secondary position.

Further reading

Very little has been written about this specific area. The most useful general books are:

R. Reitberger and W. Fuchs, *Comics: Anatomy of a Mass Medium*, London: Studio Vista, 1971.
M. Barker, *A Haunt of Fears*, London: Pluto, 1985. (The final chapter deals with Korean war comics.)

James Aulich

6

Cartoon Representations of the Vietnam War in the British Press

Cartoons and 'the free press'

Forces at work in the British press – most dramatically over the past three decades – have resulted in the operation of covert censorship masked by ideas of 'individualism' and 'independence' which are, according to Stuart Hall, 'central to the way power and ideology are mediated in societies like ours'.[1]

The 1960s were host to 'liberalization' in the fields of opportunity, education and sexual mores in a society popularly conceived as having reached a stable consensus. Indirectly this led to the virtual elimination of the left-wing press as proprietors became increasingly dependent on advertising aimed at an upwardly mobile, middle-class and young audience endowed with spending power. Hence what was in fact a socially and politically heterogeneous group with wide-ranging views, underwent a process of homogenization as the production of news and comment was narrowed to reduce the risk of causing offence and alienating parts of the market. Opinion, therefore, became stereotyped, less representative of the divisions within society and increasingly responsive to the assumed consensus.

By 1977 the Royal Commission on the Press expressed concern at the lack of diversity and indicated an inherent problem in the fact that three-quarters of the British press was owned by five business groups, only one of which had interests solely confined to journalism. The others had extended beyond cultural production and were, therefore, doubly vulnerable, being dependent on advertising and subject to more general market forces. In view of this and Britain's subject status in relation to the US, the failure of the British press to address the issues behind the war sufficiently was hardly surprising.

During the 1960s owners tended to favour the delegation of responsibility to professional editors who yet worked within frameworks of implicit understanding. Today, the involvement of proprietors in editorial policy is often more direct – as in the case of Tiny Rowland's stance over the reporting of his investments in Zimbabwe in his newspaper *The Observer* (and the consequent departure of his editor).

This creates pressures very apparent to those at the sharp end of newspaper production. Gerald Scarfe (an artist whose work figures prominently in this study) recently made clear the consequences of such developments when he described his own position in terms of the professional who does not waste time on a drawing he knows will be turned down. In brief, self-censorship.[2]

Scarfe's comment gives the lie to notions of the individualism and independence of the writer and artist in our free press – even though, ironically, the cartoonist is often seen as its ideal personification. Allegedly the cartoonist has the role of the iconoclast to whom nothing is sacred and whose satire exposes corruption, reveals folly and decries man's inhumanity to man. It is a strictly authorial medium, identified by the name of the cartoonist: 'Scarfe' appears in the *Sunday Times*; 'Steadman' in *Rolling Stone*; 'Jensen' in the *Sunday Telegraph*; and 'Vicky' in the *Evening Standard* or the *New Statesman*. It relies on the convention of the 'individual' artist and the uniqueness of vision. In other words, the 'independence' and 'freedom' of the cartoonist is crucial to the perception of the cartoon. These characteristics are reinforced by the autonomy traditionally granted to the cartoonist who often answers directly only to the editor.

Yet the cartoon, whether drawn from the popular or the more élitist and sophisticated departments of the press is formally conservative, rarely taking advantage of modernist techniques like photomontage.[3] Despite the emphasis on the grotesque and the fact that caricature proceeds by paradox, distorting 'reality' in order to tell the 'truth', the newspaper cartoon conforms monotonously to hierarchical representational conventions established in the eighteenth century. The pictorial language of the cartoonist is figurative and often relies on the direct translation of figures of speech into a visual mode. The cartoon is constructed in language and absorbed in convention, it conveys a message and like any linguistic code it has the capacity to lie.

Like the papers and periodicals they appear in, cartoons are now taken for granted as part of our normal, natural landscape. They are historically specific and emerge from a concatenation of event, in this case the Vietnam War, and person, usually an authority figure. They share many characteristics with the news story, as Jeremy Tunstall has described it:

> The type of dramatic political event most likely to become news is conflict between leading personalities over issues which can be easily dramatised as relevant to large numbers of audience members.[4]

Bearing in mind the prominence of cartoons in the formal construction of 'news' (they are often on or opposite the editorial page), Freud's comment on caricature is worth recalling here:

Fig. 1 Vicky: 'We'll knock hell out of 'em!', *New Statesman*, 23 April 1965.

> Caricature, parody and travesty . . . are directed against people and objects which lay claim to authority and respect, who are in some senses exalted. . . . By making our enemy small, inferior, despicable or comic we achieve in a roundabout way the enjoyment of overcoming him – to which a third person bears witness by his laughter.[5]

The laughter cartoons on Vietnam usually provoked was a sort that did indeed mock, criticize and vent aggression against eminent figures. If these *personalized* depictions worked to display and displace the frustrations and fears of large sections of the readership, they also meant that the war itself was rarely a primary target. The war inevitably assumed a secondary importance in the mind of the observer.

There are historical, institutional and formal explanations for the general inadequacy of the medium in tackling the national economic and political impulses behind the fact of the war. Far from being a visionary beacon, the cartoonist is more often than not unwittingly complicit in this failure, because his satire is directed not against the institutions and structures of power, but those individuals who are their temporary tenants and whose ridicule entails a trivialization of the economic and historical causes of the war.

Changing attitudes

Until 1964 and Harold Wilson's Labour government, Vietnam was not an issue that featured in the British press with any great regularity or urgency.

Fig. 2 Vicky: 'The British Government's attitude is now so clearly a reflection of Washington's that it can have no standing as a mediator whatever', *Evening Standard*, 11 November 1965.

However, Wilson's support of Lyndon B. Johnson's bombing of the North was seen by his opponents at both ends of the political spectrum as an exercise in cynicism since, in return, he could expect American support for British policy in Malaysia and Indonesia.

Much to the delight of the conservative press the Anglo-American 'special relationship' served to bestow a world role on the British government through British and Commonwealth peace initiatives in an area where there was a potential for a superpower conflict. At the same time it emphasized Britain's insularity and independence from Europe. Vicky depicts a diminutive Wilson next to Johnson in the backyard of the White House, symbolic of world power, in 'We'll knock hell out of 'em' (Fig. 1) and quotes Phan van Dong's comment that, 'The British government's attitude is now so clearly a reflection of Washington's that it can have no standing as a mediator whatever', in his depiction of Wilson in the guise of three wise monkeys unable to see, hear or speak of the B52 flying overhead (Fig. 2). The failure of Wilson's efforts provoked elements of the left-wing and liberal press like the *New Statesman* to ask 'When is the government going to offer the smallest whisper of criticism of American policy in Vietnam?'[6] Gerald Scarfe in a particularly virulent cover for *Private Eye* drew Wilson licking Johnson's bare behind (Fig. 3). But

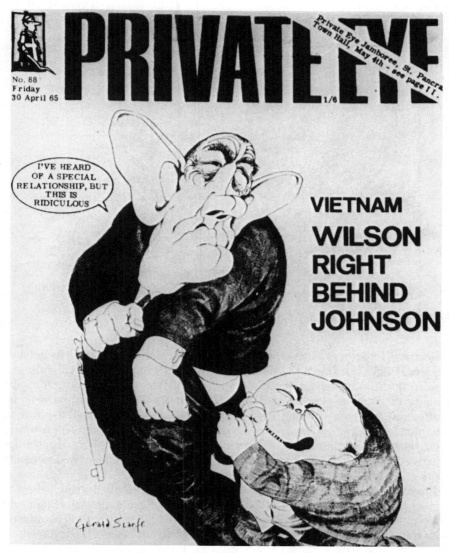

Fig. 3   Gerald Scarfe: 'Wilson right behind Johnson', *Private Eye*, 30 April 1965.

Vietnam remained only one among many newsworthy issues confronting the
government. Vicky, for example, shows Wilson and his Foreign Secretary
George Brown discovering barrels of gunpowder in the cellars under the
Houses of Parliament, in a parody of the Guy Fawkes story, variously labelled
Vietnam, Rhodesia, Defence and Immigration.[7]

By 1966 media interpretations of events in Vietnam were moving against

Fig. 4 J. Jensen: uncaptioned, *Sunday Telegraph*, 25 April 1965.

official indifference. US involvement was seen as morally correct in its defence of democracy; but less so with respect to Diem's authoritarian regime and disaffection among an increasingly war-weary American public. Domestic trouble in America was treated by Jensen in the figure of Johnson as an ineffectual fireman pointing his dripping hose at the blaze of the war in Vietnam, while casting his eyes over his shoulder to see his pants on fire with race riots in Alabama (Fig. 4). As the Marxist historian Eric Hobsbawm observed in 1971, all was not well in this 'capitalist abundance, and nowhere more obviously than in its stronghold, the U.S.'.[8]

Pressure from the left-wing of the Labour party eventually forced Wilson to dissociate the British government from American raids against Hanoi and Haiphong in the summer of 1966. Within a year the *Daily Telegraph* could note with 'shock' American indifference to British opinion. Wilson's move effectively removed Vietnam as a point of political contention on the left until Nixon's intensification of the bombing in 1970. The war was perceived as a more uniquely American affair. During 1968 the war was little more than a factor in the Presidential campaign. Described as the 'longest run up to the elections he will ever have travelled' in the *Sunday Telegraph*, 2 weeks later Jensen drew a parched Johnson crawling in the desert surrounded by vultures variously described as 'Hawks' and 'Doves' (Fig. 5). Richard Nixon's relation to the war was perceived as being no less equivocal, as Emmwood awards the winner of the election race the dead weight of a medal inscribed with the words,

Fig. 5 J. Jensen: uncaptioned, *Sunday Telegraph*, 20 August 1967.

'Vietnam and Civil Rights' in 'The Winner?' As such he echoes his newspaper's editorial line – *The Daily Mail* – talking of:

> not simply the ending of the Vietnam war but the ending of the American Empire. . . . The war, quite simply, has cost too much

and of an 'America floundering and sinking deeper into self-doubt', while from Saigon emanated 'the smell of defeat'.[9]

The general tone of the press had settled against American involvement, focussing on the 'tragedy' and the 'meaninglessness' of the war. In February 1968 even Peregrine Worsthorne, the highly conservative editor of the *Sunday Telegraph*, queried if America should not ask herself whether the Communist successes had not undermined the moral basis for continuing the war against

> the dreadful certainties of napalmed babies and ancient cities in ruins. . . . Blanket support does more harm than good, since it rings embarrassingly false, and leaves the anti-Americans with all the convincing tunes.

The following month Edward Kennedy added his voice and legitimacy to the anti-Vietnam chorus.

In a particularly revealing cartoon from 1969 Jensen depicts Nixon and Ho Chi Minh charging at each other in civilian clothes while Ho cries 'Sure I altered the rules – but there's no need for you to follow them!' Ho's gun has a bayonet,

Fig. 6 J. Jensen: 'Sure I altered the rules – But there's no need for you to follow them!', *Sunday Telegraph*, 4 March 1969.

Nixon's an olive twig labelled 'Paris Talks'; the fact that Nixon is armed demonstrates his own duplicitous nature in tune with the racial stereotyping of his counterpart. The challenge offered by the war to the rhetoric of American models of democracy and freedom is expressed inadvertently, but congruent with the establishment discomfiture at American overkill in a cause felt to be just (Fig. 6).

The 1970s saw a lessening of coverage as American troops withdrew under the 'successful' Vietnamization programme. It was quite simply no longer an issue. Massive intensification of bombing could stimulate no protest from the British government. Calley's trial for the murder of Vietnamese civilians evinced in the press the story of the small American pitted against the power of the privileged in a demonstration of the moral bankruptcy of American foreign policy. The cartoons 'Daddy what did *YOU* do in the Great War?' by Scarfe and 'What did you do in the war daddy?' by Jensen illustrate this particularly well. The slogan originally devised during the First World War in order to inculcate guilt for not fighting, now has the opposite effect, and supports the view of the GI as prey to larger forces as he sits 'haunted' by his memories, that have made him the victim of the contradictions of his liberal conscience (Figs 7 and 8).

Stereotyping

The cartoon, then, as it follows the historical course of the war, offers no more than a slightly humorous commentary from within the confines of the media's

Fig. 7   Gerald Scarfe: 'Daddy, what did *YOU* do in the Great War?', 1971.

Fig. 8   J. Jensen: 'What did you do in the war, Daddy?', *Sunday Telegraph*, 4 April 1971.

Fig. 9   Vicky: 'It came to pieces in my hands', *Evening Standard*, 27 August 1963.

Fig. 10   Vicky: 'We don't think this is the way to win', *Evening Standard*, 4 September 1963.

conventional construction of the war. Indeed, on the level of stereotyping political leaders, especially American Presidents, the cartoonist hijacks popular prejudices which serve as little more than a mask for an unquestioning response to the ideological correctness of American involvement.

During the Kennedy era the American President was conventionally seen in cartoon as a benign presence in civilian clothes handling, for example, his precious collection of oriental porcelain in Vicky's 'It came to pieces in my hand' (Fig. 9); or dressed in white, he is represented as an armed but much maligned and manipulated dupe of the dressed-in-black, back-stabbing *femme fatale* Mme Nhu, notorious for her remarks about 'barbecued monks'. American involvement is seen to be the benevolent victim of the treacherous and essentially evil oriental (Fig. 10).

By the time of the Johnson administration the President was most often found in the guise of a cowboy. The cowboy epitomizes the improvised nature of the enterprise and the idea of the frontier spirit engaged in an aggressive but moral battle of good against evil, imposing the power of reason and the will of the individual on the chaos of unreason and the irrationality of Asian mentality which is unable to resist the Communist threat. This is very much in tune with contemporary commentary. Peregrine Worsthorne, for example, could

Fig. 11   Garland: 'Aping his master. Imitation is the sincerest form of flattery', *Daily Telegraph*, 23 May 1966.

condemn Diem for his repressive measures and yet justify his and American action in the name of the noble struggle for survival of a democratic nation state.

The cowboy establishes the principle of Johnson's moral rightness very early on in the conflict. By 1966 this was further reinforced by the depiction of the President as a GI, dual inheritor of the moral weight earned in the Second World War battles against the 'evil empires' of Hitler and Hirohito and the more problematic role as international peace keeper in an era Dwight MacDonald had dubbed an age of 'impossible alternatives'. The means required to defeat totalitarianism was so catastrophic as to defy democracy itself. Something of this is addressed when Garland focussed on the true cost of the war when he drew for the *Daily Telegraph* a GI bride for Johnson not as 'War on Poverty' but 'War in Vietnam'.[10]

The question of moral rightness is often concealed beneath the mocking of Presidents when they are depicted as misguided or blundering, particularly when considered in the light of Freud's analysis of the significant violence of the clumsy action that might also be seen to project unconscious desires and motives. Vicky's 'It came to pieces in my hand' (Fig. 9) shows Kennedy smashing an object of some value, literally a piece of porcelain, allegorically Vietnamese self-determination. But this depicted *clumsiness* conceals the carefully orchestrated anti-Communism of the machinery of state. Another cartoon by Vicky has Johnson walking in the dark[11] and Garland finds him as a physically uncoordinated Gulliver figure trampling the political landscape of South Vietnam (Fig. 11). Only political *blundering* is apparent: what is masked is an unerring systematic imperialistic impulse. The cartoonist's challenge is

Fig. 12 J. Jensen: 'Don't panic folks, I'll be right back', *Sunday Telegraph*, 3 May 1970.

muted and the observer's frustration at his own powerlessness is gratified in laughter from a false sense of superiority.

These popular archetypes chosen by the cartoonist participate in what Barthes diagnosed as contemporary and discontinuous myth; existent in discourse but unable to sustain a narrative, it constitutes a 'phraseology', a corpus of phrases and stereotypes. Myth disappears but the mythic remains, 'all the more insidious' and 'present wherever stories are told'.[12]

Predictably in this parade of stereotypes, the real Vietnamese rarely appear, reports from the battle zone usually addressing the reader from an American point of view. In Vicky's 'It came to pieces in my hand' (Fig. 9) they are objectified and commodified into valuable objects. They are reduced to diminutive irritants by Garland (Fig. 11) and Scarfe (Fig. 15). In the face of Nixon's onslaught they are dehumanized to the extent that they become a man-trap in Jensen's 'Don't panic folks' (if simultaneously a sign of grudging respect) (Fig. 12). By 1972, in line with the tenor of press reporting, they have become sympathetic victims in Waite's 'It's either New Year's Day, or another Presidential Election' (Fig. 13).

In sum, the raw material of historical events has all but disappeared. These figurative interpretations of events, encapsulated in the caricatures of the main political protagonists simultaneously exclude the war, mobilize popular archetypes and provide a remarkable homogeneity in the repertory of images, presences and absences. Politicians in their bungling are ultimately perceived as rather feeble characters whose power is subject to the defusing mockery of

Fig. 13   Waite: 'It's either New Year's Day, or another Presidential Election', *Daily Mirror*, 30 December 1972.

the common man: the military and the industrial system that support them are effectively removed from the scene. Their eloquent absence is similar to that of the anti-Vietnam war protestors whose collective action cannot be accommodated. Even Vicky, well known for his left-wing views, marginalizes them by reducing them to an anonymous mass at the right-hand edge of 'We'll knock hell out of 'em!' (Fig. 1). Here lies what Barthes might term an *historia* of dismissals: 'Public opinion is defined by its limits, its energies of exclusion, its censorship.'[13] While appearing to be critical the cartoon obfuscates the role of the American industrial and military war machine, the suffering of the Vietnamese people, and the exacerbation of the spiritual crisis in the *pax Americana* caused by the war. It follows closely the contours of dominant readings in a manner contrary to ideological allegations about cartoons as a humanitarian call in a dehumanized wilderness.

Cartoons for the educated reader

The art of the cartoonist operates in a kind of pictorial vernacular, divorced from the so-called literalism of the photograph or the intellectual sophistication and sensual power of the art object. It might be regarded as a form of pictorial slang where frustrations, fears, angers and a sense of mischievousness are expressed as they are in spoken language, much abbreviated and to the point. There is, however, a distinction to be made between cartoons commonly found in the popular press and those found in the quality press. The former tend to belong to a modern tradition of cartooning typified by Low and exemplified in the mass circulation dailies. The latter tend to be superficially more complex, lending themselves to more ambiguous readings and belong to an Enlightenment tradition of cartoon identified with Gillray. Such cartoons confirm the status of the educated reader without grappling with the war any more effectively or pertinently than their popular counterparts.

Consider Jensen's 'Black Dove' (Fig. 14), executed for the right of centre and highly respectable *Sunday Telegraph*. It refers to the peace initiative of Dr Nkrumah who was invited to Hanoi by Ho Chi Minh in the wake of Harold Wilson and Harold Davies of the Commonwealth Peace Mission. The three are depicted sitting dejectedly on the branch of a tree accompanied by two more hopeful doves as a pointer to unknown future developments. Peregrine Worsthorne writes on the same page of Wilson's 'efforts to peddle his unsaleable peace initiative' and comments on conditions in Vietnam where:

> The Communists today control three quarters of South Vietnam, and are gaining ground all the time. The idea of the Commonwealth Peace Mission or Mr. Harold Davies (first dove on the right), still less Dr Nkrumah being able to charm the North Vietnamese leader into foregoing these advantages – is too fanciful to be taken seriously.

The meaning is directed by the context in which it appears but it can still be read in a number of different ways. It can be seen in terms of the history of cartoon and Low's use of similar imagery in 'The Owl's Welcome' in relation to arms control talks between England and Germany; from the point of view of art history as a reference to Goya's diabolism in *Ridiculous Folly* or as a sarcastic colouristic inversion of Picasso's *Dove of Peace*; as a visual interpretation of the proverb. 'A bird in the hand is worth two in the bush'; as ornithology and the sight of birds roosting, achieving nothing; as an example of racism implicit in Nkrumah's stereotypical bewildered expression, compounded by the irony of the title; or even as a Biblical, Christian reading of the dove bringing hope to Noah adrift in the Ark. The polysemous character of the image adds complexity and confers an apparent authority on the observer who perceives meanings according to his educational and cultural status within the

Fig. 14   J. Jensen: 'Black Dove', *Sunday Telegraph*, 18 July 1965.

social fabric. The range of potential readings available to the reader is determined by his relationships to structures of class, race, sex and education and the cartoonist can be seen to conspire, if not altogether consciously, in the assertion of such cultural differences or distinctions. The apparent homogeneity of representations of the war begins to break down as the critical power of the cartoonist mobilizes diverse connotations. Barthes claims we are subject to a *pax culturalis* that conceals the nature of culture as the pathological site *par excellence*, host to 'an inveterate war of languages; languages exclude each other; in a society divided (by social class, money, academic origin), language itself divides'.[14]

The response, for example, to a drawing by Scarfe, bordering on the obscene, published in the *New Statesman* (Fig. 15), prompted two letters. The first, likening it to grafitti, found that it does 'nothing more than reveal the unhealthy state of the originator's mind'; the second found it 'the best short summary of it [the war] I have seen'.[15] It is apparent that even in a small circulation socialist weekly where a unified readership could reasonably be expected, this is not the case. Barthes writes of that 'stupid expression mass culture'; for him culture is quite literally excruciating in an area where:

> Boredom, vulgarity, stupidity are various names for the secession of language . . . this secession not only separates men from each other, but each man, each individual in himself is lacerated.[16]

The assertion of difference within the general homogeneity of representations of the war can also be seen to rest with style. 'Black Dove' is almost

Fig. 15   Gerald Scarfe: 'Symbolic Caricature', *New Statesman*, 10 February 1967.

schematic. Dramatic contrasts of light and dark are complemented by a cursory
line designed to convey as much information as necessary, as economically as
possible. The simple silhouette of the tree and branch is foregrounded against
an empty background (in many other similar cartoons a distant horizon). The
emphasis is upon caricature as a humorous device and a deliberate 'artlessness'
which nevertheless does little to conceal the hand of the individual cartoonist.

Scarfe in the drawing discussed above tries to grasp the historical predicament by showing something of the complexity of the war in preference to the
polysemous qualities of the image. The drawing was used as an illustration to
the books page alongside the article 'Viewpoints on Vietnam' by Gavin Young.
Its context would suggest a much higher cultural charge than the editorial page
of the *Sunday Telegraph*. The cartoonist referred to it as a 'symbolic caricature'
and it relies on the anecdote concerning Johnson's orchestration of the war
from a lavatory seat. Centre-right General Nguyen Khanh who toppled the
junta that had ousted Diem leaves the stage; below Johnson leads the way with
a crooked candle and pulls strings to control the movements of General Ky. At

his feet the Buddhists express their discontent with their raised bare bottoms. Opposite, Ho Chi Minh sits on the shoulders of a ravaged female personification of North Vietnam while a giant Johnson defaecates bombs over an equally ravaged personification of South Vietnam. In the centre another caricature of Johnson steps on a peasant hut and holds a stone tablet inscribed with the treachery of his own duplicity. A comparable complexity can also be found in Garland's 'Aping his Master. Imitation is the Sincerest form of Flattery' for the *Daily Telegraph* (Fig. 11), but it has little of the effectiveness of the Scarfe which is less tied to a specific event. The obscenity of the imagery and the violence done to women, while shocking, carries memories of Gillray's vitriolic response to the inhumanity of the Terror in 'Un petit Souper à la Parisienne, or a family of Sans-Culottes'. Scarfe's line is also self-consciously 'arty'; he makes use of cross-hatching to produce variations in the contrasts between light and dark. His figures are not baldly presented but emerge from a complex *mêlée* that might be described as a psychological landscape. The literal obscenity of his anal fascinations is extended into allegory where the defilement of the female personifications as refugees from a pastoral vision is not confined to the indiscriminate violence of war but comments upon the spiritual barrenness of a classical ideal of wholeness.

The suggestion here is that the cartoonist can offer therapy on a social level and not merely the individual catharsis Scarfe over-modestly asserts: 'My art, for me, is a great way of explaining myself, a great way of getting rid of all these angers and frustrations.'[17] Alette Hall, in her article on the cartoons of the Jimmy Carter presidential campaign, describes the cartoonist as a natural Freudian, projecting unconscious desires, fears and motives. 'Cartoons', she writes 'as an enduring part of culture, should provide clues to an overall apprehension of society.'[18] As Freud has indicated: 'throughout the whole range of the psychology of the neuroses what is sexual includes what is excremental'.[19] In this guise the cartoon becomes the site for the expression not of individual frustration so much as a collective guilt on behalf of its educated middle-class audience.

Scarfe's work has been published primarily in organs such as *Punch, Private Eye, New Statesman* and the *Sunday Times* (then under the enlightened editorship of Harold Evans) and all are aimed at a well-educated and liberal middle-class audience disdainful of both the popular and conservative press. Similarly, his fellow traveller Ralph Steadman has appeared in *Black Dwarf, Rolling Stone, Private Eye, New Statesman* and the *New York Times*, all of which took early and strong lines against the war in true left-liberal tradition. Significantly, only the *Sunday Times* and the *New York Times* are dependent on advertising to any great extent. Their drawing style is self-consciously 'arty', and the 'violence' of their scratching and blotting conforms to a destructive cliché of creative expression typical of the period. It carries connotations of subjective self-expression in conformity with bourgeois conventions of artistic production and is in tune with the cultural expectations of their audience. Their cartoons are closer to 'drawing' in the high cultural sense and refer back to the elaboration of the sixteenth-century broadsheet as 'food for thought, contemplation and conversation'.[20]

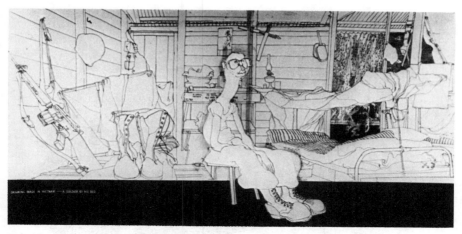

Fig. 16   Gerald Scarfe: 'The Private Soldier', *Daily Mail*, 8 September 1966.

Both Scarfe and Steadman have tried to extend the medium of the cartoon beyond the barren confines of the stereotypical by reference to a tradition which begins with Goya's *Disasters of War*. First, it belongs to high bourgeois culture; secondly, it treats that which is psychological and diabolical in human nature; thirdly, it is able to do this by reference not only to other art but first-hand observation. In this respect cartoons take on an unusual power when they spill over from their customary 'editorial' position of exercising comment to reportage and the production of news.

In 1966 Scarfe was sent to Vietnam with the journalist Richard West by the liberal editor of the *Daily Mail*, Mike Randall. West's words were by no means uncritical of the Americans and Scarfe's drawings executed in hotel rooms from pencil sketches made on the spot stepped terribly out of line, as he did the ordinary Vietnamese the honour of doing their caricatures. Scarfe humanizes the Vietnamese as the acidity of style found in symbolic caricature fails in the face of a reality too great.

Scarfe produced ten finished drawings in the short time he was there, seven of which were published with accompanying articles by West. Scarfe is aware that the cartoon is not simple but makes use of words as well as the image in the context of the page and the publication as a whole:

> over the years I've learned my craft. . . . I make it as punchy as possible . . . as direct as possible because in a newspaper you're fighting with so many other elements that are trying to gain your attention . . . headlines, articles by other people, advertisements, they are all designed to catch your eye.[21]

The Private Soldier (Fig. 16) shows a rather pathetic image of the American fighting man who has just seen his comrades obliterated by a misdirected napalm attack from his own side. Look at the whole page, however, and the

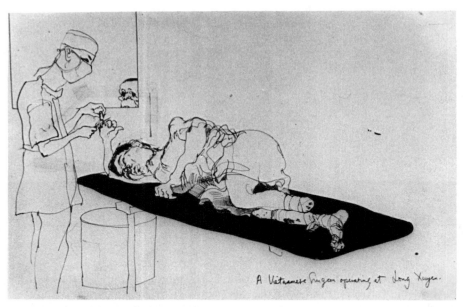

A Vietnamese Surgeon operating at Long Xuyen.

Fig. 17   Gerald Scarfe: 'The Wounded', *Daily Mail*, 14 September 1966.

more conventional image of the fighting man as an heroic man of action is reasserted in the advertisement for Marlon Brando's film *The Chase* – 'A Breathless Explosive Story of Today'. Scarfe's compassionate image is subverted by the conventional stereotype. The picture 'The Wounded' (Fig. 17), of a Vietnamese mine casualty who stiffens into a pose for Scarfe as the surgeon amputates his fingers, is subtly countered by the advertisement in the bottom right-hand corner of the page for BUPA (a private medical corporation). Compassion is redirected from the reality of the war and on to the fears of the observer for his own well-being. A caricature of a family of Vietnamese farmers from the Mekong Delta, 'The River People', who have suffered from the impact of the war, is countered by questions concerning the observer's prosperity in the advertisement which asks 'Are you a two set family, yet?'

The Buddhists in 'The Buddhist Feast', the South Vietnamese government in 'The Elections' and the Dickensian corruption of life in Saigon in 'The Children' are legitimate targets.[22] 'The Opium Den' which deals with the taboo subject of drugs, 'The Bar', in fact a brothel showing American construction workers, and the 'Troop Carrier' (Fig. 18) presented a brutalized image of Americans in Vietnam and, for that reason, Scarfe thought, remained unpublished. Nevertheless, Keith Mackenzie, the art editor of the *Daily Mail*, claimed 'Gerald Scarfe lost the *Mail* 50,000 in circulation.'[23]   Steadman's reportage is compromised in a different way. Like Scarfe his images transcend political caricature and by their treatment of the anonymous participants in the conflict touch life as it is lived. The drawing 'Four More Years' (Fig. 19)

Fig. 18 Gerald Scarfe: 'The Troop Carrier', unpublished drawing, September 1966.

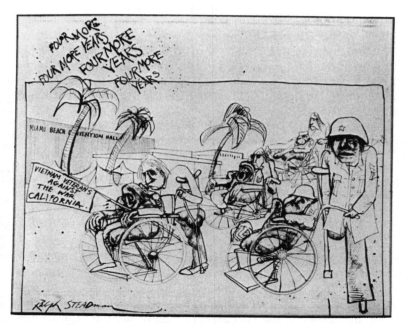

Fig. 19 Ralph Steadman: 'Four more years, Four more years', *Rolling Stone*, 28 September 1972.

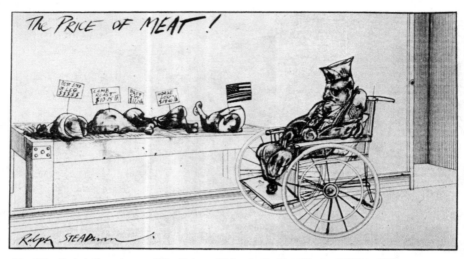

Fig. 20   Ralph Steadman: 'The Price of Meat', *Rolling Stone*, 10 May 1972.

exaggerates and distorts in a manner familiar from caricature, and focusses on the mutilated and crippled 'Vietnam Veterans Against the War' as part of a report written by Hunter S. Thompson, from the Miami Beach Republican Convention. Because of their opposition to the war, their recently acquired status as 'baby-killers', and their denial of the American Dream in their disfigurement, Steadman attempted to redress the balance. He drew attention to their predicament and added to their voice of protest in line with the general anti-war sentiment of the left liberal press in 1972 and in the pages of *Rolling Stone*, where it was effectively marginalized since it was dedicated not to 'news reporting' and 'informed comment' but to music and entertainment. For that it is all the more easily dismissed.

There is, however, a deeper psychological motive that might explain the effectiveness of the drawings on a purely visual level. Baudelaire had discovered in laughter all that is human and all that is diabolic; he called it:

> a token of an infinite grandeur and an infinite misery . . . it is certain that human laughter is intimately linked with the accident of an ancient Fall, of a debasement both physical and moral. Laughter and grief are expressed by the organs in which the command and the knowledge of good and evil reside – I mean the eyes and the mouth.[24]

The visual and the verbal are the territory of the cartoon and, like the laugh, it is not always the result of something funny but it is often a spontaneous reaction in the face of some deeply felt anxiety, as for example in 'The Price of Meat' (Fig. 20). Barthes discovered in culture the pathological area *par excellence* where lies inscribed the alienation of man from himself. Cartoons such as these might be regarded as an expression of collective guilt on behalf of the left liberal community in the light of its failure to prevent or stop the war.

The sophisticated cartoons of the periodical and (occasionally) the quality press evoke an introverted guilt. More generally and more often, their counterparts in the popular press work through caricatured individuals, venting the frustration and powerlessness of the wider population. Either way, the systematic causal affairs of state, economy and polity remain out of view.

Notes

1. Stuart Hall, quoted in James Curran and Jean Seaton (eds), *Power without Responsibility: The Press and Broadcasting in Britain*, London: Methuen, 1985, p. 276. I am in debt to this publication and James Curran, Jake Ecclestone, Giles Oakley and Alan Richardson (eds), *Bending Reality. The State of the Media*, London: Pluto, 1986 for much of the general information on the ideological structures of the press included in this chapter.
2. Gerald Scarfe in a transcript of an interview with the author published in part in *City Life*, Manchester, 4 September 1984.
3. Vicky, Ralph Steadman, Steve Bell and Ray Lowry have all used the technique at irregular intervals.
4. Jeremy Tunstall, quoted in Colin Seymour-Ure, 'How Special are Cartoonists?', *Twentieth Century Studies: Politics in Cartoon and Caricature*, Canterbury: University of Kent, 1976, p. 12.
5. Sigmund Freud, *Jokes and their Relation to the Subconscious*, Harmondsworth: Penguin, 1983, p. 147..
6. *New Statesman*, 21 April 1965.
7. Vicky, no caption, *Evening Standard*, 11 November 1965.
8. See Eric Hobsbawm, quoted in Curran and Stanton, *Power without Responsibility*.
9. Editorial, *Daily Mail*, 7 November 1968.
10. Garland, *Daily Telegraph*, 12 April 1966.
11. Vicky, *Evening Standard*, 11 November 1965.
12. Roland Barthes, *The Rustle of Language*, Oxford: Basil Blackwell, 1986, p. 66.
13. Ibid., p. 58.
14. Ibid., p. 101.
15. Letters to *New Statesman*, 17 and 24 February 1967.
16. Barthes, op. cit., p. 101.
17. Scarfe interview.
18. Alette Hall, 'The Carter Campaign in Retrospect: Decoding the Cartoons', *Semiotica* 23 (3/4), 1978.
19. Sigmund Freud, *The Psychopathology of Everday Life*, Harmondsworth: Penguin, 1985, p. 141.
20. See Ernst Gombrich, 'The Cartoonist's Armoury', *Meditations on a Hobby Horse*, London: Phaidon 1971, pp. 127–42.
21. Scarfe interview.
22. 'The River People', 'The Buddhist Feast', 'The Elections' and 'The Children' all appeared in the series 'Gerald Scarfe in Vietnam', *Daily Mail*, September 1966.
23. 'Emmwood', unpublished typescript from archive at The Centre for the Study of Cartoon and Caricature, University of Kent, Canterbury.
24. Charles Baudelaire, 'On the Essence of Laughter and, in General, on the Comic in the Plastic Arts', *Baudelaire. Art in Paris* (translated and edited by Jonathan Mayne), London: Phaidon 1964, p. 153.

Robert Hamilton

7

British Photojournalism and the Vietnam War

The currency of the photographer

In 'The Currency of the Photograph' John Tagg argues that photographs have a currency within a certain set of social relations in which they are produced, distributed, exchanged and consumed. They have a value and a meaning before they become the fixed artistic products of individual photographers, displayed in books or on gallery walls as works of art. He further argues that the process by which photographs become works of art must be reversed if we are to understand the social and historical function of the photograph, which, as he states, 'had a use, a value, an objective social validity, in short, had a currency'.[1]

In this paper I want to extend Tagg's notion of currency to the social body of the photographer, and in particular to British photojournalists working during the Vietnam War. My purpose in this is three-fold. First, if photographs have a social currency, so then must the photographers who produce them. They do not come to wars as fully-fledged creative individuals, names waiting to be made, reputations intact, 'great' photographs to be taken at the instant click of a shutter wherever the gaze of the photographer happens to fall. They are subject to a historically specific set of social relations: they have to earn money, they have to be accredited by military, governmental and media institutions, issued with passes and identification; they have to travel to and around wars; they have to reach specific areas to 'get the goods' for their editors, and are subject to the editorial policies and the decisions of their employers. They have a currency in that their work and reputations are subject to and constructed by that set of social relations.

Secondly, the history of photography is dominated by formalist and biographical accounts of great photographers, or the textual analyses of structuralism which frames and isolates the photograph from its moment of production in history. The notion of the currency of the photographer enables one to turn to the other side of the lens, as it were, to the presence of the photographer which destabilizes the objectivity of the framed and isolated photographs as text, and opens up the historical and social relations between photographer and photographed.

Thirdly, British photojournalists have come to occupy a special place with regard to the Vietnam War in that it might be said that the important photojournalists, in terms of reputation and production (although the two are not synonymous), were British. It should be stated here that their nationality would seem to be important in so far as it suggests an ideological distance from the aims of the American involvement in Vietnam. However, in terms of the currency, the notion of national and therefore ideological objectivity is not guaranteed. I have chosen to focus on British photojournalists because their work was crucial to the picturing of the war, and because they provide a succinct demonstration of the different kinds of photographic currency. I want to examine in particular four photojournalists: Larry Burrows, Don McCullin, Philip Jones Griffiths and Tim Page.

Larry Burrows was a staff photographer for *Life* magazine and worked, mainly in Vietnam, for 9 years until his death in a helicopter accident in Langvie, South Vietnam, on 20 February 1971. Burrows is known for his coverage with the American forces of the air and ground conflict, with stories such as 'Air War' (*Life*, September 1966) and 'Papa Yankee 13' (*Life*, April 1964), as well as work for the DMZ. By his own admission, up until 1969, Burrows supported the aims of the American involvement in Vietnam, as did *Life*, whose editorial policy began to shift in late 1967 and more noticeably after the Tet offensive. As Don Oberdorfer pointed out: 'the most consistent and enthusiastic supporter of the war among the giants of the news media was Time Inc'.[2] In February 1966, the editor-in-chief Hedley Donovon wrote the lead story in *Life* under the heading 'Vietnam: the war is worth winning'. Donovon forecast that by late 1966 or 1967, 'military action in South Vietnam would be declining and the big unit war should be over'. In June 1967, Donovon wrote another lead story for *Life* entitled 'Vietnam: slow, tough, but coming along', and by the end of that summer he announced that Time Inc. would have a new editorial policy towards the war. In October 1967, *Life* urged a pause in the bombing of North Vietnam, and stated:

> *Life* believes that the US is in Vietnam for honorable and sensible purposes. What the US has undertaken there is obviously harder, longer, more complicated than the US leadership foresaw. . . . We are trying to defend not a fully born nation but a situation and a people from which an independent nation might emerge. We are also trying to maintain a highly important – but in the last analysis not absolutely imperative – strategic interest of the US and the free world. This is a tough combination to ask young Americans to die for.[3]

The seeds of editorial doubt had been sown, and the Tet offensive of 1968 fed and watered that doubt. In 1969, Burrows published a ten-page photo and text story on the state of the war called 'Vietnam: a degree of disillusion'. The article consisted of four separate stories under the following headings: (1) The only loyalty – to field and family; (2) Morale and mass graves; (3) The despair of the sewer pipe dweller; and (4) A case of cowardice under fire. Burrows introduces the stories with this statement:

> All over Vietnam you see the faces – more inscrutable and more tired now than I have ever known them to be. Their eyes do not meet yours, because they are aware that the enemy is still, even today, all around them, watching. They are in the middle. The pressure on them is terrible and has existed for some thirty years.
>
> I have been rather a hawk. As a British subject I could perhaps be more objective than the Americans, but I generally accepted the aims of the US and Saigon, and the official version of how things were going. This spring, impressed by government statistics showing that conditions were improving, I set out to do a story on the turn for the better. In the following three months I indeed found some cause for optimism – better training and equipment in the South Vietnamese Army, more roads open and safe – but I also found a degree of disillusion and demoralisation in the army and the population that surprised and shocked me.[4]

Burrows' disillusionment, or rather the disillusion he found in the South, is by degrees, and is related to the attitudes of the South Vietnamese population which, as late as 1969, surprised and shocked him. He does not question the American involvement in Vietnam, nor the overall aims of the Saigon government – indeed he finds some cause for 'optimism'. The point I wish to make is that Burrows, his photographs and his attitude towards the war, cannot be seen in the terms in which he has come to be discussed: as a 'compassionate photographer', as in the title of the book Time Inc. published of his work, or as the creator of dramatic war pictures, painstaking indicators of his 'professionalism'. The currency of Burrows must be seen in the context of the editorial history of the institution he worked for, his close involvement with the American forces, and the degree of his disillusionment which did not go beyond *Life's* editorial disengagement with official American policy towards Vietnam. Burrows' photographic production, his presence and material support while in Vietnam, the procedures of processing, layout, editorial decisions, publication and distribution, must be seen within the context of *Life* magazine and its relations to the society in which it was produced, distributed and consumed.

Perhaps the best known of all British war photographers is Donald McCullin. For the *Sunday Times Magazine* he covered conflicts in Cyprus, Belfast, Beirut, Biafra, the Congo, Cambodia and Vietnam. There is a long list of publications by and about him, as well as many individual and group exhibitions. McCullin's reputation is not only dependent on the power of his photographs to provide visual information as to the nature of war but, also, in their carefully constructed design and sharp contrasts of tone, they are seen both as reportage and as art. His entry in the reference book *Contemporary Photographers* begins: 'Don McCullin's work emerges from photojournalism, but its importance transcends the journalistic conventions.'[5] His work is seen here as rising above these conventions and thus aspiring to the status of art.

On 24 March 1968, the *Sunday Times Magazine* published a 12-page feature by McCullin on the Marines' fight to retake the city of Hue. Called 'This is how it is', the feature consisted of 12 photographs with commentaries by McCullin. Each photograph is supplied with a brief account of what is happening in the picture. For example, the text accompanying the picture of a dead Vietcong soldier states:

> The Marines search the dead VCs for documents. Then you find out they're really just somebody's husband or father. They all carry neat medical kits and you never find any of them without a little toothbrush.[6]

If every picture tells a story, McCullin's is factual, humanitarian, but also anecdotal. Furthermore, each photograph and caption is presented as an isolated incident and there is little or no connection between the events depicted, except that of McCullin's presence. Neither is there any indication of the strategic importance of the battle for Hue or the effects of street fighting on its position in the context of the Tet offensive. It is assumed that the readers of the *Sunday Times* already understand these things, or that Sunday morning is neither the time nor the place for a political, social or historical account to help explain the photographs. They are served up for consumption, not as a detailed photographic record of the battle for Hue, but as aesthetically powerful photographs, taken not only by a journalist, but by a 'great' photographer, who 'combined cool, effective professionalism with a rare compassion'.[7] Tom Picton, in discussing this aspect of McCullin's work, states:

> Don McCullin is a transitional figure between journalism and art.
>
> McCullin's pictures are tidy and brilliantly composed, abstracted down to a single person or group. They are static, denying the horror that they attempt to show with their classic simplicity.
>
> In the way that McCullin ignores politics, his pictures frequently seem isolated from the real world.[8]

Thus McCullin's currency hovers between that of photojournalist and that of artist: his work shows aesthetically and atmospherically what it might have been like to be there, rather than attempting to explain the political and historical foreground and background to the events they depict.

McCullin's photographs of Hue function as confrontation. The viewer is presented with images that are meant to shock, but not necessarily to inform. However, in their removal from a specific context and historical situation, and containment within the covers of the *Sunday Times Magazine*, the pictures are afforded an ambiguity of interpretation by the gap between journalism and art. They can be read as horrific photographs from a far-off battlefield, and it is not necessary to understand the full context of Hue in order for the pictures to have the desired effect; or they can be seen as the latest photo assignment of a well-known (to the *Sunday Times* readership at least) war photographer, as indicators of McCullin's growing reputation. This second reading is reinforced by a short interview with McCullin by Francis Wyndham entitled 'A Sort of Madness', which appears after McCullin's photoessay. The interview seeks to find biographical evidence as to why McCullin is 'compulsively attracted by violence and death', which is more personal and complex than 'the excellence of his pictures'.[9] McCullin's development as a photographer is worked on and to some extent defined by the development in the 1960s of the *Sunday Times Magazine*. The function of the colour supplement moved perceptibly away from previous models of picture magazines such as *Life* and the *Picture Post*. As Hunter Davies, former editor of the *Sunday Times Magazine*, succinctly put it: 'Colour magazines rarely tried to be important, to evaluate or explain. They just showed.'[10] It is within this currency and the privileging of McCullin as a 'great' photographer, as 'the *Sunday Times* star', that his powerful photographs must be historically evaluated and understood.

Unlike Burrows and McCullin, Philip Jones Griffiths did not work for a specific publication. Through the photographic agency Magnum, he sold his work to any publication that would accept it. However, the nature of his work precluded many publications showing it, and he was often told that his photographs were too harrowing for the American market. In an interview in 1977, he stated:

> The incredible thing is, the first two years in Vietnam I tried to sell the pictures – I had to make a living, I had to exist. I made more money covering Jackie Kennedy in Cambodia in one week than I did the whole two years I was in Vietnam . . . what I really came up against was the fact that back in '66 you could only really be a photojournalist in Vietnam if you were prepared to toe the line; I mean very few publications of the time would take any other pictures than those which fitted the official Washington line, so that in a sense, considering the time I spent there and the pictures I took, I really got very few published. So quite early on in Vietnam I realised the thing to do was a book . . .[11]

In 1977 Collier Books published *Vietnam Incorporated*,[12] with text, photography and design all by Jones Griffiths. It is a substantial photographic and textual document covering not only the fighting but also the lives of the Vietnamese population, the role of the village, the military use of computers and the 'Pacification' programme, victims and prisoners, relocation, prostitution, politics, the effects of napalm, and the state of Vietnamese hospitals. Susan Sontag, in *On Photography*, stated: 'Photographs cannot create a moral position, but they can reinforce one – and can help build a nascent one.'[13] Jones Griffiths, emphasizing Sontag's point, uses his photographs in conjunction with design, layout and text to make his position clear. Nor is that position moral outrage, but rather a thorough and explicitly political intervention that raised the role photojournalism could play and the awareness of its audience to the complex totality of what was happening in Vietnam. However, it should be noted that by 1971 publishers had perceived a market for views opposed to the American involvement in Vietnam. Even the traditionally conservative Hollywood pandered to the growing 'anti-war/youth' market, from 1968 onwards. Michael Paris, in his paper 'The American Film Industry and Vietnam', states that:

A *Newsweek* survey, published in 1970, revealed that 62% of regular film-goers were aged under thirty years; precisely the age group that had been or would be going to Vietnam, and the group most active in the peace movement. Understandably, this audience wanted a cinema which was relevant and reflected their own doubts about the war.[14]

Thus cultural products that directly or indirectly opposed the war were marketable. The currency of Philip Jones Griffiths, unlike that of Burrows and McCullin, must be understood within the context of the production and publication of *Vietnam Incorporated*, which bypassed the editorial constraints of the major Western press apparatus and, therefore, avoided the ideological barriers that stifled much of the photographic production of the Vietnam War.

Tim Page was one of the photojournalists described by Henry Kamen of the *New York Times* as non-professionals, who 'came without real involvement, came with the vocation of being onlookers'[15] and who became correspondents or photographers. Accreditation was a simple process needing only two letters from an agency or newspaper saying that they would be prepared to use the photographer's material. Page came to Vietnam in the early 1960s at the end of the hippie trail across Asia. *Life* magazine used his photographs of the battle at Chu Lai. Philip Knightley, in his book *The First Casualty*, states that if a correspondent 'was prepared to take risks, he could find himself rich overnight'.[16] Page was, and in 18 months earned some $28,000 – however, at the cost of being wounded, almost fatally, several times. No other photographer has become so associated with the Vietnam War as has Tim Page.

Interest in Page's work, somewhat forgotten as the American involvement in the war was wound down, was rekindled with the publication of Michael Herr's *Dispatches*, which was followed by an exhibition of Page's work at the Institute of Contemporary Art and a lecture by Page in 1979, together with a BBC documentary. *Tim Page's Nam*,[17] published in 1983, collected together a good many of Page's photographs as well as a commentary by him and an introduction by William Shawcross. There is little or no connection between photograph and text, which in itself paints a romanticized picture of a rock'n'roll war, littered as it is with snatches of the lyrics from popular songs of the time: the thrills and spills of riding in helicopters and 'playing with tanks' are reinforced by the heightened colour reproductions of the hardware of war and those who use it. Page does not consider it necessary to ask why or how or for whom the war was taking place, only that it was exciting. Of 1968 Page enthused:

It was one of those years, good and bad all balled up into one rolling stone. '68, the year of the election, or revolt, the Airplane, Doors and Sergeant Pepper, Tet and Mini Tet, Khe Sanh; an incredibly mad year.[18]

Ten years after the American withdrawal, 1983 was a good year to glamourize the war.

Page has come to hold a privileged cultural currency over other photographers of the Vietnam War. His book is readily available, while the book on Burrows and *Vietnam Incorporated* have both long been out of print, and McCullin has never done one specifically about Vietnam.

Furthermore, Page's currency has been extended to cover not only Page-as-photographer, but also Page-as-character – young, spaced-out, reckless and hip (this point is covered more fully in the section entitled 'Shooting from the Hip' – see p. 143). This characterization has become important to the representation of photojournalists and correspondents, particularly in films about Third World trouble spots, the most recent example of this being Oliver Stone's *Salvador*.

The point I wish to make is that through the notion of a currency, one is able to encompass the full production of the discourse of photojournalism, both producer and product, and cultural effect, without privileging 'creative' human agency over the institutional modes of representation.

Institutions and practices

There can be no doubt as to the powerful effect photographic images had on how the war was perceived and the role they played in the radical shifts in public opinion with regard to the war. However, I do not think that images are self-evidently anti- or pro-war. It does not follow that by showing the 'horror' of war, the image is necessarily anti-war. It is dependent on the context in which it is used. For instance, in the case of Philip Jones Griffiths, text, design and layout are important factors that contribute to how an image or series of images is read. Nor is the issue of the effectivity of the images as clear-cut as I have previously implied. Images can have many different readings and a multiplicity of effects. When considering the effectiveness of photography on public opinion, a complex set of relations would appear to be at work. Photography surely affected opinion, but also, as opinion shifted, the perception of opinion by the media, through filters like editorial policy and audience research, would have had a reciprocal effect on what photographers produced and what picture editors would accept for publication. Thus the reporting of the Tet offensive not only affected people's attitudes towards the war, but also shifted post-1968 editorial policies and audience expectations of the pictures and reports received from Vietnam. Furthermore, before one draws any conclusions about the possible effects of photography on public opinion, one has to consider the range of institutional constraints and procedures that photographers had to negotiate before their work appeared on the printed page.

Philip Knightley states that after 1964, Vietnam '. . . became a war like no other, a war with no front line, no easily identifiable enemy, no simply explained cause'.[19] Knightley's assessment of the difference of the Vietnam War points out two constraints on photographing the war. The first was one of comprehension. The war put forward a set of problematic propositions about sovereignty, self-determination, the role of Vietnamese nationalism and the perceived rise of 'the red menace', which photography as a medium could not or would not deal with. As Larry Burrows admitted, he 'generally accepted the U.S. and Saigon, and the official version of how things were going'.[20] Overall this was true of most photojournalists in that their stories, critical or not, revolved around the US military presence in Vietnam. The camera pictured the war from the American side. This can be explained in part by the fact that their photographs were for an American market. However, one has to consider a second and much more physical and geographical constraint. As Knightley pointed out, Vietnam was a war without a front line. It was a war of insurgency and counter-insurgency. In covering this disparate nature, photojournalists had to rely on the American military for travel to and accommodation at the various war zones, as well as being accredited by the military in order to be eligible for assistance. Furthermore, the military command could control, to some extent, what could be photographed. As the My Lai story showed, there were operations that photojournalists were not allowed to cover. The photographs from My Lai were taken by Ron Haeberie, an army combat photographer with the Public Information Office of the 11th Brigade of the 23rd Infantry Division, based at Duc Pho. While direct military censorship did not exist, there were physical and geographical, as well as operational, constraints on what could or could not be photographed.

While the presence of the photographer in Vietnam was subject to certain conditions, their presence could also affect those being photographed. Philip Jones Griffiths, referring to a photograph of a man holding his wounded child, taken in Cholon in 1966, stated:

> He ran towards me and I moved back as I took pictures, and the man knew darned well what I was doing. And if you look at the picture carefully, you'll see how unnatural it is to carry a kid in your arms like that. He's not carrying him; he's holding him out to me.[21]

In this way, Jones Griffiths points out that the camera is not an invisible, objective eye. Those who are subject to its gaze can act for that gaze, their actions moulded by their awareness of the presence of the camera or of the photographer.

There existed, then, a diverse set of internal relations within Vietnam which affected the work of photojournalists and the material conditions within which they worked. There was, at the same time, a set of external relations which further determined what was consumed within the pages of the various illustrated magazines. Photojournalism is a distinct practice from news photography or TV reportage. That is not to say that it is a homogeneous practice, with unified and fixed procedures. Under the general framework of photojournalism, there existed a diversity of practices, from full-time representatives of magazines such as Burrows and McCullin, through photographers sent by the various picture agencies (Black Star, Gamma Sygma and Sipa), such as Jones Griffiths of Magnum, to freelancers such as Page, who would sell their work direct to the media institutions. The procedures by which work was commissioned, processed, offered to and accepted or rejected for publication, were also various, and were related to the systems of assignment and soliciting of work by the expanding variety of individual magazines. But the one major restriction between photojournalist and publisher was editorial policy and process.

Within Vietnam, photojournalists were given a high degree of freedom of movement and reporting (although I have tried to show that this had its limitations). Where pressure and restrictions could be brought to bear upon what was shown was within the media institutions, whose political orientations and market sense of what their audience would want to see could decide whether particular photographs would be published, and the context in terms of captioning, layout and design, in which they would be used. Photographers like Larry Burrows and Don McCullin had reputations and contracts that afforded them some degree of autonomy from editorial restrictions, but those such as Jones Griffiths found it difficult to get work accepted because it was often at odds with established editorial views of how Vietnam should be represented. Furthermore, pressure could be brought to bear on editorial policy by US government institutions which, while desiring publicity, attempted to restrict adverse criticism. For example, in 1966 the Assistant Secretary of Defense (Public Affairs) issued a letter urging restraint by the media in showing the faces of wounded men before their relatives could be informed, as well as:

> . . . photographs that may stir up unpleasant thoughts such as those of maimed bodies, obvious expressions of agony, serious shock or circumstances that cast doubt on the patient's chances of recovery.[22]

In general, the media resisted such direct interference. However, they often imposed a system of self-censorship in response to what David Dellinger, in *Vietnam Revisited*, defined as 'the two realities of our technically free press':

> The first reality is the business needs of the gigantic corporations that dominate the public's normal access to the news. They depend on corporate advertisers for profits and on governmental 'information' for a substantial portion of what is presented as news. The second reality is the belief of most large publishers and TV executives that their own self-interest and that of the country require a perpetuation of the status quo.[23]

The Vietnam War is generally regarded as an 'uncensored war'. While the degree of freedom given to photographers and correspondents was greater than it had been in previous conflicts (and since – governments such as the British in Northern Ireland and the Falklands and, more recently, the South African regime at home, have learned the lesson of Vietnam well in regard to news management), there were serious limitations. By concentrating on the photographic products of the war, it is all too easy to allow the procedures of production and the constraints placed upon them to fade from the light of history. I have sought here to argue that for a full understanding of the photojournalists of the Vietnam War, attention to the historical context is as important as the text. Although my argument has been in general terms, and the points of it are simple ones, I think they are worth consideration in an area where there is much historical spadework to be done, and new relations between photojournalism, its institutions and procedures, its practitioners, geographical and spatial considerations, governmental and editorial restrictions must be brought into view.

Shooting from the hip: the photojournalist as character

The notion of the currency of the photographer is important to our understanding of producer, product and cultural effect. It is the 'cultural effect' of the photojournalist of the Vietnam War that I want to examine here. The representation of the photojournalist as character was formed in and defined by the Vietnam conflict, and in particular by the continuing cultural currency of Tim Page.

I want to take as my starting point what might appear to be a marginal and relatively obscure point of entry. Towards the end of the film *Apocalypse Now*, there appears the tertiary character of a photographer, played by Dennis Hopper. His narrative function is to provide a link, or act as a go-between, for the two main characters, Captain Willard, played by Martin Sheen, and Colonel Kurtz, played by Marlon Brando. Hopper appears bedecked with cameras, beads and a headband, and his speech is littered with the 1960s Americanism, 'man'. There are three points to be drawn from this characterization. First is the construction of 'hipness' through Hopper's costume and mannerisms. Gilbert Adair marks Hopper's character as being 'a throw-back to the 60s'.[24] Second is the construction of the notion of 'concern' which is embedded in Hopper's role as go-between. He is 'concerned' to point out to Willard the importance of Kurtz's project, and is equally 'concerned' to understand that project. Hopper ultimately fails at explanation and understanding, through a failure of language. He says to Willard: 'I dunno, man, maybe if I was better at using words I could explain.' This condenses a third characteristic of the photographer, that of his medium being primarily visual and non-verbal; photography itself is privileged as a visual medium. This point would appear to apply to photography in general; however, in the film it applies to photojournalism specifically. Hopper says, in introducing himself to Willard, that he is a photojournalist, which separates that genre from other forms of photography.

Through the construction of the Hopper character, the film defines the meanings of photojournalism and the Vietnam War as first, visual, lying outside language; secondly, as a 'concerned' practice; and thirdly, as a medium whose practitioners are 'hip'. The historical sources of these meanings lie outside the temporal confines of the film. The notion of photography being a purely visual medium which simply reflects or captures reality, and therefore pictures 'truth', is deeply embedded in the historical discourse of the medium

since its invention in the nineteenth century, and has further been accommodated and defined within the discourse of Modernism itself. The second notion,
that of 'concern', can be traced back in the discursive formation of photojournalism as a separate practice, or set of practices, which is not purely
'aesthetic' but which functions as documentation, and those documents had the
intention and power of invoking social change or alteration – photojournalism
was therefore a 'concerned' practice. The third notion, that of 'hipness', relates
specifically to the practice of photojournalism and the Vietnam War, and it is
the introduction of this third term which separates the discourse of the Vietnam
photojournalist, in its conjunction with the other two terms, from previous
models of photojournalism and the photojournalist.

In his introduction to the book *Tim Page's Nam*, William Shawcross writes:

> The mad journalist who is waiting at the top of the river in the film
> *Apocalypse Now* was the creation of Page's friend Michael Herr and is
> based partly on Page.[25]

Shawcross indicates the source of Hopper's characterization of the photojournalist as Tim Page via Michael Herr's account of him in *Dispatches*.[26] (Herr also
wrote the narration of *Apocalypse Now*.) To define further the third term,
'hipness', it will be necessary to explore Herr's account. He states:

> There were more young, apolitically radical, wigged-out crazies running
> around Vietnam than anybody ever realized; between all of the grunts
> turning on and tripping out in the war and the substantial number of
> correspondents who were doing the same thing, it was an authentic
> subculture . . . and . . . Page was the most extravagant [example].[27]

In this description, Herr defines the characteristics of 'hipness' as youth,
apolitical, radical views, and 'wigged-out' madness, forming the 'authentic
subculture' of which Page was the most extravagant example: 'hipness',
therefore, signifies a young, apolitical recklessness. Furthermore, Page, the
model on which the subsequent representation of the Vietnam photographer
was based, is often written about in terms of this construction of 'hipness'.
Page's youth and recklessness are constantly referred to throughout Herr's and
Shawcross's accounts of him. Page was 20 when he became involved in
photographing the war, and had a reputation for entering combat zones which
other correspondents avoided. As a result, he was wounded several times.
According to Herr:

> People made him sound crazy and ambitious, like the Sixties Kid, a
> stone-cold freak in a country where madness raced up the hills and into
> the jungles, where everything essential to learning Asia, war, drugs, the
> whole adventure, was close at hand.[28]

To some extent Herr reproduces Page's recklessness to secure a qualitative
legitimacy to his combat photographs, but it is also pinned to the notion of
Page's youth, which is itself attached to the third characteristic of 'hipness', that
of being 'apolitical'. Herr links Page's recklessness to the developing youth

culture of the 1960s – 'like the Sixties Kid' – and from there to the Vietnam War as the playground of that generation, where 'Asia, war, drugs, the whole adventure was close at hand'. This shift is critical to the construction of Page's position as apolitical, in that the combination of youth, recklessness and adventure effectively depoliticizes the position of the photographer in the Vietnam War in order that he may be seen not as a representative of an American ideological apparatus (the press) covering America's military intervention in the affairs of another country to protect its own interests, but specifically as a 'wigged-out' crazy youth on a reckless, apolitical adventure. Page's position is therefore removed from any political interference which might occur in the construction of the photojournalist as concerned, but primarily visual, creator of powerful though independent and objective images of war.

Herr's first description of Page contains two further strategies which must be looked at. First, the idea of the Vietnam War as a 1960s youth 'trip' was not quarantined to the domain of the photojournalist (although here it was easier to sustain). Herr identifies the position of the correspondents with that of the 'grunts' [29] in that they were both 'turning on and tripping out in the war',[30] thereby implying that the infantrymen's experience of the war also comes back to the idea of an adventure or 'drug'. This performs two functions. The journalist and the grunt are collapsed into one another so as to be almost indivisible – their situation *vis-à-vis* the war is identical. It also constructs a relationship of conflict with the authority which brought them both to the war, and therefore to the second strategy of 'hipness', the creation of what Herr calls 'an authentic subculture'.

In his book *Subculture: the Meaning of Style*, Dick Hebdige[31] defines subculture as a form of resistance to the dominant culture within the framework of Gramsci's theory of hegemony. This is that the dominant class or alliance of classes cannot exert control over other classes in society simply by coercion, but must seek the consent of those classes through various political, ideological and cultural forms. However, hegemony can never be permanently secured and won; it is constantly in a state of movement, having to be negotiated and renegotiated with the subordinate classes in order that their consent to dominance may be secured and resecured. Within the process of hegemony (and it always is a process) there is the concept of counter-hegemony or resistance to power. On a cultural level, the vying for dominance has often been staged – in post-Second World War years, in the theatre of youth, in various forms of resistance or subculture. Hebdige further states:

> However, the challenge to hegemony which subcultures represent is not issued directly by them. Rather it is expressed obliquely, in style. The objections are lodged, the contradictions displayed . . . at the pro-foundly superficial level of appearances: that is, at the level of signs.[32]

During the Vietnam War the journalist and the grunt developed their challenge to authority, at this level of appearances, in the way they dressed, their language, and the music they listened to. They constructed a Vietnam style, which was related to the subculture of the 1960s in America. However, in Vietnam this took on a specific form. Military attire was juxtaposed with peace signs or other anti-war references signifying, perhaps, opposition to authority, to the war or to militarism. But the meaning of these signs is dependent not on their presence but on their juxtaposition with the signs of authority, the war and the military – such as uniform, combat fatigues, weapons and helmets. The Vietnam style or subculture is formed by the combination of representations of resistance and authority, and not resistance to authority. This point is important, as the troops and the journalists were in Vietnam not in a subcultural position, but in one of securing the dominance of their culture over another, namely the Vietnamese. The task of the Americans was often stated as that of winning hearts and minds. Constructing the notion of a Vietnam 'subculture' among the troops and journalists effectively disguises their hegemonic function.

The term 'hipness', then, performs specific tasks. It connotes youth and recklessness which, while legitimizing the quality of the combat photograph, effectively turns the war into an adventure, positing the photojournalist in an apolitical stance; and it guarantees the objective independence of his photographic production. Furthermore, the idea of the war as a *youth* adventure assimilates the journalist and the grunt as one into the construction of a Vietnam style or subculture.

Now, just as the Vietnam war itself has become a cultural commodity, removed from its specific political and historical context, to be consumed in the form of films, TV programmes, books and records, so the photojournalist, as a set of culturally constructed meanings and characteristics, has also been commodified in the form of filmic representations, as the authorial subject in books of photography, and as a 'character' in journalistic accounts of the war. In short, it is not only his photographic production that is consumed, but also his character.

The potentially oppositional role of the photojournalist is retrieved and recouped through the depoliticization of his position in the construction of the war as adventure, and more specifically in its coupling with the notion of fascination. Page was asked by a publisher to produce a book which would take the glamour out of war. Herr recounts Page's reaction:

> Take the glamour out of war! I mean how the bloody hell can you do that? . . . can you take the glamour out of a cobra or getting stoned on China Beach? . . . It's like trying to take the glamour out of sex, trying to take the glamour out of the Rolling Stones. . . . I mean, you know that it just can't be done![33]

Page may be opposed to the war, but he is fascinated by its 'glamour', its machinery, its sex, drugs and rock-and-roll, its adventure. The opposition/fascination couplet ensures that the photojournalist may be inserted into the adventure not as the producer of images with a specific political currency and market, but as an objective tourist pervading the sites of conflict, recording not only the horror, but also the beauty, as if on a Third World package tour. Shawcross, in his introduction to Page's photographs, comments:

Page's pictures show the exquisite beauty of Vietnam better than any other collection of photographs of the war I have seen.[34]

The language is that of the travelogue. Opposition becomes cultural tourism, and is rendered safe.

The photojournalist as character is becoming important to the depiction of Third World trouble spots in films. Recent examples are *The Killing Fields, Under Fire, Circle of Deceit* and *The Year of Living Dangerously*, in which main and secondary characters play out the ethical and political processes of covering wars, whether they be in Cambodia, Beirut, Nicaragua or Indonesia. Each conflict is seen through the characters of Western correspondents or photojournalists. In each, the portrayal of the photojournalist is shot through with the characteristics of concern, hipness, and recklessness. My point here is that *their* representation of the photojournalist's character is worked on and defined by the depiction and display of those characteristics which have been culturally constructed in and through the discourse of the Vietnam photojournalist. The discourse has effectively shifted the paradigm of photojournalist on which subsequent representations will depend, and by which they will be defined.

I have sought to reconstruct the status and function of the photojournalist of the Vietnam War as a specific set of cultural characteristics and meanings, on which his status as the producer of 'truth' is supported and deployed in the mechanisms of the production of knowledge in and around that conflict. The photojournalist as 'character', young, reckless, apolitical and hip, functions to secure the cultural incorporation of visual images of Vietnam, producing them as 'truth', while recouping them for consumption as adventure.

Notes

1. John Tagg, 'The Currency of the Photograph', in *Thinking Photography* (ed. Victor Burgin), London: Macmillan, 1982, pp. 120–1.
2. Don Oberdorfer, *Tet*, New York: Doubleday, 1971.
3. *Life Magazine*, October 1967.
4. *Life Magazine*, October 1969, p. 67.
5. Mark Holborn, *Contemporary Photographers*, London: Macmillan, 1982, p. 500.
6. *Sunday Times Magazine*, 24 March 1968, pp. 14–15.
7. Holborn, op. cit., p. 500.
8. Tom Picton, 'The Photographer as Hero', in *Camerawork*, 1977 (July), p. 11.
9. Francis Wyndham, 'A Sort of Madness', *Sunday Times Magazine*, 24 March 1968, p. 20.
10. Quoted in Martin Slavin, 'Colour Supplement Living', in *Ten Eight*, No. 20, p. 10.
11. Quoted in Picton, op. cit., p. 10.
12. Philip Jones Griffiths, *Vietnam Incorporated*, New York: Collier, 1971.
13. Susan Sontag, *On Photography*, London: Allen Lane, 1977.

14. Michael Paris, 'The American Film Industry and Vietnam', in *History Today*, 1987 **37** (April), p. 21.
15. Quoted in Philip Knightley, *The First Casualty*, London: André Deutch, 1975, p. 386.
16. Ibid., p. 387.
17. Tim Page, *Tim Page's Nam*, London: Thames and Hudson, 1983.
18. Ibid., p. 26.
19. Knightley, op. cit., p. 349.
20. *Life Magazine*, October 1969, p. 67.
21. Quoted in Rainier Fabian and Hans Christian Adam, *Images of War*, London: New English Library, 1985, p. 38.
22. Ibid., p. 326.
23. David Dellinger, *Vietnam Revisited*, Boston: South End Press, 1986.
24. Gilbert Adair, *Hollywood's Vietnam*, London: Proteus 1981, p. 162.
25. William Shawcross, Introduction to *Tim Page's Nam*, London: Thames and Hudson, 1983, p. 7.
26. Michael Herr, *Dispatches*, London: Pan, 1978.
27. Ibid., p. 189.
28. Herr, op. cit., pp. 189–90.
29. American term for infantrymen.
30. Herr, op. cit., p. 189.
31. Dick Hebdige, *Subculture: The Meaning of Style*, London: Macmillan, 1979.
32. Ibid., p. 17.
33. Herr, op. cit., p. 199.
34. Shawcross, op. cit., p. 13.

W. D. Ehrhart

8

Soldier-poets of the Vietnam War*

In the spring of 1972, a slim volume of poems appeared called *Winning Hearts and Minds* (First Casualty Press), its title taken from one of the many official slogans used at various times to describe the American pacification and relocation programme in South Vietnam. Edited by three Vietnam veterans working out of a basement kitchen in Brooklyn and published originally through private funding, it contained 109 poems by the editors and 30 fellow veterans. With some notable exceptions, they were artless poems, lacking skill and polish, but collectively they impacted with the force of a wrecking-ball.

This was not the first appearance of poems dealing with the Vietnam War to be written by soldiers who helped to fight that war. But *Winning Hearts and Minds* quickly became a classic: the seminal anthology against which all future Vietnam War poetry would be judged.

'[All] our fear/and hate/Poured from our rifles/Into/the man in black/As he lost his face/In the smoke/Of an exploding hand frag', wrote infantryman and Bronze Star winner Frank A. Cross, Jr. 'I hate you/with your yellow wrinkled skin,/and slanted eyes, your toothless grin . . ./Always when the the time is wrong; while friends are moaning', wrote ex-Marine Igor Bobrowsky, holder of two Purple Hearts. 'I'm afraid to hold a gun now', wrote Charles M. Purcell, holder of the Vietnamese Cross of Gallantry, 'What if I were to run amuck here in suburbia/And rush out into the street screaming/"Airborne all the way!"/And shoot the milkman.'

Most of the poems in *Winning Hearts and Minds* are carried by raw emotion alone, and most of the soldier-poets were not really poets at all, but rather

---

* W. D. Ehrhart is himself a major figure in the field of poetry on Vietnam. While for obvious reasons his own work is not discussed in this chapter, examples of his poems may be found in the Appendix.

soliders so hurt and bitter that they could not maintain their silence any longer. Some, however, stand out more sharply than others. Bobrowsky, Cross and Purcell contribute powerful poems. Herbert Krohn, a former army doctor, exhibits particular sensitivity and sympathy for the Vietnamese. In 'Farmer's Song at Can Tho', he writes:

What is a man but a farmer
Bowels and a heart that sings
Who plants his rice in season
Bowing then to the river.
I am a farmer and I know what I know.
This month's harvest is tall green rice.
Next month's harvest is hordes of hungry beetles.
How can peace be in a green country?

Co-editor Jan Barry (the other two editors were Basil T. Paquet and Larry Rottmann), who had served in Vietnam back in the days when US troops were still called advisers, speaks of earlier occupations by the French, Japanese, Chinese and Mongols 'In the Footsteps of Ghenghis Khan', but concludes:

Unencumbered by history
our own or that of 13th-century Mongol armies
long since fled or buried
by the Vietnamese
in Nha Trang, in 1962, we just did our jobs[.]

Barry is perhaps the single most important figure in the emergence of Vietnam veterans' poetry, not only for his own pioneering poems, but especially for his tireless efforts to encourage and promote the work of others.

But the two most noteworthy poets in the collection are Paquet and Michael Casey. Of the dozen or so poems Paquet contributes, three or four must rank as among the very best Vietnam war poems ever written. Literate without being literary, Paquet was, at the time, far and away the most skilful and practised of the soldier-poets. His 'Morning – A Death' is a masterpiece, capturing at once the new, sophisticated battlefield medicine of Vietnam and the ancient, ageless human misery and futility of all wars:

You are dead just as finally
As your mucosity dries on my lips
In this morning sun.
I have thumped and blown into your kind too often.
I grow tired of kissing the dead.

Casey, a former military policeman, works exclusively with the truncated matter-of-fact speech rhythms that mirror the Vietnam grunts' favourite phrase: 'There it is' – no further explanation offered. 'School children walk by', he writes in 'On Death':

Some stare
Some keep on walking
Some adults stare too
With handkerchiefs
Over their nose

No jaw
Intestines poured
Out of the stomach
The penis in the air
   It won't matter then to me but now
I don't want in death to be a
Public obscenity like this

With the passage of time, Casey's poems seem less substantial than former medic Paquet's, but back then they were deemed good enough to earn him the Yale Younger Poets Award, and his collection *Obscenities* appeared almost simultaneously with *Winning Hearts and Minds*.

Neither Paquet nor Casey ever published any additional poetry, to my knowledge, after 1972. But for others in the volume, and for Vietnam-related poetry in general, *Winning Hearts and Minds* proved to be only the forerunner for a body of poetry that, 14 years later, is still growing. Many of the poets, like Paquet and Casey, surfaced briefly, then disappeared. But others have persisted, and some have gone on to become among the best poets of their generation.

Even before 1972 ended, D. C. Berry's *saigon cemetery* appeared from the University of Georgia Press. Another former medic, Berry offers a vision of the war in which 'hope' (and almost everything else) appears in lower case:

the boy's ma said may
be he's one of the Lord's
pretty flowers'll rise
resurrection day –
  'God woman ain't
no dead bulb gonna rise this May
never! God
   pity you Martha!'

In many of Berry's poems, lines, pieces of lines and words are scattered across the page like dismembered body parts, mimicking that all-too-frequent reality of the war.

Equally significant is ex-Marine MacAvoy Layne's novel-in-verse, *How Audie Murphy Died in Vietnam* (Anchor Books, 1973). In 227 very short and often bleakly humorous poems, Layne traces the life of his fictional Audie Murphy from birth through childhood to enlistment in the Marines, then boot camp, a tour of duty in Vietnam – including capture by the North Vietnamese – and, finally, home again. Some of the poems are as short as 'Guns':

When the M-16 rifle had a stoppage,
One could feel enemy eyes
Climbing
His
Bones
Like
Ivy.

None is longer than a single page. Though few, if any, could stand up alone without the support of all the others, their cumulative effect is remarkable and convincing.

More durable a poet – indeed, one of the very best – is John Balaban. His first book-length collection, *After Our War* (University of Pittsburgh, 1974), deservedly won the Lamont Award from the Academy of American Poets.

Balaban is an anomaly: a soldier-poet who was not a soldier. Indeed, he opposed the war and became a conscientious objector. But he chose to do his alternative service in Vietnam, first as a teacher of linguistics at the University of Can Tho, then as field representative for the Committee of Responsibility to Save War-Injured Children. Later returning to Vietnam independently in order to study Vietnamese oral folk poetry, he spent a total of nearly 3 years in the war zone – learning to speak Vietnamese fluently and even getting wounded on one occasion – and he is as much a veteran of Vietnam as any soldier I have ever met.

Because of his unique situation, however, Balaban brings to his poetry a perspective unlike any other. 'A poet had better keep his mouth shut', he writes in 'Saying Good-by to Mr. and Mrs. My, Saigon, 1972':

Unless he's found words to comfort and teach.
Today, comfort and teaching themselves deceive
and it takes cruelty to make any friends
when it is a lie to speak, a lie to keep silent.

While Balaban's poems offer little comfort, they have much to teach. Years before Agent Orange was widely acknowledged for the silent killer it is – the deadly seed sewn in Asia only to take root at home among those who thought they'd survived – Balaban wrote in 'Along the Mekong':

With a scientific turn of mind I can understand
that malformations in lab mice may not occur in children
but when, last week, I ushered hare-lipped, tusk-toothed kids
to surgery in Saigon, I wondered, what had they drunk
that I have drunk.

And his 'The Guard at the Binh Thuy Bridge' is a frightening exercise in quiet tension – the way it was; the war always a hair-trigger away, just waiting to happen:

How still he stands as mists begin to move,
as morning, curling, billows creep across
his cooplike, concrete sentry perched mid-bridge
over mid-muddy river.

Anchored in red morning mist a narrow junk
rocks its weight. A woman kneels on deck
staring at lapping water. Wets her face.
Idly the thick Rach Binh Thuy slides by.
He aims. At her. Then drops his aim. Idly.

Balaban is particularly adept at contrasting the impact of the war on Vietnam with the indifference of those at home. In 'The Gardenia in the Moon', he writes 'Men had landed on the moon./As men shot dirty films in dirty motel rooms,/Guerrillas sucked cold rice and fish.' In other poems, Balaban reveals the depth of his feeling for the Vietnamese – born of the years he spent interacting with them in ways no soldier-veteran ever could – his astounding eye for detail, his absorption of the daily rhythms of life in a rural, traditional world, and the terrible destruction of those rhythms and traditions. In 'Orpheus in the Upper World', he offers perhaps an explanation for the hundreds and even thousands of poems written by those who fought the war:

For when his order had burst his head,
like sillowy seeds of milkweed pod,
he learned to pay much closer watch
to all things, even small things,
as if to discover his errors.

Not all the poems in *After Our War* deal with Vietnam. But if some of the non-Vietnam poems occasionally reveal the graduate student labouring to flex his intellectual muscle, they also reveal the poet's ability to transcend Vietnam and reach out to the wider world around him.

America's bicentennial year brought the publication of Bryan Alec Floyd's *The Long War Dead* (Avon, 1976), a collection of 47 poems, each given the name of a fictitious member of '1st Platoon, U.S.M.C.'. Floyd, a Vietnam-era Marine, did not actually serve in the war zone. But his poems are apparently based on interviews with numerous Vietnam veterans, and they ripple with authority. 'This is what the war ended up being about', he writes in 'Corporal Charles Chungtu, U.S.M.C.':

we would find a V.C. village,
and if we could not capture it
or clear it of Cong,
we called for jets.

Then the village
that was not a village any more
was our village.

Floyd's poems have marvellous range, giving voice to those who supported the war and those who detested it, lashing out with equal vehemence at American generals and north Vietnamese diplomats, the anti-war movement and the failed war. He succeeds, like no other poet I know of, in offering the full breadth of feelings and emotions of those who fought the war.

Equally important was a new anthology, *Demilitarized Zones* (*DMZ*) (East River Anthology, 1976), co-edited by Jan Barry and a second *Winning Hearts and Minds* (*WHAM*) contributor. Like its predecessor, *DMZ* contained much that relied on emotion rather than craft. But it offered additional work by *WHAM* poets Barry, Cross, Krohn, Purcell and others, as well as new work by Balaban and Berry.

It also introduced a handful of good newcomers. Ex-infantryman Steve Hassett contributes half a dozen poems, including his eerily ironic 'Christmas', in which 'The Hessian in his last letter home/said in part/"they are all rebels here/who will not stand to fight/but each time fade before us/as water into sand"'.' Former Airman Horace Coleman writes of his 'Saigon daughter' in 'A Black Soldier Remembers':

> She does not offer me one of the
> silly hats she sells Americans and
> I have nothing she needs but
> the sad smile she already has.

In 'Death of a Friend', ex-artilleryman Doug Rawlings writes: 'his death/begs me to follow/pulls me toward him/my hands grow weak/and/cannot break/the string'. There are also excellent poems by Gerald McCarthy and Bruce Weigl, both of whom would later publish book-length collections of their own.

A third major book to appear during the bicentennial year was Walter McDonald's *Caliban in Blue* (Texas Tech Press, 1976). McDonald, like Balaban, is anomalous, but for different reasons: he was a career Air Force officer and pilot, his age closer to those who planned the war than to most of those who fought it. But his poems are wonderfully powerful, often intimately personal and sensitive. In 'Faraway Places', he writes:

> This daughter watching ducks knows
> nothing of Vietnam,
> this pond her only Pacific,
> separation to her
> only the gulf between herself
> and ducks that others feed.
>
>   Strange prospect
> to leave such gold he thinks.
> There is no gold for him
> in Asia.
>
>   Possession
> turns on him like swimming ducks,
> forcing his touch again.

She does not feel his claim
upon her gold
that swirls upon her face but cannot blink
her eyes
so full of ducks.

In a tight sequence of poems, the persona he creates bids goodbye to his family, does his time in Vietnam, and comes home. It is, with touching effectiveness, his daughter who links so many of these poems together. In 'Rocket Attack', he first describes the death of a young Vietnamese girl, then cries out:

Daughter, oh God, my daughter
may she never
safe at home
Never hear the horrible
sucking sound a rocket makes when it

– and there the poem ends, abruptly as consciousness at the moment of impact. Finally, home at last, 'The Retired Pilot to Himself' wonders:

Bombs so long falling; after falling,
what release?

     O for tonight –

my child
with benediction
sidling heel and toe in graceful
rhapsody,
acceptance of herself.

In one particularly striking poem, 'Interview with a Guy Named Fawkes, U.S. Army' he captures – as well as any young 'grunt' could – the grinding frustrations of guerrilla war:

– you tell them this –
tell them shove it, they're
not here, tell them kiss
my rear when they piss about
women and kids in shacks
we fire on. damn.
they fire on us.

what do they know back where
not even in their granddam's days
did any damn red rockets glare.

In addition, a number of very good non-Vietnam poems in *Caliban in Blue* attest to McDonald's great skill and expanding field of vision.

The following year brought McCarthy's solid collection, *War Story* (The

Crossing Press, 1977). The first section of the book is a sequence of 22 untitled poems set mostly in the war zone, but as the book progresses, the poems become richer and more haunting as the full impact of the war slowly settles in upon the former Marine. In 'The Sound of Guns', he writes:

> At the university in town
> tight-lipped men tell me the war in Vietnam is over,
> that my poems should deal with other things[.]

> At nineteen I stood at night and watched
> an airfield mortared. A plane that was to take
> me home, burning; men running out of the flames.

> Seven winters have slipped away,
> the war still follows me.
> Never in anything have I found
> a way to throw off the dead.

It would be another two years before Weigl would publish his first book-length collection, *A Romance* (University of Pittsburgh, 1979). Two earlier chapbooks had already offered tantalizing hints of Weigl's ability, and when *A Romance* appeared, it immediately confirmed that promise.

Again, one finds the particular hallmark of the very best of the soldier-poets: scattered among the war-related poems are numerous excellent poems on other topics, suggesting an ability to transcend Vietnam. Indeed, of the 36 poems, only 10 deal with the war. Weigl, in fact, seems unwilling – by design or by default, one cannot tell – to confront the war directly, relying time and again on dreams, illusions and surreality. 'Sailing to Bien Hoa' is typical:

> In my dream of the hydroplane
> I'm sailing to Bien Hoa
> the shrapnel in my thighs
> like tiny glaciers.
> I remember a flower,
> a kite, a mannikin playing the guitar,
> a yellow fish eating a bird, a truck
> floating in urine, a rat carrying a banjo,
> a fool counting the cards, a monkey praying,
> a procession of whales, and far off
> two children eating rice,
> speaking French –
> I'm sure of the children,
> their damp flutes,
> the long line of their vowels.

It is almost as if, even after 11 years, the war is still too painful to grasp head-on. Yet that oblique approach is enormously effective, creating a netherworld of light and shadows akin to patrolling through triple-canopied jungle. In 'Mines', he writes:

Here is how you walk at night: slowly lift
one leg, clear the sides with your arms, clear the back,
front, put the leg down, like swimming.

And in 'Monkey', a complicated five-part poem, he writes:

I like a little unaccustomed mercy.
Pulling the trigger is all we have.
I hear a child.

I'm tired of the rice
falling in slow motion[.]

Each one of these ten poems, scattered as they are among the others, is like stepping into a punji pit or triggering a tripwire.

Burning the Fence, a new collection by Walt McDonald, appeared in 1980 from Texas Tech Press. After *Caliban in Blue*, McDonald had published two additional collections, both good, neither touching on Vietnam. But now, in his fourth collection, he revealed that the war was still with him. In 'The Winter Before the War', he talks of raking leaves in late autumn, the approach of winter, the first snow and ice-fishing, concluding:

the fireplace
after dark
was where we thawed.
Chocolate steamed
in mugs we wrapped
our hands around.
Our children slept.
The news came on.
We watched
each other's eyes.

Only in 'Al Croom', in fact, does he write of Vietnam directly, and the word 'Vietnam' appears nowhere in the collection. But the war is there, nevertheless, like a dark and brooding presence.

It had now been nearly 8 years since Balaban published *After Our War*, but he had not been idle. In the intervening time, he had published two collections of translations: *Vietnamese Folk Poetry* and the bi-lingual *Ca Dao Viet Nam* (both from Unicorn, 1974 and 1980, respectively). And in 1982, his *Blue Mountain* (also from Unicorn) ably demonstrated the growth of his own poetry over the years. Here are poems ranging from the American West to the southern Appalachians, from Pennsylvania to Romania, along with eloquent elegies to friends and family members.

Still, lingering memories of Vietnam persist. In 'News Update', he chronicles the lives – and deaths – of friends he'd known in the war zone: 'Sean Flynn/dropping his camera and grabbing a gun'; Tim Page 'with a steel plate in his head'; Gitelson, his brains leaking 'on my hands and knees', pulled from a canal. 'And here I am, ten years later', he muses:

written up in the local small town press
for popping a loud-mouth punk in the choppers.
Oh, big sighs. Windy sighs. And ghostly laughter.

In 'For Mrs. Cam, Whose Name Means "Printed Silk",' he reflects on the
dislocation of the refugee Boat People:

The wide Pacific flares in sunset.
Somewhere over there was once your home.
You study the things which start from scratch.

And in 'After Our War', he writes:

After our war, the dismembered bits
– all those pierced eyes, ear slivers, jaw splinters,
gouged lips, odd tibias, skin flaps, and toes –
came squinting, wobbling, jabbering back.

After observing wryly that 'all things naturally return to their source', he
wonders, 'After our war, how will love speak?'
   But there is finally here, in these poems, a remarkable promise of hope, a
refusal to forget the past and 'go on', wilfully oblivious to history or the lessons
that ought to have been learned. In 'In Celebration of Spring', he insists:

Swear by the locust, by dragonflies on ferns,
by the minnow's flash, the tremble of a breast,
by the new earth spongy under our feet:
that as we grow old, we will not grow evil,
that although our garden seeps with sewage,
and our elders think it's up for auction – swear
by this dazzle that does not wish to leave us –
that we will be keepers of a garden, nonetheless.

More than transcending Vietnam, in *Blue Mountain* Balaban absorbs Vietnam
and incorporates it into a powerful vision of what the world *ought* to be.
   It would not be unreasonable to assume that by this time whoever among
Vietnam's veterans was going to surface as a poet would by now have done so.
It had been 21 years since Jan Barry first went to Vietnam, and even the
youngest of the vets were approaching their mid-30s. But the appearance in
1984 of D. F. Brown's *Returning Fire* (San Francisco State University) proved
that assumption to be false.
   Former medic Brown is particularly interesting, having remained in the army
from 1968 to 1977, and one can only wonder why he stayed in and why he got
out. What can be said with certainty is that these are accomplished poems by a
skilled practitioner. All of them deal with Vietnam and its aftermath. 'I can tell
true stories/of the jungle', he writes in 'When I Am 19 I Was a Medic':

I sleep strapped to a .45,
bleached into my fear.
I do this under the biggest tree,
some nights I dig
in saying my wife's name
over and over.

    I never mention
the fun, our sense of humor
embarrasses me. Something
warped it out of place
and bent I drag it along –
keep track of time spent,
measure what I think we have left.

In 'Eating the Forest', he speaks of 'soldiers/trained to sleep/where the moon sinks/and bring the darkness home'. In 'Still Later There Are War Stories', he warns: 'We grow old counting the year/in days, . . . The jungle/loaded, nobody/comes away in one piece.' And in 'Coming Home', he notices:

Someone has stacked his books,
Records, souvenirs, pretending
This will always be light
And zoned residential[.]

The shortest poem in the book is 'L'Eclatante Victoire de Khe Sanh':

The main thing
to remember
is the jungle
has retaken the trenches –

think it forgiven
look on it healed
as a scar.

The longest poem, from which the book's title is taken, runs over three pages. In between are some of the best poems to come out of the war. Whether Brown will eventually expand his reach to include other subjects and themes remains to be seen, but *Returning Fire* is a strong beginning.

Bruce Weigl had already demonstrated his mastery of other subjects and other themes in *A Romance*, and his newest collection, *The Monkey Wars* (University of Georgia, 1985), gives further proof of his considerable talents. Only 6 of these 34 poems, in fact, deal with Vietnam, two others referring to the war in passing. Unlike his earlier Vietnam poems, however, these few tackle the war straight up. Absent are the dreams and illusions, the surreality. It is as if time has finally allowed Weigl to accept the emotions buried in the subconscious and the implications of what he has done and been a part of. In the tellingly brutal and straightforward poem, 'Burning Shit at An Khe', he describes in painful detail the repulsive task of cleaning makeshift outhouses:

> I tried to light a match
>   It died
> And it all came down on me, the stink
>   And the heat and the worthlessness
> Until I slipped and climbed
>   Out of that hole and ran
> Past the olive drab
>   Tents and trucks and clothes and everything
> Green as far from the shit
>   As the fading light allowed.
> Only now I can't fly.
>   I lay down in it
> And finger paint the words of who I am
>   Across my chest
> Until I'm covered and there's only one smell,
>   One word.

Even more chilling is 'Song of Napalm', in which he tries to appreciate the wonder of horses in a pasture after a storm:

> Still I close my eyes and see the girl
> Running from her village, napalm
> Stuck to her dress like jelly,
> Her hands reaching for the no one
> Who waits in waves of heat before her.
>
> So I can keep on living,
> So I can stay here beside you,
> I try to imagine she runs down the road and wings
> Beat inside her until she rises
> Above the stinking jungle and her pain
> Eases, and your pain, and mine.

But the poem continues, 'the lie swings back again', and, finally:

> . . . she is burned behind my eyes
> And not your good love and not the rain-swept air
> And not the jungle green
> Pasture unfolding before us can deny it.

Perhaps because he has come to terms with the worst, he can also now remember with a certain amusement 'The Girl at the Chu Lai Laundry', who wouldn't give him his uniforms because they weren't finished:

Who would've thought the world stops
Turning in the war, the tropical heat like hate
And your platoon moves out without you,
Your wet clothes piled
At the feet of the girl at the laundry,
Beautiful with her facts.

These are wonderful poems, made more so by their juxtaposition with touchingly beautiful non-war poems like 'Snowy Egret' and 'Small Song for Andrew'. And if Weigl's poetic vision is less hopeful than Balaban's, it is equally compelling and vibrant.

Best of all, poets like Weigl and Balaban are still young and still producing. One hopes for the same from Brown, McCarthy and others. A poem of McDonald's appeared recently in *The Atlantic*. And other poets may yet emerge. Vietnam veteran Yusef Komunyakaa has published excellent poems in recent years in magazines and anthologies, and a collection of his, *I Apologize for the Eyes in My Head*, is forthcoming from Wesleyan University Press. Who knows what else awaits only the touch of a pen or the favour of a publisher?

There remains, for now, only to speculate on why Vietnam has produced such an impressive body of poems (not to mention short stories, novels and personal narratives) – especially considering the relative paucity of poems arising from other modern American wars. Korea produced almost nothing at all. From the Second World War, one can think of only a handful of poems like James Dickey's 'The Firebombing', Randall Jarrell's 'The Death of the Ball Turret Gunner', and sections of Thomas McGrath's *Letter to an Imaginary Friend*. The contrast is even more remarkable when one considers how very few members of the Vietnam generation ever actually served in Vietnam in any capacity at all. Where then do these poems come from?

Surely it has to do with the peculiar nature of the war itself. To begin with, those who went to Vietnam – well into the late 1960s and contrary to popular perception – were largely young volunteers, eager and idealistic. The average age of American soldiers in Vietnam was 19½ (in the Second World War, it had been 26). They had grown up in the shadow of their fathers' generation, the men who had fought 'the good war' from 1941 to 1945. Most had been in grade school or junior high school when John F. Kennedy had declared that 'we will bear any burden, pay any price' in defence of liberty. They were young enough to have no worldly experience whatsoever, they had absorbed the values of their society wholesale, and they had no earthly reason prior to their arrival in Vietnam to doubt either their government or the society that willingly acquiesced in their going.

All of that was about to change forever. Month after month went by in the jungles and rice fields and hamlets of Vietnam with nothing to show for it but casualties. Men fought and died for nameless hills, only to walk away from them when the battle was over. Men taught to believe that American soldiers handed out candy to kids found themselves killing and being killed by those very kids. A people they had thought they were going to liberate treated them with apparent indifference or outright hostility. Progress was measured in grisly official body counts, and any dead Vietnamese was a Vietcong. Torture, assault and battery, malicious destruction, murder and mayhem – the very things young Americans had always been taught only the enemy did – were widespread and tacitly or openly sanctioned. Worst of all, as time passed, it became obvious even to the most naive 18-year-old that the war was going nowhere.

And because the war dragged on and on in ever-escalating stalemate for weeks and months and years, there was more than enough time for soldiers to *think* about the predicament in which they found themselves. Who in the hell was fighting whom? Why? And for what? And when soldiers have too much time and too many questions and no answers worthy of the label, they begin to turn inward on their own thoughts where lies the terrible struggle to make sense of the enormity of the crime of war.

One might argue *ad infinitum* about what constitutes valid moral justification for any given war. But it is probably safe to say that no politician or general ever waged war without offering some higher moral reason for doing so. Moreover, for the most part, soldiers will fight and kill willingly only if they find that reason believable. Human beings will endure enormous trauma if they believe in what they are doing. But the explanations given by those who'd sent the soldiers to fight in Vietnam became ever more surreal and absurd until they were revealed for what they were: nothing but empty words, bereft of reason or any semblance of higher moral authority.

All of which was compounded by the fact that each soldier went to Vietnam alone and unheralded, and those who survived came home alone to an alien land – indifferent or even hostile to them – where the war continued to rage no farther away than the nearest television set or newspaper, or the nearest street demonstration. Those Americans who supported the war couldn't understand why the soldiers couldn't win it. Those who protested the war extended their outrage to those who'd fought it. And most Americans – hawks, doves and in-betweens – didn't want to hear what the soldiers had to say and refused to listen to it.

In short, those who had been asked and ordered to pull the trigger were left alone to carry the weight of the entire disaster that was America's war in Indo-China. The American people turned their backs on the war long before it ended. Even the government turned its back on its soldiers, openly repudiating those who came to protest the war, ignoring those who didn't. Veterans' Administration (VA) benefits were a paltry disgrace – and even the little that was offered had to be fought for tooth and nail. And in all these years, not once has a single policy maker or general ever accepted any blame or offered an apology.

Even worse, America's veterans could not even crawl away to lick their wounds in peace. Without even the illusion of a satisfactory resolution, the war ground on for years after most veterans had come home, and the fall of Saigon has been followed by one reminder after another: the boat people, the amnesty issue, Agent Orange, delayed stress, the occupation of Cambodia, the bombing of the Marine barracks in Beirut, the mining of Nicaragua's harbours. And the initial rejection of Vietnam veterans, and the long silence of the 1970s which followed (during which time Vietnam veterans were routinely stereotyped as drug-crazed, emotionally unbalanced misfits), have only given way to Rambo, Chuck Norris and the sorry spectacle of America's Vietnam veterans driven to build monuments to themselves and throw parades in their own honour.

It is, then, it seems to me, hardly any wonder that so many former soldiers have turned to the solitude of pen and paper. Under such conditions as these, there has been more then enough reason and plenty of time for once-idealistic youngsters to consider long and hard the war they fought, the government and the society that sent them to fight it, and the values they had once believed in. While many of these writers might be loathe to call themselves anti-war poets, few if any have anything good to say about their experience in Vietnam.

In 1963, John Kennedy said in a speech at Amherst College, 'When power corrupts, poetry cleanses.' Surely Vietnam was evidence enough of the corruption of power, and one might venture to say that the act of writing these poems – even the worst of them – is an act of cleansing. One would like to think that the soul of the nation might somehow be cleansed thereby, but that is hardly likely. More realistically, one hopes that in writing these poems, the poets might at least have begun to cleanse their own souls of the torment that was and is Vietnam. Surely, in the process of trying, the best of them have added immeasurably to the body and soul of American poetry.

Editors' Note

As the author has not discussed his own work in this essay which originally appeared in *The Virginia Quarterly Review* (Spring 1987), the editors wish to comment briefly on W. D. Ehrhart's own contribution to Vietnam War poetry. An ex-Marine sergeant and Vietnam veteran, Ehrhart is a major figure in the literature of the war. He contributed poems to *Winning Hearts And Minds: War Poems by Vietnam Veterans* (McGraw Hill, N.Y. 1972), a seminal anthology of veteran poetry, and co-edited with Jan Barry *Demilitarised Zones: Veterans after Vietnam* (Perkasie p.a. 1976). He is also editor of *Carrying the Darkness: American Indo-China – the poetry of the Vietnam War* (Avon, N.Y. 1985), the best anthology of Vietnam War poetry which includes work by most of the poets discussed in this essay.

He is the author of three nonfiction books about Vietnam: *Vietnam-Perkasie: A combat Marine's Memoir* (Zebra Books, N.Y. 1983), *Marking Time* (Avon, N.Y. 1986) and *Going Back: An ex-marine returns to Vietnam* (McFarland Co. North Carolina, 1987). Most of his own Vietnam-related poems can be found in his most recent collections *To Those Who Have Gone Home Tired: New and Selected Poems* (Thunder's Mouth Press, N.Y. 1984) and *The Outer Banks and Other Poems* (1984).

Appendix

W. D. Ehrhart has written some of the most distinguished poems to emerge from the Vietnam War, works such as 'A Confirmation', 'The Blizzard of Sixty Six' and the controversial protest poems, 'To Those Who Have Gone Home Tired' and 'The Invasion of Grenada'. His Vietnam poems display considerable range, and extend from representations of the conditions encountered by soldiers, as in 'Night Patrol'; verse concerned with the Vietnamese, such as 'Farmer Nguyen', and more reflective yet angry analyses of why and how the war was fought, which is the theme of 'A Relative Thing'. His poems are, in general, within the American vernacular tradition, and are written in sparse, 'unliterary' free verse. His frequently understated style with its economy of utterance is appropriate for his radical, oppositional themes and his poetry conceals its artistry and craft. 'The Invasion of Grenada', for example, a succinct and low key meditation on the Vietnam Veterans Memorial, is impressive because of its restraint: like many of his poems, it is terse, unsentimental and thus gains an austere power. It seems to catch in its flat cadences a tough realism and, through its accessible and direct mode of address, a genuine voice of conscience.

The Invasion of Grenada

I didn't want a monument,
not even one as sober as that
vast black wall of broken lives.
I didn't want a postage stamp.
I didn't want a road beside the Delaware
River with a sign proclaiming:
'Vietnam Veterans Memorial Highway.'

What I wanted was a simple recognition
of the limits of our power as a nation
to inflict our will on others.
What I wanted was an understanding
that the world is neither black-and-white
nor ours.

What I wanted
was an end to monuments.

In Ehrhart's poem, lament and elegy are impressively transcended by a rhythmically dignified call to action. The poem resists high flown images, achieves a remarkable plainness of diction and its statement is therefore intensified. More than any other poet of his era Ehrhart seems to be a spokesman for the anti-war veteran who is haunted by the war and now lives (as he writes in 'Letter')

. . . among a people
I can never feel
at ease with anymore:

To achieve redemption, healing and emotional solace Ehrhart does in his poetry what all good poets do after wars: he writes poems sympathetic to his former enemy, thus acknowledging his own guilt, and he retreats to the open countryside to cleanse the wounds of shame. Two of his best poems, 'Letter' and 'A Confirmation', take up these respective positions. In 'Letter' he writes in colloquial locutions and bare speech patterns to the North Vietnamese soldier who seriously wounded him in Hue-City in 1968. The thrust of the poem is to implore his former enemy to recover from the conflict, to restore the 'green land/I blackened with my shadow'. As in most of his poems the concise final lines clinch the poem's meaning in memorable unvarnished language,

> Remember Ho Chi Minh
> was a poet: please,
> do not let it all come down
> to nothing.

A similar relaxed, discursive mode characterises what is probably his finest poem, 'A Confirmation: For Gerry Gaffney'. Tonal colouring and, in particular rhythm, give this magnificent poem its 'American frontier' feeling. Two war comrades meet in the wilderness, long after the war, and attain communion,

> In a kind of awkward silence
> in the perfect stillness of the shadows
> of the Klamath Indians.

In 'A Confirmation' continuity is restored to the veteran through the magical intervention of nature that purges the sorrow. In such a context understanding is fostered,

> The wind moves through the Douglas firs,
> and in the perfect stillness of the shadows
> of the Klamath Indians, we test
> our bonds and find them, after all
> these years, still sound-knowing
> in the awkward silence we will always share
> something worth clinging to
> out of the permanent past of stillborn dreams:
> the ancient, implacable wisdom
> of ignorance shattered forever, a new
> reverence we were never taught
> by anyone we believed, a frail hope
> we gave each other, communion
> made holy by our shame.

In conclusion we include two of W. D. Ehrhart's poems reprinted with the author's permission from *To Those Who Have Gone Home Tired: New and Selected Poems* (1984).

Guerrilla War

> It's practically impossible
> to tell civilians
> from the Vietcong.
>
> Nobody wears uniforms.
> They all talk
> the same language,
> (and you couldn't understand them
> even if they didn't).

They tape grenades
inside their clothes,
and carry satchel charges
in their market baskets.

Even their women fight,
and young boys,
and girls.

It's practically impossible
to tell civilians
from the Vietcong;

after awhile,
you quit trying.

                    W. D. Ehrhart

Making the Children Behave

Do they think of me now
in those strange Asian villages
where nothing ever seemed
quite human
but myself
and my few grim friends
moving through them
hunched
in lines?

When they tell stories to their children
of the evil
that awaits misbehavior,
is it me they conjure?

                    W. D. Ehrhart

Laurence Coupe

9

'Tell Me Lies About Vietnam': English Poetry and the American War

The achievement of the American poets in responding to, and challenging, the war in Vietnam has been well documented. But very little has been written about the position in which English poets were themselves placed: far more closely implicated than in any previous international conflict by virtue of media coverage (despite the fact that this was not their war as such), they were forced not only to decide where exactly they stood but also to find an appropriate artistic perspective of their own.

For evidence that English poetry was indeed affected by Vietnam, we might refer to the questionnaire conducted by Ian Hamilton's *The Review* in April 1968.[1] Three poets were in favour of US policy, and 3 did not know quite what to think; but 17 were against. Kingsley Amis's outspoken support – 'The American war needs stepping up, not scaling down' because 'Communist aggression must be resisted' – led to heated exchanges with his former 'Movement' friend Donald Davie. In the pages of *Encounter* they accused each other of ignorance and irresponsibility.[2] So Vietnam clearly did matter to some English poets, one way or another. Indeed, it seemed to matter more to the poets than to the British Labour Government. In October 1964 Harold Wilson had been elected prime minister by a small majority, so his backbenchers were prepared initially to be lenient about his failure to voice any opposition to America. But even after being re-elected by a large majority in September 1965 he was still refusing to speak up, and the left-wing Labour weekly was forced to ask in a leading headline, 'What IS the Labour Government's Vietnam Policy?'

One English poet in particular seemed to know the answer. Earlier that year Adrian Mitchell's 'To Whom It May Concern' appeared in the same journal. It concluded as follows:

You put your bombers in, you put your conscience out.
You take the human being and you twist it all about

So scrub my skin with women
Chain my tongue with whisky
Stuff my nose with garlic
Coat my eyes with butter
Fill my ears with silver
Stick my legs in plaster
Tell me lies about Vietnam.[3]

Those 'lies', implicit in the silence of Wilson, were meant here to be exposed by the poet as the products of a corporatist conspiracy. Nobody wanted to know about the true horror of the war because it was in nobody's interest. The government needed to placate the US because of their manipulation of the International Monetary Fund, and the consequent threat to the security of the new 'classless' consumer society sponsored by Wilson. Businessmen wanted continuing trade and profits, and the accompanying good life. The working class was meanwhile too busy catching up with the joys of consumerism to take any effective joint action.

It is a comprehensive attack; and it further indicates that the war was certainly having its impact within the English poetic community. Moreover, that community was prepared, where necessary, to take its stand and make its challenge to the prevailing orthodoxy.

'To Whom It May Concern' was one of the poems performed at Michael Horovitz's 'Albert Hall Incarnation', a mass 'happening' occasioned by the visit to London in 1965 of the American 'Beat' poet Allen Ginsberg. About 6000 people were present; most of them enthusiastically applauded Mitchell's refrain, 'Tell me lies . . .' But one of the minority who remained unimpressed was Edward Lucie-Smith. He reflected on the event in the pages of *Encounter*:

There was a triumph, which one might have wished otherwise. Adrian Mitchell, already well known for his political verses and for his powers as a reader of them, declaimed a clever but more than slightly smug poem about Vietnam, and was rewarded with the biggest ovation of the evening. Yet there was an awareness that this was applause without catharsis, that the spectators were applauding the echo of their own sentiments and willing themselves to be moved without truly being so – the stock response at work.[4]

What Lucie-Smith was objecting to was not so much the element of protest, or even the urge towards the popularization of poetry (he himself was to go on to edit an anthology of the Liverpool 'pop' poets Henri, McGough and Patten), but the amount of self-discipline involved. What was intended to represent natural indignation at global inhumanity was in practice the uneasy consolidation of a self-congratulatory community: a community which felt itself to be aloof from vulgar consumerism yet which subscribed to its own pseudo-alternative equivalent.

In what follows, I shall situate and consider the idea and ideal of poetry put forward by Horovitz and Mitchell; their affinities with, and differences from, American 'Beat' poetics as practised by Ginsberg; and the further weaknesses which are revealed in such work as 'Tell Me Lies' when one considers the response of other English poets to the American war in Vietnam.

'trying to talk directly'

Antony Easthope has noted that an impulse behind the English romantic movement was the denial of rhetoric, which was understood as an external application of devices to poetry. Wordsworth, for instance, wanted his poems to be as close to free, natural utterance as possible: 'the spontaneous overflow of powerful feelings' (albeit 'recollected in tranquillity'). Easthope argues that this was wrong-headed, since there can be no language which is either free or natural: rhetoric is a condition of discourse.[5]

If we take this aspect of English romanticism, then we can see the subsequent American tradition as to some extent continuous with it. Whitman sought what Wordsworth had sought: a way of exploring and presenting the self with all the appearance of spontaneity. In this, they were implicitly subscribing to that poetic which M. H. Abrams was to call the 'expressive' orientation.[6] The poetry was to be explained and justified by its fidelity to the experience and emotion of the poet. But as the American tradition extended, and outgrew English romanticism, it found that if it was to be radically mimetic – discovering the mysteries of a new-found land – it could not help but engage with the problematic which we might call, following Abrams, the 'objective' orientation (that which attends to the 'words on the page'). The burden of English tradition – the sequence of its literary objects – was as burdensome as any 'fate' Emerson had found lurking behind American nature. Thus from Poe to the 'New Critics', the struggle to sustain the present workings of genius meant the struggle with past (especially English) works of genius: through and beyond them, with language itself.

When we reach the recent past of American poetry, we find that that struggle goes on. The Vietnam War did not distract the poets from this crucial engagement; on the contrary. James F. Mersmann has shown that the Ginsberg of *Planet News* (1968) is not essentially distinct from the Ginsberg of *Howl* (1956). In both cases the self-consciousness about language, the deliberate engagement with the matter of rhetoric, informs the poetry. Only it has become obsessive to the point of 'madness' in the later work, written after visiting the war. The poet hears, in Mersmann's summary:

> phantom voices in the air, the television, radio and airport that deal in 'black magic language'. It is a language of body counts, rationalization, prevarication, obfuscation, advertisement, money, materialism, 're-sponsibility', punishment, fear, and death. The deaths that swirl from this vortex of judgement and language are physical (the carnage of the Vietnamese countryside), psychological and spiritual (the tormented souls of America's poets, and all the souls 'held prisoner in hungertown' dying from inhibition and lacklove).[7]

This is the same Ginsberg who visited London and inspired the happening at the Albert Hall: a complex figure, as concerned about the perils of language as those of 'lacklove'. But Horovitz's 'Afterwards' to his anthology of English (and Scottish and Irish) Underground poetry, *Children of Albion*, emphasizes only one side of the master's achievement. Having condemned the English 'Movement' of the 1950s for its 'conformist programme, which defined poetry as "the words on the page", [and which] proved a two-dimensional concept-cage', he hails 'the unfetter'd insurrection of Ginsberg'. It is a theme also taken up by Adrian Mitchell, whom Horovitz quotes as follows:

> . . . one by one and four by four, poets broke out of their cells. Edith Sitwell tried. Dylan Thomas made it and was punished to death. Ginsberg and Ferlinghetti and Yevtushenko opened the gates and out we rushed, blinking and drinking in the light. . . . I want poetry to bust down all the walls of its museum/tomb and learn to survive in the corrosive real world. The walls are thick but a hundred Joshuahs are on the job.[8]

What is striking about this brief history, apart from the bizarre and sentimental resumé of Thomas's decline, is the assumption of poetry as progressing by virtue of its distance from formal obligation. The trope of the prison-house, reminiscent of Nietzsche, is deployed as if it conveyed, contrary to Nietzsche, a simple and natural truth. Of such rhetoric we can either say that it is blind to its own rhetoricity, or else that it is an illustration of the rhetorical technique favoured by Chaucer's Frankin, *diminutio* or self-effacement. The latter seems unlikely, and Mitchell's naivety contrasts sharply with the kind of talent represented by, among the others cited, Ginsberg.

Having decided that he and his friend are in all respects very close to their American paradigm, Horovitz proceeds to situate Mitchell's 'To Whom It May Concern':

> The critics are scared . . . because we are doing something very simple – trying to talk directly and honestly to people about the things which matter most to us . . .[9]

It is as if the 'objective' orientation had never concerned poets like Ginsberg. Moreover, when we attend to invocations of earlier traditions, we see that Horovitz is still arguing as if the brief denial of rhetoric by Wordsworth had never been challenged within English poetics, as if romanticism meant a few paragraphs in the 'Preface' to *Lyrical Ballads*. Even Blake becomes simple:

> We're confronting ourselves, jumping and pushing (our minds) as high as we can – 'without fear', knowing there's nothing to fear; taking up, with Ginsberg and with each other, the eternal themes of Inferno, Purgatory and Paradise, the marriages of heaven and hell, reason and energy, conscious and unconscious – in new systems of our own making; supplemented – in their application – by the voices of all bards 'Who present, Past and Future see'.[10]

Here we have a representative appropriation of literary history, Blake stands for the authenticity of speech, for bardic 'expressivity', at the service of a naive mimesis. Mitchell similarly rewrites romanticism, this time in verse:

Blakehead, babyhead,
Your head is full of light.
You sucked the sun like a gobstopper . . .
Always naked, you shaven, shaking tyger-lamb,
Moon-man, moon-clown, moon-singer, moon-drinker,
You never killed anyone.
Blakehead, babyhead,
Accept this mug of crude red wine –
I love you.[11]

Rhetoric is not a problem: as long as poets may 'talk directly', the world may be redeemed.

Rhetoric of course was the very condition of the Underground's success. There were two Albert Hall 'incarnations' (1965 and 1966): specifically rhetorical occasions. Again, Mitchell declaimed an occasional poem in Hyde Park at the 'Legalize Pot' rally in July 1967. The context of persuasion was well-defined, but the poet wished to go further. Many of the participants were carrying flowers, which he acknowledged as standing 'for love'; but he wanted to relate marijuana to the even more pressing issue of Vietnam. Thus 'a vague gas of love' was not enough and, he demanded:

A love so explosive that its tremors
Will shake out of the sky
The bombers which at this minute
Are murdering Hanoi . . .
A love so hot that it can melt the armaments
Before they melt the entire country of Vietnam
And maybe the inflammable sea
The inflammable earth
The inflammable sky
And the inflammable people of the earth.[12]

Whatever the poet thought he was doing here – 'trying to talk directly?' – the poem inevitably deploys rhetorical tropes and schemes and commonplaces. The initial declaration – 'These flowers are for love' – establishes the *ethos*, the authority and sympathy of the orator's voice. He then bases his argument on one of Aristotle's approved *topoi*: the proving of one's position by weighing up with its possible opposite. If love will solve our present global problems, then all those problems must be caused by war. Thus may he move from *ethos* to *pathos*, which in turn involves the moving of the audience through a mood of drug-induced quietism to a delight in violence and apocalypse.

When the distance between emotional persuasion and truth, between rhetoric and dialectic, becomes as invisible as this, the very least that occurs is self-deception; the very worst, mass-deception. Horovitz quotes Mitchell in an interview with George Macbeth, speaking about his relation to the Vietnam War:

> *Mitchell*: Well, peace and war affects me as a British citizen: and the way that war is going, it seems to me to influence Britain. I feel people in Britain are just as involved in the Vietnam War as people in America are. They've got less power to do anything about it.
> *Macbeth*: They can't be drafted into an army to fight there though?
> *Mitchell*: No. They can't yet. And I don't think they'll have to fight in Vietnam. But they're going to have to fight a white man's war, which is what this whole thing is – what this war is. And it's leading up to a global white man's war, eventually – maybe twenty, thirty years away if we're lucky . . .[13]

The ease with which the poet translates a specific international conflict into the language of apocalypse – even here, in an informal interview – betrays a profound insensitivity to the relation between rhetoric and politics. It also represents the tendency, typical of the Underground, to subsume the radical impulse within the Bohemian.

The radical impulse in England in the 1960s led to the major demonstrations against US policy in Grosvenor Square and Trafalgar Square in 1968. It was such occasions that prompted Raymond Williams to move from alliance with the academic 'new left' to a sympathetic apprehension of the necessarily forceful 'ultra-left':

> It is necessary to say soberly and quietly that the decay and corruption of the political system, and the intolerable violence now actually directed against the poor of the world will go on being fought by all effective means; and that unless the demonstrations grow into a new and open political movement, that fight will be ugly. Under a strain like this, it's time, not simply for those of us who are demonstrating, who want a new democratic politics, but for the society itself, a society more and more openly based on money and power, to change and be changed.[14]

This is an entirely different tone and stance from Mitchell's pronouncement, which relishes the fight rather than the necessity for change.

In this respect he relates directly to the Bohemian impulse, and so is closer to Richard Neville, for example, than to Williams. Neville, editor of the magazine *Oz*, produced a celebration of the English Underground in his book *Play Power* (1971). That phenomenon he saw as being occasioned specifically by the war in Vietnam; but having claimed as much in his introduction, he spent the rest of the book mocking 'straight' politics and celebrating a new 'life-style' of sex, drugs and rock'n'roll. The following account of his relation to the radical left gives us the tone:

> I arrived late at the home of the man behind *The Black Dwarf*. It was obviously a solemn occasion. The living room was strewn with hand-picked London militants. The man in the chair was speaking heavy Marx in a German accent. It was Mr (Deadly) Ernest Mandel, editor of

Belgium's *Le Gauche*, and a respected socialist economist. In measured tones, he precisely minimized the contribution of 'libertarian elements' in the Paris uprising and spoke of the subsequent influx of recruits to 'the party'. . . . Ken Tynan was the first to leave, in despair.[15]

(Ken Tynan, theatre critic, had staged the pornographic revue *Oh Calcutta!* and had been the first man to say 'fuck' on British television.) For Neville, 'the most memorable experiences underground' were not like that at all, but occurred

> when you connect to the music, to the light show, happening and movie simultaneously, while being stoned and fucking all at the same time – swathed in stereo headphones, of course.[16]

This logic of what we might call libertarian consumerism informs a good deal of Underground poetry, not just Mitchell's. Consider how Tom McGrath tackles the analogy between imperialism, particularly the American aggression in Vietnam, and psychic distortion. The radical impulse is subsumed within the Bohemian as he moves very rapidly from this ostensible theme to his real preoccupation: the poet's own vision of himself as emblem of guilt-free desire. There are token gestures to political reality; for example, soldiers 'blown up/for the sake of a bar of American chocolate', which is a telling enough *hyperbole*. But the key moment comes about by a shift of emphasis:

> Vietnam. Viet-nam Vie et man. . . .
> The whore I met in Soho,
> sitting on top of a dustbin of all things,
> smiling and calling to the men going past,
> endearingly, but not endearing enough
> supposedly – the men are embarrassed,
> for God's sake,
> embraced maybe, yes,
> she transmits visions of cock,
> dark rooms, trousers crumpled on the floor,
> myself beside her, tickling the tips of her breasts
> with fivers.[17]

The rhetorical context of such poetry, declaimed to a mass audience, is the reverse of radical, since the occasion of persuasion is anxiety about one's own Bohemian credibility. It certainly tends to leave Vietnam, its official occasion, far behind.

'not to say a thing'

There is one Underground poem about the war, one written by Mitchell, which may be seen as exempt from the above charges. It is 'Norman Morrison', his epitaph for the American martyr. Remarkable for its controlled, committed seriousness, the poem works by virtue of the poet's honest assumption of rhetorical responsibility. It is a formal exercise (based largely on the scheme of *anaphora*: 'He . . . He . . . He . . .') at the service of dialectic:

> He poured petrol over himself.
> He burned. He suffered.
> He died.
> That is what he did
> in the white heart of Washington
> where everyone could see.
> He simply burned away his clothes,
> his passport, his pink-tinted skin,
> put on a new skin of flame
> and became
> Vietnamese.[18]

To find poetry about the Vietnam War that matches this exceptional Underground piece, we have to turn to a 'straight' poet, D. J. Enright.

Enright began his career in association with the 'Movement', much despised by Horovitz as making a fetish of 'words on the page'. The accusation here is (in Abrams terms) one of extreme 'objectivity', a condition which the oral 'expressivity' of the Underground was supposed to be challenging. But what Enright was actually concerned with, even in those early years, was neither himself nor 'the verbal icon', but reality – his orientation was mimetic. In the 1960s he was lecturing in Asia, close to but not directly involved in the war. His themes are urgent none the less: oppression, powerlessness and suffering. As he makes Faust ask in a later volume:

> I charge you . . .
> Tell me this –
> Why is it little children suffer,
> Guiltless beyond dispute?[19]

What he will not do is provide glib prescriptions, such as 'love'. Nor is he impressed by his own capacity for 'truth'. In 'Its An Art' (1968) he takes as his theme the relation between poetry and politics, Arnoldian disinterestedness and atrocity. The occasion is the Vietnam War, though he does not reveal this until the end. As a man he may be nearer the event geographically than Horovitz or Mitchell, but as a poet he is irrelevant. After all, the war is effectively 'oblique', 'elsewhere'. It is the 'rabble of/Newspapermen' – 'Venal scribblers of/Purple passages and/Red-streaked reportage' – not the safely disinterested poets who tell the truth about his war. Thus as he finishes his formal exercise he provides mock-aesthetic justification for it, courtesy of Dr Johnson:

> Vietnam has neither made nor marred a poet.
> The art of poetry is not to say a thing.[20]

What Enright's poetry of this period offers is a refusal to mouth what Theodor Adorno calls 'the jargon of authenticity', that language of late capitalism which fosters an illusion of an autonomous, self-fulfilling subjectivity –

somehow evasive of the exigencies of society and history.[21] In the process of refusing, the poet engages in a tactical anti-rhetoric, as opposed to the rhetoric which pretends to be otherwise. The poet knows that in the act of expressing his disillusionment and guilt, those of the Western liberal professing the very cultural values of the oppressors, he runs the risk of using Vietnam as vicariously as any Mitchell, McGrath or Horovitz. So in order to do justice to atrocity he produces a scrupulously circumspect poetry that we might call 'minimalist' did that term not have such modish connotations. What is important to emphasize is that the mimetic impulse is informed by a strongly 'objective' (objective in Abrams' critical sense) alertness.

Maintaining what Adorno calls 'good reification', in the early 1970s Enright conceived of the very ease with which the Westerner pronounces on war, whether it be remote or on his own country's doorstep, as the logic of consumer capitalism. The talk in this hell is endless, concerning:

> . . . the world situation,
> The events in Vietnam, Ulster,
> Whatever's going.
> Who do you think invented politics,
> And why? At times I fancy
> That is why the world was created –
> . . . What else
> To chat about in eternity?[22]

The poet's use of this conceit, Western privilege as one infernal cocktail party, is a reminder that utterance never does elude figuration. Enright knows as much: he has already found truth within 'purple passages' and 'Red-streaked reportage'. Well might he conclude ironically that 'The art of poetry is not to say a thing.'

'objects other than ourselves'

While Enright was envisaging his inferno, James Fenton was working as a foreign correspondent in Cambodia. In 1975 he was in Vietnam, witnessing the fall of Saigon. His account was subsequently published in *Granta*. At first glance he seems to speak the subjective language of the Underground. He watches a fire with 'mixed feelings'.

> . . . the Vietcong had announced their proximity – the fire, though distant, spelled an immediate danger; nevertheless a city fire, far enough away, has a terrible splendour. The fire attracted me.

We can trace such an interest back to Fenton's avowed reasons for going to Saigon in the first place:

> . . . I wanted very much to see a communist victory. . . . I wanted to see what such things were like. . . . The point is simply in being there and seeing it.[23]

The mimetic and 'expressive' orientations are seen as in competition and it is the 'expressive' which seems to be winning. That at any rate is how a Marxist critic has interpreted Fenton's account. Complaining of the poet's 'insouciant illiteracy about Vietnam', he accuses him of being less interested in historical truth than in a 'fundamentally apolitical search for the next frisson'.[24] What this commentary on Fenton's article lacks is an understanding of the relation between rhetoric and reportage which the poet very exactly highlights. Emotional thrills were the business of the Underground poets, and Vietnam could provide them. But here the artificial construction – the scheme of *anaphora*, 'I wanted . . . I wanted' – alerts us to the fact that this is most certainly not natural 'expressive' utterance. Fenton is in effect warning us off, telling us not to take his word or experience as truth.

Thus 'The Fall of Saigon' is a repudiation of all premature totality, all attempts to homogenize the war in the service of 'authenticity'. Even the Marxist critic George Lukacs is not exempt. Fenton quotes him on the victory of the Vietcong:

> The defeat of the U.S.A. in the Vietnamese war is to the 'American way of life' as the Lisbon earthquake was to French feudalism. . . . Even if decades were to pass between the Lisbon earthquake and the fall of the Bastille, history can repeat itself.

Fenton comments:

> Stirring words, and – look – we don't have to support the Lisbon earthquake in order to support the fall of the Bastille.[25]

He is raising the issue of what is made of Vietnam at the expense of engaging with its contradictions. Thus it is as a radical but also with proper disinterested-ness that he later argues that the boat people are

> not merely 'obstinate elements' or Chinese comprador capitalists on their way to new markets. They are simple people with no hope.[26]

Fenton's suspicion of the jargon of authenticity is evident in his poems on Cambodia and Vietnam included in *The Memory of War* (1982). 'Dead Soldiers' might have been a good excuse for 'expressivity' – the poet after all 'was there', taking lunch with Prince Chantaraingsey, military governor of Kumpong Speu province, on a battlefield of all places; but it becomes instead the formal presentation of a bizarre spectacle. Continuous with the 'found poetry' of his previous volume, he gives not a flat mimesis (nor a justification of his own position) but a sense of history as coded: a mysterious language difficult but not impossible to translate. The war in Cambodia is seen as a 'family war', full of stylish rivalry and superstition:

> On my left sat the prince;
> On my right his drunken aide.
> The frogs' thighs leapt into the sad purple face
> Like fish to the sound of a Chinese flute.
> I wanted to talk to the prince. I wish now

I had collared his aide, who was Saloth Sar's brother.
We treated him as the club bore. He was always
Boasting of his connections, boasting with a head-shake
Or by pronouncing of some doubtful phrase.
And well might he boast, Saloth Sar, for instance,
Was Pol Pot's real name, The APCs
Fired into the sugar palms but met no resistance.[27]

In rhetorical terms, what seems a conventional enough *demonstration*, the recounting of an actual event in vivid terms, turns out to be a terrifying *exemplum* of the realization that history is never just a game or play but, in Fredric Jameson's phrase, 'what hurts'.

The form of 'Dead Soldiers' is bare, almost prosaic, free verse. Fenton's impersonal authority derives from his doing justice to the cultural shapes which the external world may take, not from the imposition of a world of his own imagining. Yet the persuasive impulse is there – what Abrams calls the 'pragmatic' orientation – and it is expanded in the other poems. Fenton is not one to evade the moral weight of explicit rhetoric:

One man shall smile one day and say goodbye.
Two shall be left, two shall be left to die.

One man shall give his best advice.
Three men shall pay the price.

One man shall live, live to regret.
Four men shall meet the debt.

One man shall wake from terror to his bed.
Five men shall be dead.

One man to five. A million men to one.
And still they die. And still the war goes on.[28]

Here are the tropes, schemes and *topoi* of traditional persuasion. The poet is not passing off his indictment of the historical event as free, natural utterance. In seeking to state a truth he does not assume the truth.

In 'Children in Exile', Fenton's poem about a small group of young Cambodian refugees, the form is an eccentric variation on a ballad stanza – the first and third lines of each quatrain being in free verse, the second and fourth being rhyming iambic pentameters:

They have found out; it is hard to escape from Cambodia,
    Hard to escape to justice of Pol Pot,
When they are called to report in dreams of their tormentors,
    One night is merciful, the next is not.

I hear a child moan in the next room and I see
    The nightmare spread like rain across his face
And his limbs twitch in some vestigial combat
    In some remembered place.

Oh let us not be condemned for what we are.
    It is enough to account for what we do.
Save us from the judge who says: You are your father's son,
    One of your father's crimes – your crime is you.

And save us from that fatal geography
    Where vengeance is impossible to halt.
And save Cambodia from threatened extinction.
    Let not its history be made its fault.[29]

These stanzas are enough to give the flavour of the whole poem: a firmly 'pragmatic' impulse informs clear mimetic particulars. Fenton, so far from avoiding sententiousness, gives it Augustan authority and precision: 'It is enough to account for what we do.' He deliberately deploys such devices as *anaphora* ('save us . . . save us'; 'Let not . . . let not'), *antithesis* ('One night is merciful, the next is not'), and *apostrophe* ('Oh let us not be condemned . . .'): these substantiate the conscious saying.

'Children in Exile' may serve to remind us of the original conception of rhetoric: that its affective power was designed to serve the pursuit of knowledge. Rhetoric was inconceivable apart from dialectic. Fenton's very deliberate form and diction are not only designed to give his poetry 'objective' status, but also to announce the concrete context of discourse. For it is through drawing attention to his poetry's very rhetoricity that he facilitates the reader's own intuition of what recent history has involved.

Thus Fenton follows on from Enright in the repudiation of the instant 'expressive' totality of the Underground, by which Vietnam becomes one more justification for one's own individualism. It is not part of the present purpose to explain the superiority of these two poets by pointing to the fact of their close proximity to the war. Vietnam in itself 'has neither made nor marred a poet'. But it is perhaps pertinent to place them in the same context as that provided by Philip D. Beidler in his study of American combatant poets. John Balaban, though a very different kind of Vietnam writer from Enright and Fenton, may yet strike us from Beidler's account to be engaged in something ultimately very similar:

> *After Our War* . . . is an attempt to put Vietnam 'in context' in the largest sense of that expression, to project memory into creative union with the sense of high and fully achieved imaginative comprehension that has traditionally marked the major art of a given age.
>
> The key term in the process for Balaban – although he never uses it outright – is something like *culture* as writers such as Ezra Pound and T. S. Eliot seem to have commonly conceived of the term in the years following 'their' war. Balaban's book, like many of the works of these distinguished predecessors, is an unabashed attempt to recreate the function of culture as a sustaining matrix of vision, a medium of understanding that may still restore us to whatever is left of a sense of whole relation to the world, a context of common human value and meaning.[30]

We might sustain the connection by referring to an interview which Fenton gave to Grevel Lindop in 1984. When asked if he thought there was still a function for a poet in changing people's political view of the world, he replied. 'I don't think you can ask poetry to do too much.'[31] What he means by this soon becomes clear. He is against the critical notion that 'the better somebody writes about the war, the more the poem draws attention to the poet rather than the ostensible subject matter'. But he is not interested, on the other hand, in 'writing about the poem itself or about the inability of poetry to communicate, or writing about the self-referential nature of art'.

Like Enright, only more systematically, he is concerned to make poetry serve and support our engagement with the world. If his predecessor sometimes edges towards the self-referential in seeking to reduce poetry's claims to autonomy, Fenton is quite clear:

> What we want is simply: poet A writing about subject B. The two things are distinct and we want our poetry to point to objects other than ourselves.[32]

'Objects other than ourselves': it is a good criterion, providing we allow here for the poet's dramatic clarity of exposition. Fenton's own poetry is no simple matter, though its rationale may seem so. His vision is both objective and 'objective': both dialectical and rhetorical, both true to history and true to the culture which he has uncomfortably and yet deliberately inherited as a poet. The contrast with the Underground could not be more extreme.

Notes

1. 'Poets on the Vietnam War', *The Review*, 1968, No. 18 (April), pp. 28–44.
2. *Encounter*, 1969 (October), pp. 87–93; 1969 (December), pp. 94–6.
3. Later reprinted in Michael Horowitz (ed.), *Children of Albion: Poetry of the 'Underground' in Britain*, Harmondsworth: Penguin, 1969, p. 212.
4. Edward Lucie-Smith, 'A Wild Night', *Encounter*, 1965 (August), pp. 64–5.
5. Antony Easthope, *Poetry as Discourse*, London: Methuen, 1983, pp. 122–5.
6. M. H. Abrams, *The Mirror and the Lamp*, Oxford: Oxford University Press, 1953, pp. 3–29.
7. James F. Mersmann, *Out of the Vietnam Vortex*, Lawrence: University of Kansas Press, 1974, p. 71.
8. Horowitz, (ed.), op. cit., pp. 315–17.
9. Ibid., p. 334.
10. Ibid., p. 343.
11. Ibid., p. 219.
12. Ibid., pp. 365–6.
13. Ibid., p. 359.
14. Raymond Williams, 'Why do I demonstrate?', *Listener*, 25 April 1968, p. 523.
15. Richard Neville, *Play Power*, St. Albans: Paladin, 1971, p. 15.
16. Ibid., p. 10.
17. Horowitz (ed.), op. cit., pp. 202–3.
18. Ibid., p. 223.

19. D. J. Enright, *A Faust Book*, Oxford: Oxford University Press, 1979, p. 16.
20. D. J. Enright, *Unlawful Assembly*, London: Chatto and Windus, 1968, p. 13.
21. Theodor Adorno, *The Jargon of Authenticity*, London: Routledge and Kegan Paul, 1973.
22. E. J. Enright, *Sad Ires*, London: Chatto and Windus, 1975, p. 24.
23. James Fenton, 'The Fall of Saigon', *Granta*, 1985, No. 15 (Spring), pp. 72–81.
24. Benedict Anderson, 'James Fenton's Slideshow', *New Left Review*, 1986, No. 158 (July–August), p. 89.
25. Fenton, op. cit., p. 112.
26. Ibid., p. 114.
27. James Fenton, *The Memory of War and Children in Exile: Poems 1968–1983*, Harmondsworth: Penguin, 1983, pp. 26–8.
28. Ibid., p. 23.
29. Ibid., pp. 30–1.
30. Philip D. Beidler, *American Literature and the Experience of Vietnam*, Georgia: University of Georgia Press, 1982, pp. 129–30.
31. 'James Fenton in Conversation with Grevel Lindop', *P N Review*, 1984, No. 40, p. 30.
32. Ibid., p. 32.

Further reading

Adorno, Theodor, *The Jargon of Authenticity*, London: Routledge and Kegan Paul, 1973.
Ali, Tariq, *1968 and After*, London: Blond and Briggs, 1978.
Anderson, Benedict, 'James Fenton's Slideshow', *New Left Review*, 1986, No. 158 (July–August), pp. 81–90.
Bayley, John, 'The Verse of Accomplishment' (review of *The Memory of War* by James Fenton), *Times Literary Supplement*, 27 August 1982, p. 919.
Hewison, Robert, *Too Much: Art and Society in the Sixties*, London: Methuen, 1986.
Marwick, Arthur, *British Society Since 1945*, Harmondsworth: Penguin, 1982.
Smith, Stan, *Inviolable Voice: History and Twentieth Century History*, Dublin: Gill and Macmillan, 1982.
Thwaite, Anthony, 'The Two Poetries', *Listener*, 5 April 1973, pp. 425–54.

John Storey

10

Rockin' Hegemony: West Coast Rock and Amerika's War in Vietnam

Prelude: beautiful history

> In England they seemed to misunderstand flower power. I pointed out it was a political, radical movement trying to stop an immoral war in Vietnam.
>
> Eric Burdon[1]

> It happened in San Francisco. . . . We created something there. We didn't know what we were doing. . . . Me and Eric Burdon and others would be up all night and day talking about music, playing records and arguing. . . . It's beautiful history.
>
> John Lennon[2]

In 1966, the English rhythm'n'blues singer Eric Burdon, late of The Animals, moved to California 'to struggle for more psychedelic, innovative sounds'.[3] The result was the album *Winds of Change*, made and released the following year. *Winds of Change* represents Burdon's contribution to the music of 'the West Coast revolution'.[4] Two songs taken from the album became Top Ten hits in the American charts: *Sky Pilot* and *San Franciscan Nights*. As is often the case with 'outsiders' and 'converts', Burdon's work during this period provides a keynote instance of the concerns and practices of West Coast counter-cultural rock. *San Franciscan Nights* and *Sky Pilot* reproduce the defining lyrical/ideological features of counter-cultural rock: its celebration of counter-cultural life-style, and its anti-war politics. They in fact do more than this; both songs not only generate the counter-culture's politics, they also display its cultural practices, the 'psychedelic' and 'innovative sounds' which had partly attracted Burdon to the West Coast.

The anti-war politics of *Sky Pilot* are constructed around the apparent contradiction in the Church's attitude to war (implicitly the war in Vietnam). On the one hand, it invariably supports a nation's going to war, while on the other, it preaches 'Thou shall not kill'. The narrative of the song tells of a priest who 'blesses the boys' as they prepare for battle. He reassures them, hoping 'they will find courage in the words that he's said'. He is at the close of the song left to consider the contradictions (as we are ourselves), as what is left of the platoon return. This narrative is worked into a tripartite musical structure, which in turn represents before battle, battle, and after battle. An exciting and anticipatory mood is established in the first section, imitating the feelings of those who are to experience war for the first time. Also, perhaps, mimicking the naivety (which is in fact a form of self-deception) propounded by the priest. The energy and expansiveness of this section is increased by the spiralling harmonies of the chorus, and by the use of a studio effect known as 'flanging'.[5] This then gives way to the middle section. What we encounter here is an aural collage of disparate sounds – including explosions, aircraft diving, bagpipes, machine-gunfire – suggesting the fragmentary and chaotic experience of war. Finally, the song returns to the melody of the first section. The studio effects have disappeared; Burdon's vocal is now accompanied by strings and woodwind, conjuring a mood of resigned sadness. 'Thou Shalt Not Kill' is spoken rather than sung, suggesting a wearying knowledge gained at too great an expense. The excitement of the first section reappears as accusation: the sky pilot is told, 'you'll never, never, never reach the sky'. In other words, he and his church will never overcome the contradictions. By implication the counter-culture has no such problems.

It should be clear from this short schematic account that *Sky Pilot* attempts to reproduce the counter-culture's revolution both lyrically and musically. *San Franciscan Nights* works in a similar way. Its lyrics celebrate the counter-culture, while its musical structure displays the culture's concern with drug experimentation.

The song begins with an announcement (reminiscent of the opening of *Dragnet*, an American police series popular in the 1960s) in which Burdon invites the youth of Europe to 'save up all your bread, and fly Translove Airways to San Francisco'. The song, however, is not as innovative as *Sky Pilot*; its psychedelia is mostly confined to its lyrics. Nevertheless, bass and drums manage to create a dreamy, drifting rhythm, punctured by sharp staccato acoustic guitar. This produces a sense of floating, anchored only by moments of illumination; clearly an attempt to reproduce the use of hallucinogenic drugs. What we hear is a celebration of counter-cultural life-style, images of a world in which:

> If you weren't for peace and love then you were a part of the outside world, the place beyond Haight Ashbury, which stood for Vietnam, police brutality, racial hatred, multinational rip offs and a bent Government.[6]

Vietnam: which music?

To make the connection between music and America's war in Vietnam raises the question – which music? We could talk about the music which played such an important part in the enlisted men's culture. Many accounts stress its centrality. For instance, once back in New York, Michael Herr remembered the war as a residual acid flash: 'Certain rock and roll would come in mixed with rapid fire and men screaming.'[7] Tim Page's account also highlights the importance of music: Vietnam in 1968 is remembered as much for Jefferson Airplane and the Doors as for the Tet Offensive.[8]

If our concern was the music which had been important to the enlisted men, the first thing that would become clear is that the music was in most cases not explicitly about the war, but only came to signify the war because of the context in which it was consumed: the round-the-clock Armed Forces Vietnam Network. Favourite songs included the following: *We've Gotta Get Out of This Place* (The Animals), *Homeward Bound* (Simon and Garfunkel), *Green Green Grass of Home* (Porter Wagoner), *Run through the Jungle* (Credence Clearwater Revival) and *Leaving on a Jet Plane* (Peter, Paul and Mary). The same point about context determining significance can be made with regard to the music listened to by draft resisters. The Paul McCartney song *Carry that Weight* was, for example, a favourite song of those who had taken refuge in Sweden.

Another possible area of investigation is the number of songs which have become associated with the war because they have featured in films about the war. *The End* (The Doors) in *Apocalypse Now, Who'll Stop the Rain?* (Credence Clearwater Revival) in *Dog Soldiers*, *Out of Time* (The Rolling Stones) in *Coming Home*, are three examples which readily spring to mind. I suspect that for many people when Jim Morrison sings 'This is the end' over Coppola's images of the jungle being napalmed, that the words and music can *only* be about the war. It is undoubtedly a meaning which has attached itself (or has been attached) to the song.

The most obvious area of investigation for anyone concerned with charting the relationship between music and the war is to look at the enormous number of songs written in response to the war. Beginning with Phil Och's *Talkin' Vietnam Blues*, the first protest song to mention Vietnam (April 1964), American musicians have written and sung about the war from a variety of different perspectives, in a variety of different styles: folk, country, blues, soul, rock, jazz. Every variety of American music has had something to say about the war. It has been justified and it has been attacked. Kenny Rogers sang about being proud to do his 'patriotic chore', only to lament that

It's hard to love a man
Whose legs are bent and paralysed.[9]

Buffy Saint-Marie simply sang 'Fuck the war and bring our brothers home.'[10] This was a sentiment shared by Freda Payne's Tamla Motown production *Bring The Boys Home*. Other Tamla artists expressed a similar attitude to the war. While Marvin Gaye asked *What's Goin' On*, Edwin Starr was clear that *War* was good for 'absolutely nothing'. It is not surprising, then, that the final verse of the Temptations' *Ball of Confusion* contains the lines:

People all over the world
Are shouting, 'End the War'.

Other songs concentrated on the war's effects on American domestic politics, especially resistance to the draft. Steppenwolf toasted the draft resister in his 'fight for sanity'[11]. John Lee Hooker, one of the founding fathers of rhythm'n'blues, undoubtedly articulated the concerns of many of his fellow black Americans when he sang:

I don't wanna go to Vietnam
I have my own troubles at home.[12]

Arlo Guthrie's *Alice's Restaurant Massacre* ridicules the draft procedure and suggests to its audience:

If you wanna end the war and stuff
you've gotta sing loud.

In opposition to this, Merle Haggard's *Okie From Muskogee* invites his audience to resist such 'hippie' sentiments:

We don't burn our draft cards down on Main Street
Cos we like living right and being free.

Victor Lundberg's *An Open Letter To My Teenage Son* takes such anti-hippie sentiments one step further:

If you decide to burn your draft card, then burn your birth certificate at the same time; from that moment on I have no son.

As these examples show, popular song was a terrain on which pro- and anti-war sentiments found expression. A few more examples should put the point beyond doubt.

Eve of Destruction, by Barrie McGuire, opens with a reference to the Vietnam War:

The Eastern world it is explodin'
Violence flarin', bullets loadin'
You're old enough to kill, but not for votin'
You don't believe in war
But what's that gun you're totin'?

The Spokesmen responded with *The Dawn of Correction*:

The Western world has a common dedication
To keep free people from Red domination
Maybe you can't vote, boy, but man your battle stations
Or there'll be no need for votin' in future generations.

Even death was a site of ideological struggle. To die in Vietnam was the result of political madness or the confirmation of American military values, depending on to whom you listened. *The Great American Eagle Tragedy*, by Earth Opera, takes the view that soldiers dying in Vietnam is the result of a kind of economic madness:

The king is in the counting house laughing and stumbling
His armies are extended way beyond the shore
As he sends our lovely boys to die in a foreign jungle war.

In *Ballad of the Green Berets*, Staff Sergeant Barry Sadler sings of the deaths of 'America's best'. The final verses of the song narrow the focus to one soldier who 'died for those oppressed'. His last wish was that his son should one day become a Green Beret. Death does not invite a turning away from war, but the reproduction of America's military tradition.

Another song which takes as one of its major themes the American family man as fighting and dying soldier is *Home*, by Gary Puckett and the Union Gap. The homely note is struck in the opening lines:

And every night they lie awake
And dream of Momma's chocolate cake.

But, as in *Ballad of the Green Berets*, the song eventually moves from the general to the particular, to the death of a soldier who will 'never ever see his home and his family'. More important than this visual loss, at least in terms of the apparent ideological project of the song, is the thought that he will never know 'What he's done for you and me.' He had died not for the 'oppressed' (as in *Ballad of the Green Berets*), but for the American people. What the song seems to suggest is, rather than organize against the war, it is much better to mourn its human losses and, moreover, be proud to do so. Every death of course increases the sentiment invested and makes disengagement that much harder.

Even from this very brief survey, one gets a sense of the range of songs produced in response to the Vietnam War. One interesting fact that does emerge is that for the first time in American military history the songs against war actually outnumber those in favour.[13] The principal reason for this was the music of the West Coast counter-culture. It is to this music I now wish to turn.

The counter-culture provided the main domestic opposition to Amerika's[14] war in Vietnam, and music was *its* principal ideological weapon in its struggle to dislodge the Johnson–Nixon hegemony on Vietnam. It will be my contention for the rest of this essay, that West Coast counter-cultural rock challenged the 'organized' meanings which the Johnson and Nixon administrations attempted to impose on America. I shall argue that counter-cultural rock posed an alternative way of 'reading' Amerika's war in Vietnam. It reinterpreted what it meant to be American, to be threatened with the draft, to be a soldier, to be a student, but above all, to be young and a member of an 'alternative' society in Johnson–Nixon Amerika.

To fully understand this music it is necessary to understand the counter-culture. What I have to say about the culture, then, should not be regarded as simply historical background (and therefore optional), but as the *primary* context in which the music's meaning was articulated.

The West Coast counter-culture

In Berkeley I found a culture in which rock and politics, music and the Movement, pleasure and action were inextricably linked.[15]

The West Coast counter-culture was a social movement consisting of a variety of predominantly middle-class cultural groupings – hippies, yippies, freaks, heads, flower children, student radicals, etc. – who between 1965 and 1970 attempted to establish a non-competitive, non-belligerent 'alternative' society.

It was a culture which came together on demonstrations, at love-ins, on marches and, perhaps, most of all, at rock festivals. Despite its fluidity, it is possible to distinguish between those who preferred the peace sign to the clenched fist, and spoke about Amerika's war in Vietnam in terms of moral outrage, rather than as a bloody example of American imperialism. The border separating the two groups was often extremely fluid. Individuals often straddled both, or drifted from one side to the other. At other times the differences became very marked. After the Spring Mobilization to End the War in Vietnam march in San Francisco, 15 April 1967, Country Joe McDonald of Country Joe and The Fish, made the telling remark: 'Man I learned one thing that afternoon. There's more than one revolution'[16] Bands like Country Joe and the Fish, Jefferson Airplane, The Doors and the Byrds drifted from one side to the other. In the words of Iain Chambers, they 'vibrated between the harsh edges of American politics and the utopian gestures of an alternative America'.[17] One has to be careful not to press this distinction too far. Too often this apparent rejection of politics has been misconstrued. What was usually being rejected was the conventional political structures and channels of American society. For example, before Crosby, Stills, Nash and Young played to the 15 November Moratorium Day rally at San Francisco in 1969, Stephen Stills announced to the crowd: 'Politics is bullshit. Richard Nixon is bullshit. Spiro Agnew is bullshit. Our music *isn't* bullshit.'[18] Stills is not saying he is apolitical, only that he rejects conventional politics. He would hardly say otherwise, the Moratorium being clearly a political event.

The counter-culture developed around the colleges and universities of the West Coast. Student numbers had doubled between 1960 and 1966. The total student population was, by the mid-1960s, around 6 million. 'Students were so numerous', according to Abe Peck, 'that they seemed to constitute a new social class'.[19] This is in fact the argument Theodore Roszak makes in *The Making of a Counter Culture*:

Just as the dark satanic mills of early industrialisation concentrated labor and helped create the class-consciousness of the proletariat, so the university campus, where up to thirty thousand students may be gathered, has served to crystallize the group identity of the young – with the important effect of mingling freshmen of seventeen and eighteen with graduate students well away in their twenties.[20]

It is easy to dismiss the counter-culture's 'revolution' as petty bourgeois: idealist principles, Utopian visions, yet another example of a subversive Bohemian variant of bourgeois individualism.[21] All this is clearly recognizable, but is it so clearly dismissable? A great deal can be said for the general thrust of its Utopian politics. Its solutions may indeed have been inadequate, but it did highlight *real* problems, mobilize against a *real* war.

The counter-culture was certainly not beyond criticism: if it is true, as Antonio Gramsci insisted, that ruling groups cannot wholly and absolutely absorb and incorporate subordinate groups into the dominant order, it is also true that subordinate groups cannot drop out of the dominant order. Despite its claims to being an 'alternative' society the counter-culture remained firmly sited in capitalist America, subjected to its rules and regulations. Certainly, at times, the connection seemed near to breaking point. But the tension soon eased, the profits flowed and the counter-culture withered.

West Coast counter-cultural rock: resistance

> Rock music must not be seen apart from the movement among young people to reshape their lives. . . . As such it is a profoundly *political* form of music, one that opts for a different form of social organisation, one that lets people love rather than makes them go to war.[22]

West Coast rock music was the product of men and women who had started out as folk musicians. Around 1965, following the example of Bob Dylan, they electrified their instruments.[23] The Byrds had formed in 1964, but it was only with their recording of Dylan's *Mr Tambourine Man* in 1965 that they began to exist as anything other than a collection of folk musicians. Country Joe and The Fish, The Doors, the Great Society, Jefferson Airplane, and the Warlocks (who changed their name to The Grateful Dead in 1966) all emerged in 1965. Early the following year, they were joined by Buffalo Springfield and Big Brother and The Holding Company. In 1968, as the West Coast counter-culture crumbled, its first and last 'supergroup' was formed, Crosby, Stills and Nash, becoming in 1969 Crosby, Stills, Nash and Young.

West Coast rock's folk heritage was never simply a question of music, more a way of looking at the world and the significance of music in it. A general sense that music was politics by other means was carried over from the folk circuit. This can be clearly heard in Country Joe McDonald's *I-Feel-Like-I'm-Fixin'-To-Die Rag*, undoubtedly the best anti-war song produced by the counter-culture. Using irony and hyperbole, the war effort is presented as an extension of the American Dream. The result is a song which holds up to ridicule the ugly triumvirate of capitalism, imperialism and war.

Another influence, carried over from folk music, was the belief that they belonged to an alternative community rather than an entertainment industry. For the political folk singers music had been a means of class mobilization, of organization, the muse of solidarity. For the counter-culture it was the central and unique mode of political and cultural expression. Put simply, the culture was built around the music. It was the means by which it discovered and reproduced itself. Rather than mass meetings and rallies, its organizing events were festivals and dances. Its 'coming out' party took place at the 'A Tribute to Doctor Strange' dance held in San Francisco on 16 October 1965. Significantly, the same day marked the first big West Coast demonstration against Amerika's war in Vietnam, the Berkeley Vietnam Day Committee march to the navy installation at Oakland. The Doctor Strange dance featured Jefferson Airplane, the march was 'entertained' by the band that was soon to become Country Joe and The Fish, The Instant Action Jug Band. Luria Castell, one of the organizers of the Doctor Strange dance, told Ralph Gleason, music critic with the San Francisco Chronicle, 'Music is the most beautiful way to communicate, it's the way we're going to change things.'[24] Gleason, who attended the dance, described it as 'a hippie happening, which signified the linkage of the political and social hip movements'.[25]

West Coast counter-cultural rock addressed its audience as members, or potential members of an 'alternative' society. Part of the sense of belonging involved an attitude to the Vietnam War. Without exception all the major musicians of the counter-culture sang songs opposing the war in Vietnam. The prevalence of this anti-war feeling was such that in the context of the counter-culture all songs were in a sense against the war. What I mean is this: the fact that Country Joe and The Fish sang songs against the war was enough to make all their songs seem implicitly against the war.

Opposition to the war was the central articulating principle of the counter-culture. (I use articulate here in its double sense, meaning both to express and to make connections.) Music expressed the attitudes and values of the counter-culture, while at the same time acting as a consolidator and reproducer of the culture. Beneath a variety of slogans – 'Make Love, Not War', being, perhaps, the most famous – it engaged in a counter-hegemonic struggle over the meaning of the war. West Coast counter-cultural rock provided *counter-explanations* of the war and the draft. It helped set limits on the ability of *Johnson–Nixon Amerika* to sustain its war in Vietnam. At its most powerful its Utopian politics produced a cultural practice in which the present could be judged from the perspective of an alternative future. It offered a counter-hegemonic space in which one could explore the potentialities of the present in terms of the possibilities of the future. *Unknown Soldier* by The Doors is a song very much in this Utopian mode. The song fades to the sound of celebratory bells and a jubilant voice announcing that 'The war is over'. This is classic education of desire: the depiction of an imagined situation in order to produce the desire for such a situation in actuality.[26]

The fact that the West Coast musicians were, in the main, of the same class, age and race (white, middle class and under 25) as their audience reinforced their links to the counter-culture. As Paul Kanter put it, referring both to Jefferson Airplane and the wider counter-culture: 'We're middle-class kids. We're spoiled and we're selfish and some of that hangs over. That's the way you grow up.'[27] Despite its class origins, the counter-culture attempted to overturn commercial pop's ideal of music as a private one-to-one experience. It insisted instead that music should be a collective event. Its favourite pronoun was 'we', its favourite adverb 'together'. Perhaps the band which most epitomized this spirit was Jefferson Airplane. Songs such as *Volunteers* and *We Can Be Together* perfectly illustrate this ideal.

West Coast rock advocated a culture in which the distance between producer and consumer was minimal. After the Doctor Strange dance, Paul Kantner made the following remark:

> It was like a party. The audience often far overshadowed any of the bands, and the distance between the two was not that great. Grace used to say that the stage was just the least crowded place to stand.[28]

This is a view shared by Ralph Gleason. On the Golden Gate free festivals:

> At the Free Fairs you could see people like the Jefferson Airplane wandering around, just members of the crowd like anyone else, enjoying themselves. For the first time to my knowledge, an emerging mass entertainment style insisted that its leading figures were human beings.[29]

And on the Doctor Strange dance:

> That night you couldn't tell the bands from the people. It was obvious that the bands represented the community itself.[30]

Jim Morrison of The Doors expressed the relationship thus:

> A Doors concert is a public meeting called by us for a special kind of dramatic discussion and entertainment. . . . When we perform, we're participating in the creation of a world, and we celebrate that creation with the audience.[31]

As I have already indicated, the West coast bands regarded their songs as ideological ambassadors, winning the world to the ways of the counter-culture. As Grace Slick told Ralph Gleason, 'Music makes it easier to get your ideas across . . . being anti-war, music is a pleasant way of getting your ideas across.'[32]

The musicians' assumption of this role and the audiences' acceptance that they were in fact playing such a role, gives the bands a striking resemblance to Gramsci's concept of the organic intellectual.[33] Because we are in the main speaking of bands rather than individuals, we must modify Gramsci's concept and speak of *collective* organic intellectuals. A good example of how this worked in practice can be heard in Buffalo Springfield's *For What It's Worth*, a song inspired by an early clash between the police and the counter-culture: the breaking up of a peaceful anti-war demonstration in Los Angeles. The song does not simply narrate events, but offers a warning about the possible cost of commitment to the counter-culture:

There's something happenin' here
What it is ain't exactly clear
There's a man with a gun over there
Tellin' me I've got to beware
I think it's time we STOP, children
What's that sound?
Everybody look what's goin' down.

Another example is *Draft Morning* by the Byrds. The song interrogates the draft both lyrically and musically. It poses the question: 'Why should it happen?' within a musical structure which plays the cacophany of war against the peace and tranquillity of a West Coast morning.

Other examples could be cited. But to repeat my argument, the point I am making is this: opposition to the war was genuine as articulated by the major West Coast bands at the centre of the counter-culture. They were not following fashions and fads, but functioning as collective organic intellectuals, articulating one of the culture's chief organizing principles: *Amerika's* war in Vietnam was wrong and, therefore, should be opposed and resisted.

West Coast rock: incorporation

West Coast counter-cultural rock was a music which had developed from the 'bottom' up, and not a music imposed from the 'top' down. But like all popular cultural initiatives under capitalism it faced three possible futures: marginalization, disappearance, or incorporation into the system's profit-making concerns. Counter-cultural rock's future was incorporation. By 1968, Michael Phillips, the vice-president of the Bank of California, was suggesting that all the indications were that rock was destined to become the fourth most important industry in San Francisco. What had started as a celebration of 'flowers that grow so incredibly high'[34] was being highjacked by those who

Cultivate their flowers to be
Nothing more than something
They invest in.[35]

As I said earlier, the counter-culture regarded its rock musicians as part of the community. To remain representative of the community they had to remain *part* of the community. It followed from this that involvement with the record industry was greeted with great suspicion (at least initially) by audience and artists alike. Commercial success threatened to break the links with the community. The problem was this: in order to make records musicians, however alternative, have to engage with capitalism in the form of the private ownership of the industry. If you want to continue making records you have to continue making profits. Your audience is no longer the community, but the marketplace. Moreover, musicians have no control over the use of profits, a fact that shocked Keith Richard of the Rolling Stones:

> We found out, and it wasn't for years that we did, that all the bread we
> made for Decca was going into making black boxes that go into American
> Air Force bombers to bomb fucking North Vietnam. They took the bread
> we made for them and put it into the radar section of their business. When
> we found that out, it blew our minds. That was it. Goddam, you find out
> you've helped kill God knows how many thousands of people without
> even knowing it.[36]

Such revelations pointed to a basic contradiction at the heart of the
counter-culture's music. On the one hand, it could inspire people to resist the
draft and organize against the war, while on the other, it made profits which
could be used to support the war effort.

While Jefferson Airplane sang

> All your private property
> Is target for your enemy
> And your enemy
> Is *We*

RCA made money. In other words, the proliferation of Jefferson Airplane's
anti-capitalist politics increased the profits of their capitalist record company.
This is a clear example of the process Gramsci called hegemony: the way
dominant groups in society negotiate oppositional voices onto a terrain which
secures for the dominant groups a continued position of leadership[37]. West
Coast rock was not denied expression, but its expression was *articulated* in the
economic interests of the capitalist music industry. It was a paradox record
companies were more than happy to live with. By 1968 they had well and truly
caught up with the spirit of the counter-culture and had started marketing its
music under slogans such as

> The revolutionaries are on Columbia
> The man can't bust our music (Columbia)
>
> It's happening on Capital
> Psychedelia – the sound of the NOW generation (MGM)

This kind of language even penetrated the 'business' side of the industry. The
1968 ABC distributors conference was held under the snappy slogan 'Turn On
To Profit Power'. And they certainly did – profits flowed. Between 1965 and
1970 US record sales increased from $862 million to $1660 million.[38]

The changing nature of the counter-culture's rock festivals provides another
telling narrative of its incorporation and defusion. The West Coast counter-
culture's first festivals took place between 1965 and 1967. They were free
open-air concerts held in Golden Gate Park, San Francisco, with attendances
ranging from 10,000 to 15,000 people. The Human Be-In, held on 14 January
1967, attracted 20,000 people. Besides inspiring Jefferson Airplane to write
Won't You Try/Saturday Afternoon, and the Byrds to write *Tribal Gathering*,
the event also inspired the Monterey Pop Festival, the first 'commercial'
counter-cultural festival of any note. The festival was intended as a counter-
cultural happening, a display not just of its music, but its values. It was billed as

'Three days of music, love and flowers' (16–18 June 1967). The intended tone was struck by David Crosby, then of the Byrds, who spoke against *Amerika's* war in Vietnam and praised the wonders of LSD. What it became, however, was a showcase for the A&R men (they usually were men); a marketplace for the purchase of profit-making talent. On the bill were Country Joe and the Fish, The Byrds, Big Brother and The Holding Company, Jefferson Airplane, Jimi Hendrix, etc. They played for expenses only, the profits supposedly going to finance free clinics and ghetto music programmes. A total of 175,000 attended, $500,000 was raised but, apparently, and unfortunately, the money went astray.[39]

Two years later, on 15 August 1969, Woodstock happened. Only 50,000 were expected, but 500,000 turned up. Woodstock is usually regarded as the greatest achievement of the counter-culture. It was a new beginning. Not a festival, but a *nation*. All its optimism is present in Joni Mitchell's song *Woodstock*, recorded by Crosby, Stills, Nash and Young in 1970:

> I dreamed I saw the bomber death planes
> Riding shotgun in the sky
> Turning into butterflies
> Above our nation.

The optimism soon faded. If Woodstock was the beginning of anything it was the beginning of the realization that the 'political' wing of the counter-culture was now very much the junior partner in the movement. This knowledge had, perhaps, already been grasped after the events in Chicago the year before. It is surely significant that the yippies managed to attract only 10,000 to lobby the 'Demokratic Death Convention', while the organizers of Woodstock attracted 500,000. This point was compounded when Abbie Hoffman, while trying to make an appeal on behalf of the imprisoned White Panther, John Sinclair, was knocked from the stage by Pete Townsend of the Who. Where Hoffman failed others had some success. Country Joe McDonald got the audience to join him in a 'fuck-the-war' chant. Not satisfied with this, mid-way through his solo performance of *I-Feel-Like-I'm-Fixin'-To-Die Rag*, he appealed for more commitment from the crowd:

> Listen people, I don't know how you expect to ever stop the war if you can't sing any better than that. There's about 300,000 of you fuckers out there. I want you to start singing. Come on!

Besides revealing the divisions within the culture the festival again showed the extent to which the counter-culture was open to commercialization. While those on stage celebrated the size of the counter-culture's community, the record companies celebrated the size of the rock market. Monterey had been viewed by the industry as a showcase for new talent. Woodstock was a successful exercise in market research.

Liberation News Service called Woodstock 'a victory for the businessmen who make a profit by exploiting youth culture'.[40] Bill Graham, ex-manager of Jefferson Airplane, made a similar comment: 'The real thing that Woodstock accomplished was that it told people that rock was big business.'[41] If the revelations about Woodstock were not exactly the end of the counter-culture, December 1969 seemed very much like it. On 1 December the draft lottery was introduced[42]. According to Abe Peck, this had immediate results:

> Many of those who'd protested because the war wasn't worth *their* lives now held numbers keyed to their birthdates that were high enough to keep them civilians, and many now said goodbye to the Movement.[43]

Worse was to follow: the first 8 days of December witnessed the indictment of Charles Manson and his 'family' in Los Angeles for murder. The charges were heard amidst, to quote San Francisco's 'underground' paper *Good Times*, 'a public frenzy of hate and fear not only against Manson but also against communes and longhairs in general'.[44] *Rolling Stone* even felt obliged to pose the question: 'Is Manson a hippie?'[45]

The event, however, which perhaps hurt the counter-culture the most happened on 6 December at the Altamont Speedway, outside San Francisco. While the Rolling Stones performed, Meredith Hunter, an 18-year-old black youth, was stabbed and beaten to death less than 20 feet from where Mick Jagger was dancing and singing. Hunter had 16 stab wounds and various head abrasions, resulting from kicks. Earlier the same day, Hell's Angels had attacked another black youth. Marty Balin of Jefferson Airplane had gone to his assistance only to be beaten unconscious.

With the counter-culture in disarray, many who had dropped out of *Amerika*, now considered dropping back in. The dilemma is dramatized in David Crosby's wonderful mixture of humour and paranoia, *Almost Cut My Hair*. In Crosby's song, loyalty to the counter-culture overcomes the temptation to cut and run.

Coercion, the other side of the consent-winning strategies of hegemony, further limited options as the new decade began. On 4 May 1970 four students demonstrating at Kent State University against Nixon's further escalation of the war into Cambodia were shot dead by National Guardsmen. Other demonstrators were met with similar violence. Twelve students at the State University of New York were wounded by shotgun blasts. Nine students at the University of New Mexico were bayonetted. Two students were killed and 12 others wounded at Jackson State University. Nixon's response was to call anti-war students 'these bums, you know, blowing up campuses'.[46]

Crosby, Stills, Nash and Young's response was the Neil Young song *Ohio*.[47] It begins:

> Tin Soldiers and Nixon comin'
> We're finally on our own
> This summer I hear the drumming
> Four dead in Ohio.

West Coast counter-cultural rock acted both as a symbol and a focal point of the counter-culture's opposition to *Amerika's* war in Vietnam. Of course the music alone could not stop the war; West Coast rock's achievement was to help to hold together a culture which made the making of war in Vietnam that much more difficult to justify in America.

Legacies

The collapse of the West Coast counter-culture following the incorporation of its music, and the ending of the war, brought about an inevitable decrease in songs relating to the conflict.

In the 1980s, two contradictory impulses have led to something of a revival: (i) the new political climate making Vietnam something of which to be 'proud', rather than 'ashamed', and (ii) the view that US policy in Central America is laying the basis for a new Vietnam.

The new political climate has undoubtedly created an audience for the music of the Vietnam veterans. Men such as Michael Martin and Tim Holiday, who got back from Vietnam only to go back there every night, 'Torn between the need to remember/And the good reasons to forget'.[48] Such music is beginning to surface after the silences and historical amnesia of the past decade. The process has undoubtedly been helped by the success of Bruce Springsteen's *Born in the USA*. Bob Dylan has also broken his silence on the war. On a recent LP, *Empire Burlesque* (1985), there is a track called *Clean Cut Kid* which deals with the difficulties faced by the returning veteran.

What is interesting about Springsteen's work on the war is how it is for him a means of talking about the present. *Born in the USA* is as much a song about working under US capitalism as it is a song about the problems of a Vietnam veteran. On a promotional video for his recent cover version of Edwin Starr's *War* (1986), Springsteen again mobilizes the war to talk about contemporary America. This time the focus is on American involvement in Nicaragua. The video opens with a shot of a father and son watching a TV news report of the fighting in Vietnam. As Springsteen begins to introduce the song, we see a montage of shots linking what happened in Vietnam with what is happening in Nicaragua today. Springsteen's voice provides a commentary on the images:

> If you grew up in the sixties, you grew up with war on TV every night, a war that your friends were involved in. . . . I wanna do this song tonight for all the young people out there. . . . The next time they're going to be looking at you, and you're going to need a lot of information to know what you're going to want to do. Because in 1985, blind faith in your leaders or in anything will get you killed. What I'm talking about here is *War* . . .

Springsteen then does a very powerful 'live' version of Starr's classic anti-war song. As the music fades we see again the room in which father and son watched the news reports from Vietnam; the reports are still coming, only now the father watches alone. Springsteen's song and video offers a counter-explanation of events in Central America. When he says to his audience 'You're going to need a lot of information', we hear an echo of the politics and practices of the West Coast counter-culture. The situation is of course very different. Not just a different war, but a different audience – a market, rather than an 'alternative' community. Moreover, Springsteen is expressing his personal political concerns (not of course unshared), rather than articulating the views of an active and organized collectivity.

General note

This essay is based on *Almost Cut My Hair*, a paper given to the EVAC project. A reduced and revised version was read at the First International Conference on the Cultural Effects of Vietnam. The essay has benefited from comments made on both occasions. I therefore wish to take this opportunity to thank all those who made me rethink and rework my ideas. I especially wish to thank Alan Fair, Jeff Walsh and Alf Louvre for their editorial help and support. But most of all, I wish to thank Katie Scott, without whose help the essay would not have been written. Finally, the essay is for Sarah who one day might read it.

Notes

1. Eric Burdon, *I Used To Be An Animal, But I'm All Right Now*, London: Faber and Faber, 1986, p. 159.
2. Quoted in Tony Palmer, *All You Need Is Love*, London: Wiedenfeld and Nicolson and Chappell, 1976, p. 249.
3. *I Used To Be An Animal, But I'm All Right Now*, p. 169. The term psychedelic to describe rock music has three possible meanings: (a) music written under the influence of hallucinogenic drugs, especially LSD; (b) music which attempts to signify the drug experience; and (c) music which attempts to reproduce in the listener something like the experience of taking hallucinogenics.
4. Ibid., p. 170.
5. Flanging thickens the sound, producing on *Sky Pilot* a sense of the music spiralling upwards.
6. *I Used To Be An Animal But I'm All Right Now*, p. 161.
7. Michael Herr, *Dispatches*, London: Pan, 1978, p. 202.
8. Tim Page, *Nam*, Introduced by William Shawcross, London: Hudson and Thames, 1983, p. 26.
9. *Ruby, Don't Take Your Love To Town* by Kenny Rogers and the First Edition (Reprise).
10. *Moratorium (Bring Our Brothers Home)* on *She Used To Wanna Be A Ballerina* (Vanguard).
11. *Draft Resister*, on *Monster* (Dunhill/Stateside).
12. *I Don't Wanna Go To Vietnam*, recorded in 1968, can be found on the 1982 compilation *Tantalizing With The Blues* (MCA Records).
13. See *All You Need Is Love*, p. 199.
14. Amerika with a 'k' instead of the customary 'c' was the preferred spelling of the counter-culture. It was meant to signify America as a Kafkaesque nightmare.
15. Simon Frith, *Sound Effects: Youth, Leisure, and the Politics of Rock*, London: Constable, 1983, p. 4.

16. Quoted in Abe Peck, *Uncovering The Sixties: The Life and Times of the Underground Press*, New York: Pantheon Books, 1985, p. 61.
17. Iain Chambers, *Urban Rhythms: Pop Music and Popular Culture*, London: Macmillan, 1985, p. 94.
18. Quoted in Serge R. Denisoff, *Sing a Song of Social Significance*, Ohio: Bowling Green University Press, 1972, p. 157.
19. *Uncovering the Sixties: The Life and Times of the Underground Press*, p. 20. In addition to this, for most of the 1960s, 50 per cent of the population was under 25 years of age. The counter-culture thus had a very large constituency to which to appeal.
20. Theodore Roszak, *The Making of a Counter Culture*, London: Faber and Faber, 1971, p. 28.
21. See Richard Middleton and John Muncie, 'Pop Culture, Pop Music and Post-War Youth: Countercultures', in *Popular*, Culture Block 5, Unit 20, Milton Keynes: Open University Press, 1981, p. 88.
22. Jonathan Eisen (ed.), *The Age of Rock: Sounds of the American Cultural Revolution*, New York: Vintage Books, 1969, p. xiv.
23. Dylan material was the starting point for most of the West Coast musicians who electrified their instruments in the mid-1960s. His own anti-war songs – *Masters of War, A Hard Rain's A Gonna Fall, With God on our Side* and *Blowin' in the Wind* – undoubtedly encouraged the counter-culture's own attitude. It is difficult to exaggerate Dylan's influence.
24. Quoted in Ralph Gleason, *The Jefferson Airplane and the San Francisco Sound*, New York: Ballantine Books, 1969, p. 3.
25. Ibid., p. 6.
26. The Doors' Utopian politics did not lose sight of the horrors of the present: *Unknown Soldier* was promoted with a film of Morrison spewing blood.
27. Quoted in *The Jefferson Airplane and the San Francisco Sound*, p. 131.
28. Quoted in Gene Sculatti and Davin Seay, *San Francisco Nights: The Psychedelic Music Trip, 1965–1968*, London: Sidgwick and Jackson, 1985, p. 48.
29. *The Jefferson Airplane and the San Francisco Sound*, p. 38.
30. Ibid., p. 9.
31. Quoted in Lee Baxandall (ed.), *Radical Perspectives in the Arts*, Harmondsworth: Penguin, 1972, p. 386.
32. *The Jefferson Airplane and the San Francisco Sound*, p. 159.
33. According to Gramsci, social groups always produce their own organic intellectuals, men and women whose function is to provide 'leadership of a cultural and general ideological nature'. See Antonio Gramsci, *Selections from Prison Notebooks*, London: Lawrence and Wishart, 1971, p. 150.
34. John Lennon's *Lucy in the Sky with Diamonds* on the Beatles' *Sergeant Pepper's Lonely Hearts Club Band*.
35. *It's Alright, Ma (I'm Only Bleeding)*. This is the published version in Bob Dylan's *Writings and Drawings*, London: Panther, 1974, and not the one performed on *Bringing It All Back Home*.
36. Quoted in Dave Harker, *One For the Money: Politics and Popular Song*, London: Hutchinson, 1980, p. 103.
37. There is a vast amount of literature on Gramsci's key concept. Tony Bennett *et al.* (eds), *Culture, Ideology and Social Process* (Milton Keynes: Open University Press, 1981), provides a good introduction. See also Tony Bennett, 'Introduction: Popular Culture and "the return to Gramsci" ', in *Popular Culture and*

Social Relations (eds Tony Bennett *et al.*) Milton Keynes: Open University Press, 1986.

38. See *One For the Money: Politics and Popular Song*, p. 223.
39. The Grateful Dead saw the festival as a 'sell out' of the counter-culture's values. They refused to attend, and instead played for free outside the event.
40. Quoted in Jon Weiner, *Come Together: John Lennon in His Time*, London: Faber and Faber, 1985, p. 103.
41. Ibid., p. 104.
42. The Congressional Quarterly Almanac explained the new system thus: 'Under the new induction system the period of prime draft eligibility is reduced from seven to one year. A registrant's period of maximum eligibility begins on his nineteenth birthday and ends on his twentieth. Men not drafted during these twelve months are assigned a lower priority and would be called up only in an emergency.'
43. *Uncovering the Sixties: The Life and Times of the Underground Press*, p. 200.
44. Ibid., p. 227.
45. Ibid., p. 227.
46. Quoted in *Come Together: John Lennon In His Time*, p. 135.
47. *Ohio* was released within 24 hours of the killings. Neil Young now introduces it in concerts as 'an old folk song'.
48. My knowledge of Martin and Holiday's work derives from two demo tapes sent to the EVAC project by Lydia Fish, State University College, Buffalo.

Discography

As I have argued, West Coast counter-cultural rock was both implicitly and explicitly against *Amerika's* war in Vietnam. It produced two kinds of anti-war song, those which attacked the war directly, and those that by affirming the values of the counter-culture attacked the war implicitly. What follows is a small selection from both categories.

Buffalo Springfield (1967). *For What It's Worth* on *Buffalo Springfield* (Atco/Atlantic).
Buffalo Springfield (1969). *Four Days Gone* on *Last Time Around* (Atco/Atlantic).
The Byrds (1966). *I Come And Stand At Every Door* on *Fifth Dimension* (CBS).
The Byrds (1968). *Draft Morning* on *The Notorious Byrd Brothers* (CBS).
Country Joe and the Fish (1967). *I-Feel-Like-I'm-Fixin'-To-Die Rag* on *I-Feel-Like-I'm-Fixin'-To-Die* (Vanguard).
Country Joe and the Fish (1968). *Untitled Protest* on *Together* (Vanguard).
Country Joe and the Fish (1969). *Maria* on *Here We Go Again* (Vanguard).
Crosby, Stills and Nash (1969). *Long Time Gone* on *Crosby, Stills and Nash* (Atlantic).
Crosby, Stills, Nash and Young (1970). *Almost Cut My Hair* on *Deja Vu* (Atlantic).
Crosby, Stills, Nash and Young (1971). *Ohio* on *Four Way Street* (Atlantic).
The Doors (1968). *Unknown Soldier* on *Waiting For The Sun* (Electra).
The Doors (1968). *Five to One* on *Waiting For The Sun* (Electra).
Jefferson Airplane (1967). *Rejoyce* on *After Bathing at Baxters* (RCA).
Jefferson Airplane (1969). *We Can Be Together* on *Volunteers* (RCA).
Jefferson Airplane (1969). *Volunteers* on *Volunteers* (RCA).

198

J. Storey

Further reading

Chambers, Iain, *Urban Rhythms: Pop Music and Popular Culture*, London: Macmillan, 1985.
Denisoff, R. Serge, *Sing a Song of Social Significance*, Ohio: Bowling Green University Press, 1972.
Eisen, Jonathan (ed.), *The Age of Rock: Sounds of the American Cultural Revolution*, New York: Vintage Books, 1969.
Frith, Simon, *Sound Effects: Youth, Leisure, and the Politics of Rock*, London: Constable, 1983.
Gleason, Ralph, *The Jefferson Airplane and the San Francisco Sound*, New York: Ballantine Books, 1969.
Harker, Dave, *One for the Money: Politics and Popular Song*, London: Hutchinson, 1980.
Middleton, Richard and Muncie, John, 'Pop Culture, Pop Music and Post-war Youth: Countercultures', in *Popular Culture*, Block 5, Unit 20, Milton Keynes: Open University Press, 1981.
Peck, Abe, *Uncovering the Sixties: The Life and Times of the Underground Press*, New York: Pantheon Books, 1985.
Sculatti, Gene and Seay, Davin, *San Francisco Nights: The Psychedelic Music Trip, 1965–1968*, London: Sidgwick and Jackson, 1985.
Weiner, Jon, *Come Together: John Lennon In His Time*, London: Faber and Faber, 1985.

Jeffery Fenn

11

Vietnam: The Dramatic Response

The dramatic response to the Vietnam conflict materialized in several distinct forms as it reflected the changing public consciousness of the development and prosecution of the war. The dramatic playscripts of the theatre that reacted to the Vietnam War spanned the period from the early 1960s to the late 1970s, and showed a significant evolution in style and attitude as the early demonstrations of political protest on the part of radical theatre groups gave way to a more intense and considered treatment of the experience. The return of the Vietnam veterans, several of whom turned to play writing and produced some of the best dramas on war themes in American theatre history, provided the impetus for the dramatic portrayal of the significance of what the war had cost the men who fought it, and the ramifications for American society.

The initial dramatic response to the war emerged in two discrete styles. One was evident in the demonstrations of political protest that often moved outside the theatre building proper to be performed in the street. These productions were usually improvised from scenarios, and were frequently unscripted pieces that seldom survived the occasion of their performance. In many cases they were produced by theatre groups formed specifically for the purpose of protesting a particular government policy, by groups who saw the theatre primarily as a forum for political revolution, or by those who viewed it as a vehicle for the artistic expression of social criticism. Typical of such groups were The Open Theatre, The Living Theatre, El Teatro Campesino, and The Bread and Puppet Theatre. The other kind of dramatic protest emerged in the form of both short one-act and longer full-length plays that were written for the commercial theatre. These often couched their messages of social and political criticism in allegory, analogy and allusion; they covered the period from the early war years to the late 1970s, but changed markedly in tone and attitude as the war was brought home to the American public through the medium of television and by the accounts of returning veterans.

Both the theatrical demonstrations undertaken by the more radical theatre groups and the more thoughtful productions of the commercial theatre were symptomatic of the revolutionary trend in American society that emerged some time before Vietnam became a significant factor in the public conscious-ness. The racial, economic, feminist and political issues that characterized the social matrix of the early 1960s invaded the arts, and the dramas of the Vietnam War era were typified by a close questioning of American society concerning the legitimacy of its ideals, values and ethics. Social principles were re-examined under the stimulus of social stress, and the war served as a catalyst to bring the very foundations of American culture under increasingly intensive scrutiny. The Drama, given its intimate affiliation with cultural myth and ritual, consequently featured dominant themes of cultural ethnocentricity, acculturation and tribalism.

Under the stress of the Vietnam conflict, American dramatists examined the nature of American society and the effects of cultural conditioning on both the society as a whole, and on the individuals of which it was comprised. As noted by C. W. E. Bigsby: 'the horrors of that war had dislocated America's values, undermined its myths, disturbed its moral equilibrium, and eroded its language'.[1] The initial criticism reflected in the demonstration plays and the abstract works of the social protesters metamorphosed into an excruciating examination of the mores and values of a society conducting such manifestly illogical policies. American culture itself became a belligerent in the conflict and the struggle on the battlefields of Vietnam became, for the stage, a dramatic metaphor for the tensions perceived to be resident in the fabric of American society.

The deterioration and weakness of society perceived in the America of the 1960s were to become the paramount concerns of the Vietnam War plays. The situations depicted in a majority of the works are symptomatic of the general breakdown of social order and stability that afflicted both the American troops in Vietnam and the family and community at home, for the war experience exacerbated the erosion of those socio-cultural myths that had provided the basis of American social identity, cohesion and continuity. As Bigsby further observes:

> The effects are shown in terms of the shattered psyches of those who had suffered, but in some ways, the principal subject of most of these plays is America itself.[2]

The collective and individual psychological trauma of the war was most appropriately suited to interpretation through the theatrical convention of Expressionism, and few plays of the period were designed to be staged in a realistic manner.

The dominant dramatic metaphors in the plays of the Vietnam era were those of fragmentation and disintegration, both in cultural stability and identity and in the individual psyche itself. Arguably, in fact as well as in fiction, the most profound casualty of the Vietnam conflict was the erosion of American cultural mythology. In drama it was depicted through Absurdist and Surrealistic techniques, and the predominant mood was that of an existentialist despair. So many plays of this period exhibit the definitive aspects of dramatic Absurdism that they virtually form an American sub-genre of the Absurdist tradition. Themes include the basic senselessness of human action; the condition of man-alienated and isolated, void of hope and salvation, facing inevitable extinction; the failure of communication; feelings of frustration and psychic anguish and fragmentation; and most consistently and emphatically, the arbitrary nature of reality. A comedic presence associated with the grotesque is never far from the surface of the plays, which often imbues many of the works with a sense of the blackest Pirandellian farce. As Allan Lewis notes:

> The absurdity of war is too real and too terrible to be taken seriously in the theatre. If war is irrational and unbelievably mad, how can the stage present the reality of the experience in any other way?[3]

A common tendency in the plays was to couch references to Vietnam in abstraction. In many cases there seems to be a predilection for eschewing direct references to Vietnam, and for expressing commentary and criticism in an oblique and tangential fashion. Jules Feiffer's *White House Murder Case* (1970) depicts the prosecution of a war in Brazil by an American government whose prime concern is withholding details of the conflict from the American people. Robert Lowell's trilogy *The Old Glory* (1965), set at the time of the American Revolution, examined the nature of American imperialism and the misuse of power in the past. Arthur Kopit's *Indians* (1968), a play that the author admits was motivated by a statement of General Westmoreland concerning the unfortunate slaughter of innocent Vietnamese civilians, examined the consequences of a powerful culture attempting to subjugate a lesser one, and contained themes of genocide and racial prejudice.

Other plays that employed mythical settings or abstract approaches in treating the problems raised by Vietnam include Joseph Heller's *We Bombed in New Haven* (1967). This work proceeds from the premise that as the American military is always involved in a war somewhere, particular geographical references and the need for any rationalization of specific social and political issues is superfluous. The stylistic technique of Heller's play, along with Kopit's *Indians*, relies on the effect of drawing attention to the particular theatrical conventions of acting and pretending, and the deliberate confusion of the distinction between reality and illusion. By implication, social and cultural ideas of identity and behaviour are also viewed as arbitrary, transitory, pretentious and subjective. These plays and many others of similar design and tone provided commentary on the Vietnam situation and its ramifications for contemporary American society. The playwrights dealt in their individual ways with particular aspects of cultural mythology and the problems that accrue when a powerful ethnocentric society imposes itself on other cultures;

however, as they resorted to abstraction to make their point, the authors often tended to obscure their message by this type of approach.

Other plays of the Vietnam era tended to ignore what the war itself represented and used it as an historical backdrop fraught with mysterious and uncertain implications of what had actually happened. These plays treated the Vietnam experience as an awkward interruption of the lives of adolescents whose post-Vietnam problems were generally an extension of those preceding the war. Plays of this type include Stephen Metcalfe's *Strange Snow*, Michael Moody's *The Shortchanged Review*, and Lanford Wilson's *5th of July*. In these works an individual had, most typically, suffered physical and emotional traumata as a consequence of the war, but his cultural perspective was generally left intact. Here, reliance was on themes that tended to treat problems of human relationships that were exacerbated by the Vietnam experience, yet were predicated on circumstances set well within the cultural parameters of American society. The Vietnam experience was thereby essentially reduced to the signficance of an unfortunate car accident or serious illness.

The truly significant dramas dealing with Vietnam that emerged from this period were written by playwrights who had had some first-hand experience of the war and were able to dramatize the ordeal and its consequences for both the combatants and the home community. They confronted the fact of war directly and chronicled in dramatic terms its psychological horror. It is to these plays, which ultimately attempted to come to terms with the magnitude of the event and the immediate and long-lasting effects it had on the individual and collective American conscience, that one must turn in order to appreciate how theatre can deal most effectively with the portrayal of such traumatic and devastating events.

The dramas that confronted the war directly are essentially of three types and are characterized, both thematically and dramatically, along variations of the structural principles inherent in rites of passage motifs. These works manifest themselves in tripartite patterns that might aptly be classified as rites of separation, experience and reintegration. Typically, these plays document the progression of an individual through his induction into the army, the alien experience overseas, and his attempts at reintegration into the society from which he has been alienated as a consequence of his military training and experience. The destruction of the cultural signifiers that formulated the individual's perceptions before he was inducted into the military, the trauma of his experience overseas and the difficulties besetting his later reintegration into his society, comprise the major themes of these pieces.

The major variation on the rites of passage theme that typifies all of these plays is that the failure of cultural myth to support the process of transition invariably denies the success of the rite. The novitiates are left in an existential void, isolated and alienated, separated by their experience from the old order, but never fully integrated into the new. This syndrome of man attempting to regain a place in a cultural construct is prevalent in virtually all major plays dealing with Vietnam. Works incorporating the theme of separation rites are represented by David Rabe's plays *Streamers* and *The Basic Training of Pavlo Hummel*; those describing rites of experience include H. Wesley Balk and Ronald J. Glasser's *The Dramatization of 365 Days*, David Berry's *G. R. Point*, Ronald Ribman's *The Final War of Olly Winter*, and Vincent Caristi's (*et al.*) *Tracers*; while integration rites are prominent in Tom Cole's *Medal of Honor Rag*, James McClure's *Private Wars*, and David Rabe's *Stick and Bones*.

A basic thematic stance of the rites of passage plays is that both the individual and the collective consciousness are products of cultural myth-making: in expanding this concept, the works draw heavily upon the key themes of the tenuous and arbitrary nature of individual and communal identity, and the perception of individual and collective reality. The military is depicted as a self-contained social unit, as distinct from the society that engendered it as one culture is from another. Draftees undergo rites of initiation that replace existing social codes; they are effectively integrated into a new social hierarchy through a systematic desymbolization and replacement of the signifiers of their former cultures; they are assimilated into a new society which has its own distinct reality. The recruit is stripped of his pre-military identity, programmed with new parameters of desirable behaviour, and in essence is acculturated to a new social order that is predicated on a cultural mythology separate and distinct from that of the civilian world.

Both of David Rabe's 'initiation' plays, *Streamers* (1970) and *The Basic Training of Pavlo Hummel* (1971), deal with the process of induction into the military forces and the irrevocable changes that the men undergo in their incorporation into a new social unit. In the process the set of mythic constructs upon which reality is based are shown to be every bit as arbitrary and unreliable as those of the civilian world. Both of these plays explicate the concept that was to become so prevalent in the dramatic works that treated the consequences of the Vietnam experience for both the individual and his society: the stress encountered as a result of the social conflict put excruciating and irresistible pressure on the fabric of American society itself. The most typical themes of the war plays emerged in the form of both individual and social disintegration, fragmentation, alienation and isolation, and of internecine conflict.

Many of the ideas inherent in Vietnam War plays were brought together in the opening scene of *Pavlo Hummel*. A grenade, later identified as a 'M-twenty-six-A-two fragmentation' type, is thrown into a bordello in which the title character is consorting with a prostitute.[4] The grenade, it transpires, has been thrown by a sergeant with whom Pavlo, a Private, First-Class (PFC), has had an altercation concerning rights to the prostitute, Yen. 'Fragging' was a term evolved in Vietnam to describe the shooting of an officer by his own men, and was a more frequent occurrence than army officials would care to admit. The fragmentation of social order implicit in such an act corresponds well in a thematic sense to the physical dismemberment associated with the effect of a fragmentation grenade and the psychological fracturing that accompanies cultural disillusionment. The nature of the weapon and the state of Pavlo's mind create a raw irony as physical and mental disintegration occur simultaneously.

The continuing action of the play consists of a series of flashbacks which chronicle the soldier's social conditioning and the process of his basic training. The inherent expressionistic flashbacks emerge from the dying Pavlo's mind and are punctuated by a choral figure or alter ego named Ardell, a black sergeant who appears immediately after the explosion and also periodically during Pavlo's progression through military indoctrination, on which he comments.

The rite of passage to manhood associated with the army and sexual maturity is regarded as an integral part of basic training, and sexual perceptions and expression are reordered along military lines. The drill instructor draws the recruits' attention to his 'left tit-tee' over which is inscribed 'U.S. Army' (p. 14). On the muscle of his arm is the symbol of sergeant, his 'name' and identity. Recruits are referred to as 'motherfuckers', an expletive used repetitively by the sergeant and enlistees alike. The predominant marching tune, 'Ain't no use in goin' home/Jody got your gal and gone', underscores the men's sexual isolation from the women of their former society and their reliance on the army for identity and status within the context of the new social hierarchy.

Pavlo, who has been a misfit in both civilian and military life, is finally assimilated into the army when his fellow enlistees ritually dress him in his street uniform and he leaves for his home to demonstrate his new status and identity. Rabe contrasts the two realities and attitudes of civilians and the military as Pavlo's brother, Mickey, casts doubts about whether Pavlo is really in the Army, and about whether there really is a place called 'Vietnam' (p. 66). Pavlo tells Mickey embellished stories about his experiences in basic training, much in the same style as his stories to his fellow recruits about his civilian past, and Mickey responds that Pavlo has always been a 'fuckin' myth-maker' (p. 66).

Both Pavlo's civilian and military lives are portrayed as a series of disillusionments when fantasies are contradicted by the immediate reality. The central dramatic metaphor of the work involves images of attempting to find one's way and establish definitive parameters of existence. The sergeant gives an exhaustive description of how to find directions by locating the North Star (pp. 56, 97), but this physical determinant is counterpointed by an extended metaphor introduced by a Sergeant Brisbey that concerns psychological orientation. Brisbey is a patient who, Ardell explains, has stepped on a mine, a 'Bouncin Betty', which has blown off an arm, both legs, and his genitals (p. 78). Brisbey wants to commit suicide and relates that Magellan, surrounded by limitless water and sky, dropped a rope overboard to ascertain the depth of the water. Brisbey says of Magellan that because the latter cannot find the bottom, he imagines that is is over the deepest part of the ocean, but that he doesn't know the real question: 'How far beyond the rope you got is the real bottom?' (p. 89). Pavlo responds to Brisbey's existential question with an account of a sexual encounter he had, during which, in orgasm, he 'just about blew this girl's head off' (p.89). He suggests that he wouldn't have had that experience had he killed himself in a suicidal state such as the one which Brisbey manifests – a rather ironic statement given Brisbey's condition.

After being wounded three times in the line of duty, Pavlo ironically meets his end fielding the grenade thrown into the bordello by his rival the sergeant. Pavlo is physically inert as his mind flashes back to a baseball scene of his youth, and the grenade explodes. As he lies dying, Pavlo makes his own existential statement at the prompting of his alter ego, Ardell. In response to Ardell's question, 'What you think a bein' R.A. Regular Army lifer?', Pavlo responds, 'Shit.' In response to Ardell's 'And what you think a all the "folks back home", sayin' you a victim . . . you an animal . . . you a fool?', Pavlo responds, 'They all shit.' He then expands his observation into his own existentialist philosophy: 'It all shit' (p. 107).

Pavlo has found neither purpose nor substance in his military career and faces the same existential void that he found in civilian life. This play, like many others of the period and genre, deals less with the actualities of the War than with the problems of the individual in the given social structure. Problems of integration, of belonging, of identity, purpose and function are exacerbated but not caused by the external conflict. The conclusion, 'It all shit', reflects the absurdist existential condition that results when the supportive individual and collective cultural mythology fails.

A similar existential limbo underlies the thematic impulse of Rabe's *Streamers*. The plot develops from the situation of inductees being held in a 'holding company', a transitional stage between the completion of basic training and assignment overseas.[5] The unit ensconced in a barracks room is a microcosm of American society forced into a crucible by the dictates of military necessity and the ever-present war. The army experience brings into acute focus social anxieties and tensions that are normally diffused in the broader social context. Vietnam exists only as a background rationale for the presence of American men in a military environment.

The title and central metaphor of *Streamers* is derived from a parody of Stephen Foster's song *Beautiful Dreamer*. 'Beautiful Streamers' is sung by two alcoholic Regular Army sergeants who have come to accept the inevitability of army life; the lyrics are a verbalization of bravado, for they evoke the image of the thin ribbon of fabric that trails from a parachute which has failed to deploy. Human experience is limited to the short intense moment that lies between the safe cocoon of the aeroplane and the impact that signals the end of mortal existence. The image owes much to Beckett, as the umbilical cord or 'streamer' symbolizes the link between the womb of the aeroplane and the tomb of the earth. As Vladimir observes in *Waiting for Godot*:

> Astride of a grave and a difficult birth. Down in the hole, lingeringly, the grave-digger puts on the forceps. . . . The air is full of our cries.[6]

Within the confines of the claustrophobic barracks environment, social distinctions and inequalities that are normally suppressed or diffused in the larger society are exacerbated and break through to the surface. The enlisted men represent a cross-section of American society: blacks are represented by Roger and by Carlyle, a ghetto black; whites by Billy and by Ritchie, an upper-class homosexual. Carlyle and Ritchie both represent objects of social rejection since they have both been abandoned by their fathers, but Carlyle is the fragmentation-inducing force. He is filled with hate for American society as a consequence of being alienated because of race, education and social status. Latent homosexual instincts and racial prejudices surface, and in response to Billy's taunts of 'Sambo! Sambo!' Carlyle stabs him fatally in a parody of sexual intercourse,[7] and later, similarly kills one of the sergeants, Rooney, who has come looking for his friend Cokes.

Rooney and Cokes epitomize superannuated and decadent ageing veterans of the Second World War, the backbone of the Regular Army. Cokes, an old master sergeant, is a choral figure and a key character in the play. He represents the continuity of American culture as his career spans three wars, but he exists in a hazy alcoholic world; he is dying of leukaemia and is blissfully unaware that the room has turned into a shambles around him. His existential philosophizing is ironic in the context of the bloody barracks room – he rationalizes life and death in fatalistic terms – and the play ends with his sitting on an army cot in a drunken stupor, mouthing senseless sounds in accompaniment to the theme song (p. 66). Cokes is, in fact, a 'beautiful dreamer'. Reality for him is defined by the parameters of army existence and by the fact that there is a war somewhere for him to fight. He does not differentiate between 'krauts', 'gooks' or 'dinks', or the European, Korean or Vietnam wars. He is totally acculturated to the military social order, and for him any world outside it does not exist.

It is significant that the unit is a holding company: the enlisted men are held awaiting assignment in a transition camp, neither civilian nor active army; they have surrendered their inherent individuality, but have not attained full military identity and status. In this limbo-like, indeterminate and transitory world, basic human prejudices and anti-social proclivities find expression without the conditioned restraint effected by an enduring social order. The men have been stripped of the protective myths of the civilian world but find that there is no compensatory mythology, other than the drunken utterings of the two sergeants, to provide for the establishment of philosophical, racial or sexual comradeship within the army structure itself. Again, cultural myth has failed and the rites of passage implicit in the induction of young men into the military are ineffective for many of the novitiates because the new cultural matrix inculcates the dilemmas of the old, but lacks the stability of a society conditioned by time and tradition. The men have not yet been 'baptized' by the experience of war, which alone is capable of molding them into an homogeneous society.

One of the few full-length plays dealing with Vietnam that is set entirely in that country is David Berry's *G. R. Point* (1975). Berry, in the Author's Preface, gives a clue to an understanding of the principles involved when cultural myth dissolves in confrontation with experience beyond the confines of familiar culture: 'Remember that this environment strips away pretense, subterfuge, and dissembling. It is a survival situation.'[8]

As with *Pavlo Hummel* and *Streamers*, the central metaphor of the work arises from mental and physical fragmentation, and the psychological readjustment that is necessary when perceptions of reality and parameters of behaviour are distorted in extraordinary situations. *G. R. Point* is structured as a rite of passage played out in the context of the Vietnam experience. The action of the play develops in a Graves Registration Unit (the G.R. of the title) and involves men whose duties are the reclamation and identification of American dead. The duties of the men involve the reassembling of corpses that have been blown to pieces and the placing of identity and invoice tags on them for shipment back to the United States. Deacon, a member of the G.R. unit, states its motto: 'You frag 'em, we bag 'em' (p. 11).

The disruption of psychological equilibrium that accompanies the fragmentation and disintegration of cultural myth and reality is manifested on many levels. The physically fragmented bodies are the 'objective correlative' of the shattered psyches of the men who are engaged in packaging the dead. Truth is defined as arbitrary and relative when reality is dependent on geographical orientation: many soldiers refer to the United States as 'the real world', but a pragmatic mortuary worker, Zan, explains: 'This is the real world: this about as real as you'll ever find' (p. 23).

Other men, referring to the incidence of drug-taking as a means of escape, refer to Vietnam as 'Disneyland West' (p. 16). The disintegration of order in the American forces is recalled in reference to the 'fragging' of officers. A G.R. man, Tito, explains to the new arrival Micah: 'One sixteen round in the back of your head. . . . We get about five of them mystery murders a month in G.R.' (p. 14). Uninitiated men are referred to as 'cherries', and Micah is warned 'You ain't back in the world. You got to lose your cherry real fast on some things' (p. 14).

As a rite of passage, the action of the the work follows the arrival and departure of its central figure, Micah, and deals with the process by which Micah and the men become conditioned, or acculturated, to the new environment. The battlefield experience forms the men into a homogeneous society that was lacking in the transitory camps of basic training, but alienates them forever from the culture that engendered them. When confronted with the kind of work performed by the unit, Micah, a college graduate who was drafted but enlisted instead to avoid the infantry, announces: 'I intend to remain civilized' (p. 11).

Attempting to impose his social ethics on the other members of his unit, Micah becomes involved in a confrontation with a black soldier, Deacon, when the latter sexually abuses a female Vietnamese camp follower. As the action of the play progresses, however, Micah is overwhelmed by the passions occasioned when his unit has to defend itself under attack, and he experiences orgasms when he participates in the destruction and killing. Combat for Micah releases the repressed sexuality that is implicitly part of the conditioning of his culture, and he comes to enjoy the sexual diversions of the camp that he had previously decried.

The war experience brings Micah to a heightened state of consciousness and unleashes in him emotions that have been suppressed in his former culture: 'For the first time in my life, I feel completely awake' (p. 42). His psychological awareness is intensified in another way when an American tank mistakenly fires into a bunker that is occupied by his friends; he subsequently performs a macabre dance of grief with Zan's corpse in a body bag. His ultimate disillusionment comes as a consequence of his sadistic recounting to his mother of the events befalling him in Vietnam; she is stricken by guilt and suffers a cerebral haemorrhage. She has claimed that she would gladly change places with him if it were humanly possible, and ironically does so when her death redeems Micah by winning him an early termination of his overseas tour. Micah has effected a transference of guilt by allowing his mother to be privy to his experience.

Much of the conflict and anxiety that provides the dramatic tension in the playscripts associated with Vietnam is generated through the frustrations that arise from the clash of cultural perspectives. *G. R. Point*, as a play of war experience, focusses on sexual themes that are extensions of the complexes evident in both the plays of initiation and the 'homecoming' works that deal with rites of reintegration. With the breakdown of psychological equilibrium associated with alien experiences, sexual instincts emerge which have been culturally repressed. The homecoming plays typically focus on how cultural attitudes complicate the process of reintegration, when the veterans' altered perspectives impede the psychological adjustment that is necessary for harmonious reunion on the part of both the returnees and the extended society.

Two homecoming plays that involve failed attempts at reintegration are David Rabe's *Sticks and Bones* (1969) and Tom Cole's *Medal of Honour Rag* (1975). The protagonists of both plays ultimately submit themselves as sacrificial victims to society when it becomes evident to them that they are irrevocably culturally alienated, superfluous, and threatening. The effect of the Vietnam experience on culturally conditioned sexual attitudes is evident in *Sticks and Bones*, while in *Medal of Honour Rag*, the stresses of existence in a non-combat environment generate intolerable psychological problems for a returnee who has won his country's highest military award.

Rabe's play deals with the return of a blind American serviceman, David, who is denied reassimilation with his culture when knowledge of his miscegenation in Vietnam disrupts the psychological equilibrium of the family unit. The cloistered perceptions of middle-class America are expressed in the stereotypical cultural analogue of the television family of Ozzie and Harriet, where David and Rick are sons. David's return generates culture shock for he poses a threat to the family's stability and continuity when his physical state and proximity force them to confront unpleasant realities. David's first observation when he enters his former home is that 'It doesn't feel right.'[9] His arrival cripples the ability of the family to function when his blindness evokes guilt in Ozzie over his non-combatant role in the Second World War; and Harriet's maternal instincts dissolve in the act of vomiting when she hears that David has made love to an Oriental woman.

The crisis in the work occurs when David's liaison with Zung, a Vietnamese girl, becomes the focus of the family's attention. Zung appears surrealistically throughout the play when her presence is invoked in David's fond reminiscences and Ozzie's rabid denunciations. When Zung's influence in David's life is finally recognized by the family, she materializes before Ozzie, and he strangles her. The family then turns to David and ritually provides him with a razor, towels and a bowl to catch his blood: his brother Rick helps him cut his wrists, and the group looks on in satisfaction. *Sticks and Bones* thus culminates in a rite of exorcism, as the family, identifying David as a diabolical threat to their well-being, expel him from their society in a scapegoat ritual.

The dilemma of maintaining cultural cohesion and stability in the face of the threat posed by the returnees underlies the conflict in virtually all of the plays that deal with Vietnam. Both within the individual and between him and his society, personal and cultural traumata are intensified by the unpopular nature of the war and its ignominious conclusion. Many plays, like Tom Cole's *Medal of Honour Rag*, Emily Mann's *Still Life*, and James McLure's *Pvt. Wars*, resemble adaptations of case studies undertaken by psychiatrists working with returnees; others, such as Terence McNally's *Bringing It All Back Home* and Ronald Ribman's *The Burial of Esposito* are short plays that treat the response of a family to the return of the bodies of their dead sons. The works have similar themes since they, like other Vietnam plays, deal primarily with problems of adjustment to a new cultural situation.

The dramatic response that addressed social problems inherent in American society during the Vietnam period was essentially an extension of contemporary social criticism. The significant dramas reflected cultural stresses and were largely a product of creative artists who either experienced the horrors of war themselves, or who had intimate contact with those who had undergone the ordeal. The consistency that characterized the playscripts of the period lay in the questioning of the tenets, values and ethics of American society. Where cultural myth provides the epoxy necessary for social and individual psychological equilibrium, failed cultural mythology has for the individual and collective social unit a devastating effect in terms of social stability, cohesion, identity and continuity. The destruction of that myth in the face of inconsistencies with an external reality (in the case of America, the Vietnam War), and the associated disintegration and fragmentation of cultural givens, was manifested in an artistic nihilism that questioned not only the values of American society, but the meaning of life itself. In the context of such cultural cynicism, rites of passage experiences must inevitably fail, since the cultural underpinnings that give such rites their efficacy are no longer capable of supporting the social myth. For both the soldier, and the citizen on the home front, the Vietnam War forced an excruciating reassessment of individual and cultural identity, and only recently has the myth, to a degree, began to reassert itself in the creation of popular cult figures such as 'Rambo' and his kind.

Notes

1. C. W. E. Bigsby, 'A Critical Introduction to Twentieth-Century American Drama', Vol. 3, *Beyond Broadway*, Cambridge: Cambridge University Press, 1985, p. 315.

2. Ibid., p. 315.
3. Allan Lewis, *American Plays and Playwrights of the Contemporary Theatre*, New York: Crown Publishers, 1970, p. 209.
4. David Rabe, 'The Basic Training of Pavlo Hummel', in *The Basic Training of Pavlo Hummel and Sticks and Bones*, New York: The Viking Press, 1973, p. 105.
5. David Rabe, 'Streamers', in *Coming to Terms: American Plays and the Vietnam War*, New York: Theatre Communications Group, 1985, pp. 5–66.
6. Samuel Beckett, *Waiting for Godot*, New York: Grove Press, 1954, p. 58.
7. David Rabe, 'Streamers', *op. cit.*, p. 53.
8. David Berry, *G. R. Point*, New York: Dramatists Play Service Inc., 1980, p. 5.
9. David Rabe, 'Sticks and Bones', *op. cit.*, p. 128.

Further reading

Balk, Wesley and Glasser, Ronald J., *The Dramatization of 365 Days*, Minneapolis: University of Minnesota Press, 1972.
Berry, David, *G. R. Point*, New York: Dramatists Play Service Inc., 1980.
Cole, Tom, 'Medal of Honor Rag', in *Coming to Terms: American Plays and the Vietnam War*, New York: Theatre Communications Group, 1985.
Grey, Amlin, 'How I Got That Story', in *Coming to Terms: American Plays and the Vietnam War*, New York: Theatre Communications Group, 1985.
McLure, James, *Private Wars*, New York: Dramatists Play Service Inc., 1980.
McNally, Terence, 'Bringing It All Back Home', in *Cuba Si!*, *Bringing It All Back Home, Last Gasps: Three Plays*, New York: Dramatists Play Service Inc., 1970.
Mann, Emily, 'Still Life', in *Coming to Terms: American Plays and the Vietnam War*, New York: Theatre Communications Group, 1985.
Rabe, David, 'The Basic Training of Pavlo Hummel', in *The Basic Training of Pavlo Hummel and Sticks and Bones*, New York: Viking Press, 1973.
Rabe, David, 'Sticks and Bones', in *The Basic Training of Pavlo Hummel and Sticks and Bones*, New York: Viking Press, 1973.
Rabe, David, *Streamers*, New York: Alfred A. Knopf, 1977.
Ribman, Ronald, 'The Final War of Olly Winter', in *Great Television Plays*, New York: Dell Publishing, 1975.

Index of names

Index of works